Blue Ridge Parkway Vistas

Blue Ridge Parkway Vistas

A Comprehensive **IDENTIFICATION GUIDE** to What You See from the Many Overlooks

TIM BARNWELL

Copyright © 2014 by Tim Barnwell
Photographs copyright © 2014 by Tim Barnwell
Blue Ridge Parkway Introduction copyright © 2014 by Deborah Morgenthal
Designed by Helen Robinson
All rights reserved
Printed in China

FIRST EDITION, FIRST PRINTING

This work is licensed only for use by the original purchaser. Making copies of this work or distributing it to any unauthorized person by any means, including without-limit email, file transfer, paper printout, or any other method, is a violation of international copyright law.

ISBN: 978-0-9711348-3-6

DISCLAIMER AND DENIAL OF LIABILITY

This book is designed for the reader's enjoyment, not as a guide for making travel or hiking decisions that might put your safety or life at risk. While great effort was made for factual accuracy, with a project of this scale and novelty there are bound to be a few errors. If you are planning to do more than take in the view from Blue Ridge Parkway overlooks, I recommend you consult numerous sources, such as topographic and road maps, guidebooks, and websites. If you are planning a hike or overnight trip, always let someone know your plans and your expected return time. Heed posted warnings and signs, don't travel on closed roads or trails, and never, ever, climb on a waterfall. Every year people are killed from a fall on a waterfall, when attempting to climb a rock face, or by swimming at a popular spot when rains have made such an adventure dangerous. Weather conditions such as rain, fog, and wet or winding roads can result in dangerous driving conditions. Neither the author nor publisher assume any liability, expressed or implied, for personal injury or property damage that happen while visiting locations mentioned in this book, or from the use of its material.

NUMINOUS EDITIONS
10 Governors Court, Asheville, NC 28805

To my wife, Kathryn, my traveling companion for many of the trips involved in this endeavor. She helped plan overnight stays, kept notes, organized materials, and put up with the long hours it took to complete the project over a five-year span.

Acknowledgements

I WOULD LIKE TO THANK THE FOLLOWING PEOPLE FOR THEIR HELP: Thanks to my friend and photo assistant, Scott Allen, for his invaluable help in optimizing my images for reproduction and for helping implement the text in the images, and for his input, advice, and feedback. Many thanks also to my friend, Nick Lanier, for helping organize the Blue Ridge Parkway list of overlooks and for his research and knowledge of the Parkway and his advice as a fellow photographer and seasonal Park Ranger.

     Special thanks to my text editor, Deborah Morgenthal, for reviewing my writing and for composing the Blue Ridge Parkway Introduction, to Helen Robinson for her beautiful book design, Kathy Sheldon for proofreading, and Todd Kaderabek for coordinating the print production end. My appreciation to Karen Searle with Eastern National for her advice and encouragement in completing this project, to Jan Alms for his design ideas early in the project, and Paul Lester for his input on map reading.

     Thanks to the North Carolina Division of Archives and History for permission to use historical images from their Blue Ridge Parkway collection, to the North Carolina Department of Transportation for providing maps of western North Carolina, and to the National Park Service office in Virginia for providing the Blue Ridge Parkway maps.

Contents

INTRODUCTION 1

BLUE RIDGE PARKWAY INTRODUCTION 11

Blue Ridge Parkway SECTION ONE 16
    Rockfish Valley overlook 18
    Raven's Roost overlook 20
    Purgatory Mountain overlook 22
    Roanoke Mountain overlook 24
    Mill Mountain overlook 25
    Cahas Knob overlook 26
    Saddle overlook 27

Blue Ridge Parkway SECTION TWO 29
    Fox Hunters Paradise overlook 30
    Air Bellows Gap overlook 32
    View Bluff Mountain overlook 34
    Mt. Jefferson overlook (looking north) 36
    Mt. Jefferson overlook (looking west) 38
    Elk Mountain overlook 40
    Grandview overlook 44
    Thunder Hill overlook 46
    Wilson Creek Valley overlook 48
    Chestoa View overlook 50
    Bear Den overlook 52
    Three Knobs overlook 54

Blue Ridge Parkway SECTION THREE 57
    Green Knob overlook 58
    Mt. Mitchell (observation platform) 60
    Craggy Gardens Visitor Center (looking east) 66
    Craggy Gardens Visitor Center (looking west) 68
    Aerial view over Black Mountain, NC, to Craggy range 70
    Lane Pinnacle overlook 71
    Haw Creek Valley overlook 72
    View of Biltmore Estate and Craggy range 73

    View Chestnut Cove overlook 74
    Bad Fork Valley overlook 75
    Hominy Valley overlook 76
    Pisgah Inn (observation deck) 78
    Cold Mountain overlook 80
    Log Hollow overlook 81
    Aerial view over Looking Glass Rock 82
    View of Shining Rock Wilderness 83

Blue Ridge Parkway SECTION FOUR 85
    Near Devil's Courthouse (looking over Pilot Mtn.) 86
    Fetterbush overlook 87
    Wolf Mountain overlook 88
    Cowee Mountains overlook 90
    Haywood-Jackson overlook 94
    Milepost 436 to Waynesville, NC (no overlook) 95
    Waterrock Knob overlook 96
    Woolyback overlook 98
    Mile High overlook (on Heintooga Ridge Road) 100
    Bunches Bald overlook 102

OTHER WNC SCENES 105
    View from Chimney Rock Park (looking north) 106
    View from Chimney Rock Park (looking east) 107
    Jump Off Rock near Hendersonville 108
    View from St. Joseph Hospital in Asheville 110
    Biltmore House Library Terrace 112
    Craggy Mountain Range from the Asheville Mall 114
    View from I-26 to Craggy Mountains 115
    Cashiers Valley from Highway 64 116

RESOURCES 118

BOOKS BY TIM BARNWELL 120

Introduction

As a native of western North Carolina, I grew up exploring the mountains—hiking and camping—and driving the Blue Ridge Parkway. As photography moved from being a hobby to becoming my profession, these trips increased in frequency and scope. Although I have always enjoyed looking at and photographing the stunning vistas offered by the Parkway, over the years I began to wonder exactly what it was that I was seeing from the many overlooks I stopped at. Like many folks, I could identify prominent peaks such as Mt. Pisgah, Cold Mountain, Lane Pinnacle, along with Mount LeConte and Clingmans Dome in the Great Smoky Mountains. But beyond that, except for those in my own "backyard," my knowledge was limited. I had a rough idea of which community was in the valley below and was aware that I was looking west, for instance, but the name of the prominent peak in the distance was a mystery. I found it frustrating that I could not identify much of what I was seeing. I searched for a book or website that would show me this information, but found nothing.

On one outing, I stopped at the Hominy Valley overlook on the Blue Ridge Parkway, between Asheville and Mt. Pisgah. A tall peak in the distance caught my attention. What was it, I wondered? I took a compass reading, and when I returned home, I got out a few maps and began the search. Immediately, other questions arose. How far was that peak from where I had stood? Was I seeing 5, 10, 15 miles—maybe more miles away? And how high was it? Certainly lower than Mt. Mitchell—at 6,684 feet, the record holder for the eastern United States, but was it 4,000 feet...5,000 feet? After much deliberation, I decided that the peak was Sandymush Bald. I was not convinced, however, as I did not recognize the shape, even though I had been driving around it for many years. This concerned me, but it was also satisfying to try to figure out with map and compass what I was viewing.

So began this project. I bought lots of maps and updated my portable GPS unit. As I became more involved, I purchased topographic computer software. I began to learn how to use National Geographic's TOPO!® Outdoor Recreation Mapping Software® for North and South Carolina, and the Virginia edition, which aided my identification efforts. Of course, as my abilities improved, so did the reliability of my findings. It wasn't until a couple of years later, when I was beginning the serious identification of peaks seen from the Hominy Valley overlook using my new skill set, that I discovered my first identification had been wrong: the peak I had originally identified as Sandymush Bald was actually Rockyface Mountain! As this had been my first attempt, I was not surprised. However, to eliminate such mistakes in the future, I began to double and triple check each finding, to be sure of the accuracy of the identification.

Even though I grew up in western North Carolina, I am always discovering something new and making connections on my hiking and driving expeditions. That is one of the joys of travel and exploration. Once I began this project, those discoveries increased exponentially. I started to develop a map in my head, as if I were viewing everything from an aerial perspective, and relationships between areas began to link up.

For instance, I realized towns that were hours apart by car were actually differentiated by just a few miles line of sight across a ridgeline. As I drove around, I could envision what was on the other side of a mountain, in the valley beyond, where the headwaters of a river originated, and why a town might have grown up in a particular spot. I was mentally able to connect areas that I had always thought of as separate, unrelated entities. By crosschecking each discovery using multiple tools over many years, I have become proficient, even expert, at this. A contiguous map of the area began to evolve in my mind, and I believe that, by studying the information presented in this book, this is possible for others to do as well. Once I had photographed that first panorama from the Hominy Valley overlook, and had created what appeared to be a unique visual method of identifying elevations, the distance between towns, the flow of rivers, the connection of highways, I was hooked. I wanted to capture this information from dozens of the overlooks I frequented. The rest, as they say, is history.

The low, warm rays of late afternoon sunlight rake across the landscape at Craggy Gardens, sculpting and delineating forms, emphasizing shape and texture.

Even though I grew up in western North Carolina, I am always discovering something new ...

These two views of Mt. Pisgah taken from downtown Asheville, NC, show how conditions can vary from extremely clear to very hazy, often from one day to the next. Cool, dry, spring and fall weather conditions tend to clear out the haze and pollution common much of the warmer months.

I realized towns that were hours apart by car were actually differentiated by just a few miles line of sight across a ridgeline.

The Challenge of the Photography

WHEN I STARTED THIS PROJECT, I USED A VARIETY OF TOOLS, including numerous maps of different scale and detail, a typical car GPS unit, a modest compass, camera and tripod, and computer topographic software. As a project of this magnitude and scope had not been done in this region of the country before, there were no other guidebooks to reference. While a few overlooks had informational displays, most were limited in their identifications and some were fraught with errors. Since I began, many of those displays have been removed (due to these errors I assume). A few remain, the best of which is an inscribed metal plaque located at the restaurant deck at Mt. Pisgah.

Initially, I figured it might take a year or so to complete this book, but due to the difficulties involved, it took more than five. There were many hurdles. Multiple trips to a location were required to decide which of several overlooks in an area offered the best view and to determine what time of day would be ideal for photography, based on the direction the overlook faced. The biggest challenge was finding clear enough days to photograph and being able to drop everything to make it there under the optimal conditions. I learned that sunny, pretty days were not the same as clear ones—those that would allow me to see 60 miles or more.

In the case of Mt. Mitchell, for instance, an extremely clear day was needed, because every mountain range seen from there is far away. I made almost a dozen forays, only to turn back as I got close and realized it was not clear enough. But perseverance paid off, and I finally did get the perfect day in mid-October one year. With binoculars, I could see the buildings of the Charlotte skyline some 90 miles away! I immediately made a new set of images to replace the working set that I'd shot on a previous trip under less-than-ideal conditions. And so it went for many of the overlooks in this book.

After I selected an overlook and arrived at the right time on a clear day, I set up the camera and began to figure out how to separate the view into two, four, or six slightly overlapping sections. I needed about half of the image to be sky, so that I could fit in the text identifications. I had already determined some of the factors to include with each peak, such as compass headings, elevations, and distance to the feature. I collected several pieces of information—the GPS coordinates from where the photograph was made, compass readings to the main peaks, and identification of anything I might recognize in the view from my years of living and traveling in the area.

Once I had the clearest photo possible, I would make a print back at my studio, sandwich it between sheets of clear acetate, and mark the points I could identify on the top overlay. Later I added these names to the actual photograph by typing in the needed identification text using Adobe Photoshop. Then I drew lines to a specific point or peak. If I found portions that were blank, I would do further investigation to identify something in that area of the image, as well.

The Process of Identification

MAKING THE IDENTIFICATIONS OF THE PEAKS I DIDN'T KNOW, which were most or all of them in the majority of views, was one of the most difficult and confounding tasks. Finding a map that had the information and features I was interested in, along with learning the topographic computer software, with its inherent shortcomings, made it a much more daunting undertaking than I had originally imagined. Initially I thought I could buy a compass, a computer program, a few paper maps, and log onto something like Google Earth and figure out most of what I needed. I soon discovered that no one source of information worked, and that computer views of the earth that didn't allow you to see the horizon line from ground level were not of use. It took a combination of maps, software, personal knowledge, many trips driving to the location, and incredible perseverance to develop the information rendered here.

Let me emphasize the driving around part: I spent a lot of time driving from each overlook to various places in the area in order to take GPS readings and visually confirm features seen from that particular overlook. As with the first view I had tried to identify, the scale of what I was seeing constantly perplexed me. How many miles away was that peak? 5, 10, 20? How far can I actually see? Are those distant ridges separate or one and the same? To keep my sanity, I would have to stop the project from time to time and try again later.

The other big surprise was that most people who lived in the various areas I was exploring were not familiar with what mountain peaks they looked at or hiked around every day. I eventually realized that I had to become the expert in order to complete the project. It took me nearly two years, but I eventually developed a working method and became more confident in my results.

If this is all the information you want before diving into using this book, I suggest you skip ahead to page 4. For those who are as obsessive about detail and process as I am, read on.

For Serious "Have to Know" Folks—Once an overlook was selected and GPS and compass readings recorded, I would find the approximate location on a large-scale map, like the 3D Topographic Raised Relief Map of the Great Smoky Mountains and Knoxville, TN. This would give me an overview of what mountain ranges might be visible from there. These maps, however, were not detailed enough for much more than that. Next, I would find a paper map with a smaller scale, identify the highest peaks that might be visible, and compare those with the photographs from the overlook. Finally, I would open the computer TOPO map and place an anchor point at the GPS coordinates of the viewpoint and another at any peak I could identify. Connecting these two points generated compass headings and line-of-sight distances I could use in the image. From there I would try to fill in the other peaks. I generated 20 to 30 lines in the TOPO program from each location, connecting the overlook to various peaks, and over the course of the project, hundreds were plotted (see photo, page 7).

I began to learn the mountains following an approach similar to the "star hopping" technique I used to teach myself about the night sky. With this method, you start with a known star and find another bright one nearby, using charts to identify it, and branch out from there. But instead of points of light, I used mountain peaks. I would start with a prominent, familiar one, and then figure out what was directly behind or in front of it, or on the opposite end of the same range. As I concentrated on a particular stretch of the Parkway, I could recognize shapes I had already identified from a previous overlook. Although seen from a different orientation, these peaks were now recognizable to me, and I could use my knowledge of them to make new links.

The more mountains I was able to identify, the easier it became to identify new ones from nearby overlooks, but it never became routine. Indeed, in many cases I would have to drive back to the location to double check overlapping ridgelines by looking through binoculars, or I might even drive through the area to be sure I was correctly identifying a particular feature. By branching out a bit at a time, I began to build a map of what I was seeing. All identifications went though many levels of confirmation before I became confident of their validity.

As to maps, each has its strengths and weaknesses, but none had all the information I required. Parkway maps might have a Milepost number for an overlook, but not the name, requiring me to constantly cross-reference other databases. I found that the various paper maps had conflicting information or were missing key facts. There might be a legend on the map covering the spot I was trying to identify, or a location would be in an area not covered well on any map. I found errors on most.

Computer topographic (TOPO) programs were better in many ways, but had their own drawbacks. They seemed to always be the wrong scale for what I needed to study. If I zoomed in at one level, I lost my surrounding orientation, and if I zoomed out to another, the scale was too small to be of use. I always needed to be in between. The 3D features available in some of these programs are useful in identifying points located within a few miles of the vantage point, but are largely useless for medium- and long-range views. And even on the short range, they are very limited, and you quickly move off their coverage as you progress along a line of sight.

The maps I found most useful are detailed in the Resources section in the back of the book (page 118), and include the Detailed Guidemap to the Blue Ridge Parkway and Surrounding Area (series of three), the National Geographic Trails Illustrated Map© series, the DeLorme Atlas & Gazetteer™ for North Carolina and Virginia, and the National Geographic TOPO computer software cited above (discontinued in 2012).

The Blue Ridge Parkway Visitor Center is located at Milepost 384 near Asheville, NC. Open year-round 9 am–5 pm, it houses a 70-seat theater, a ranger-staffed information desk, orientation services, and a retail shop offering books, apparel, CDs, and souvenirs.

The other big surprise was that most people who lived in the areas I was exploring were not familiar with the mountain peaks they looked at every day.

TOP: *The Parkway drops from Waterrock Knob on its way toward the Woolyback overlook. The peaks of the Great Smoky Mountains rise up on the horizon in the distance.*

BOTTOM: *The sun warms a rock outcropping at Grandfather Mountain, located along the Parkway near Boone.*

> What started as a simple idea to satisfy my own curiosity, developed into a five-year project ...

After the image identification elements were completed for each image, I would begin to research the area around the overlook. I gathered information that would expand on the knowledge of what mountains were visible from there. Learning the names of the mountains was just a starting point and would be of little interest if not used to place them in context to their surroundings. This might include where the rivers, lakes, towns, major roadways, and attractions were in relation to them. Having traveled, photographed, and written articles and books about this area for all of my adult life, I had intimate knowledge upon which to draw as well. I also researched notable attractions and places of particular beauty, and highlighted them with smaller photographs to accompany the main panoramic images.

What started as a simple idea, one that would satisfy my own curiosity, developed into a five-year project that required me to drive thousands of miles, spend untold hours at the computer, learn to read and understand topographic maps, figure out how to use a compass and GPS unit, as well as specialized computer software, and took hundreds of hours of research. It has resulted in a comprehensive presentation of what is visible from many of the Parkway's most impressive overlooks, something never done on this scale before. I hope you, the reader, will find this information engaging, enlightening, and easy to comprehend.

How to Use This Book

THIS BOOK IS DESIGNED FOR ALL OF US WHO HAVE THE CHANCE to drive along the Blue Ridge Parkway and stop at the overlooks to enjoy the views. In most cases, you can drive to the exact spot where the photograph was made; no hiking is required. Simply drive to the specified location, turn off your car, open the book, and begin to learn about what you are seeing. A few locations, including Mt. Mitchell, Chimney Rock Park, the Biltmore Estate, and Jump Off Rock, require a short walk to the viewpoint from their parking areas, but these paths are short and easy to access. I have also included a few aerial views to show the depth of the receding mountain ranges and how they relate and conjoin.

While a few locations have signage identifying some aspects of what can be seen from there, the vast majority does not. If you are lucky and the day is clear, it will be easy for you to match up what is labeled in the photograph to the view in front of you. Start by finding distinctive peaks or other features in both the live scene and the photograph and branch out from there. Clouds, haze, foliage, seasonality, and time of day may limit your ability to see what is shown in the photograph.

For convenience, the Blue Ridge Parkway is broken up into four sections, each beginning with a map and an index of the overlooks within that segment, along with their official name, Milepost number, and elevation. For driving reference, most of the Parkway overlooks and attractions are listed. Those highlighted in red are ones featured photographically in the book. The image titles used throughout the book are variations of these official names. Space does not allow for all Parkway overlooks to be photographed, and all views do not warrant such identification. Rather, I have chosen ones that offer especially nice views and are significantly different from overlooks nearby.

I also picked overlooks that offered the clearest vantage point and best angle on the main features. For example, the Richland Balsam overlook is the highest point along the Blue Ridge Parkway, and with signage denoting this unique spot, most visitors stop here. However, the nearby Cowee Mountains overlook offers much more expansive views, with little of the foreground trees that block large sections of the vista from

Richland Balsam. And the Cowee Mountains overlook is close enough to Richland Balsam to allow easy identification of features viewed from there as well. Indeed, the book's coverage is so extensive that views can be used to identify features from an overlook that is nearby, but not included. For example, using the identifications from the Fetterbush and Wolf Mountain overlooks, you can pick out things seen from Devil's Courthouse, as they flank it on either side.

In addition to the overlooks, I've included photographs of several spectacular vistas in western North Carolina that are a short drive from the Parkway. These appear in a separate section that starts on page 105. They are featured because they are popular destinations and offer especially nice views of the mountains through which the Parkway passes. Two of these locations, the Biltmore Estate and Chimney Rock Park, require that you pay admission to their grounds, but they are well worth the price. Both offer spectacular views and are unique destinations in their own right.

Understanding the Labeling

EACH FEATURED VISTA HAS A PANORAMIC PHOTO ACROSS THE top of two (or more) pages (some are only one page), with text included in the sky area denoting points of interest, along with its compass heading, distance, and elevation. The text panel at the bottom of each page lists the overlook name, location information, and a bit about the area surrounding the overlook. A small photo is included to highlight an area attraction or activity. I have included enough information and detail on each page that anyone, from a casual tourist to an avid hiker, can benefit from this guidebook. I have tried to offer enough interesting and useful information, without overwhelming you. Visitors unfamiliar with the area can use the book to learn about where they are and gain some sense of orientation. Those with local knowledge of an area will be able to look at the images, read the text, and trace trails, roads, and rivers they know.

Within each panoramic photograph are three or four text lines. On the top (and occasionally second) line are directional references for NORTH, SOUTH, EAST, and WEST, as well as cities and other points of interest not visible or identified within the image. Many cities and towns are either hidden within the scene or too far in the distance to be visible. All are shown in yellow text, with their compass heading and distance listed in smaller black type below. Their direction is indicated with an "up" (↑) arrow. Note that many cities listed on the top line are actually within the view, but usually hidden, as they were typically built along rivers, or railroad lines that followed riverbeds, located in the valley floors.

If you note the distance to a town or city, and look at mountain peaks along that line of sight and note their distances, many times you can figure out which valley and between what peaks they are located. An interesting fact to remember is that due to the way the mountains of western North Carolina formed, there are no natural lakes. All are manmade, created by damming rivers or ends of valleys, and didn't appear until after 1902, when Lake Toxaway, the first manmade lake in the Southern Appalachians, was built. Therefore, the older towns were not built around lakes.

On the lines below the top, city/directional one, specific mountain peaks and points of interest are shown, in large red type, with the compass heading/distance/elevation in smaller, black, text beneath. From the name, a line is drawn down to the point of interest. Mountains that extend above the horizon in the image have lines ending just above their peak, allowing for a more unbroken horizon line in the photograph, whereas features that overlap have lines directly to them to help avoid confusion. In some cases, a cross line is added to the bottom of the down/vertical lines, which indicates a wider range to a feature, rather than a specific point. These could include a range of mountains, a ridgeline, or the path of a creek, river, or road.

Many times these roads, rivers, and creeks are deep within a valley, obscured by trees or low hills, so a general description of where they are is also included in the accompanying text to enable you to visualize their location and project their path. Locations or features that are located left or right of an image's frame edge may be referenced in the accompanying text as being, "Out of frame, left" or "Out of frame, right" to provide a general sense of where they are relative to the features marked in the photograph.

Fall is an especially popular time for visitation to the Parkway. Thousands of motorists travel its winding route on a daily basis to explore the surrounding natural beauty.

TOP: *As the seasons begin to change in the spring and fall and temperatures swing wildly from night to day, fog can form in the low-lying valleys. Early mornings on these cold days are a great time to be out with your camera.*

BOTTOM: *Cloudy, even stormy, conditions can make for dynamic lighting and create unusual weather phenomenon, offering the opportunity to make stunning photographs.*

Most images span two or four pages. In the case of Mt. Mitchell, there are six pages that form a 360° panorama. In most of the photographs there is a slight overlap, with a common point noted in adjoining panels, allowing you to bridge from one to the next more easily. Below the panoramic photo is the overlook name. If there are more than two photographs from that view, they are identified as (1 of 4), (2 of 4), (3 of 4), etc.

The text section at the bottom of the page begins with basic location information, including the county and state where the overlook is situated, the GPS coordinates where the image was made, the elevation at the viewpoint, and driving directions to the location of the view. These location details are only shown on the first page of any overlook spread. The driving directions usually include a Parkway Milepost number. While the actual stone Milepost markers are located roadside every mile along the entire route of the Parkway as an aid to navigation, the overlooks rarely are located at an exact Milepost. Therefore the Parkways official list indicates their location in tenths of a mile, for instance Milepost 341.8, and these are the figures used in this book.

The text that follows details other aspects of the view as they relate to the points actually marked, including the location of main roads and rivers through the area, notes on local history and geography, information about nearby attractions, and the like. Where applicable, a note at the end of the text may reference another image in the book that offers a reverse view, from another location, back to your current viewpoint. This allows you to see how the mountains around you appear from that perspective.

In analyzing the points of interest identified in each photograph, keep in mind that there are many common names for mountains, creeks, and sections. Mountain names such as Black, Green, Rich, Grassy, Pinnacle, Rocky, Round, Hickorynut, Chestnut, Cedar, Pine, Walnut, Butt, Hogback, Little Bald, and Big Bald are commonplace, their origins based on shape, color, tree population, soil quality, and so forth. So, although you might be familiar with a "Pinnacle" mountain, the one noted in a photograph may not be the one you have in mind. It is not unusual to have something as common as a "Black Mountain" appear in adjoining photos, or even on two nearby ridgelines in the same image.

In getting to know an area, it is good to keep in mind that while a few mountains, like the conically shaped Mt. Pisgah, retain their general outline when seen from a variety of directions, most appear differently when viewed from another vantage point, which can make their identification challenging. As you drive along they may change profile, be obscured by lower hills in the foreground, or overlap with mountains behind.

Navigational Tools: Compass, Map, and GPS

A COMPASS IS A SIMPLE AND HANDY TOOL TO CARRY IN YOUR car or daypack when venturing out. It will also allow you to better utilize this book. The cardinal directions of NORTH (0°), EAST (90°), SOUTH (180°) and WEST (270°) are shown on the top line of text in each photograph to give you a better sense of the direction you are viewing from an overlook. While not noted in the images, it is handy to remember that the intermediate (intercardinal or ordinal) directions are Northeast (45°), Southeast (135°), Southwest (225°), and Northwest (315°).

In trying to establish your orientation in a scene, if you are facing north, then east is at your right shoulder, south is behind you, and west is at your left shoulder. Likewise, if you are facing east toward the morning sun, north is to your left, south is to your right, and west is behind you. When using the photographs and accompanying text to identify a point of interest, if you are looking east from an overlook (which a majority of the nicer Parkway overlooks do), and a point is described as being south of another, then it would be to the right of it in the photo, while a peak that is described as being north, would be to the left.

Remember that for us in the Northern Hemisphere, the sun rises roughly in the east (only due east on the equinoxes) and sets roughly in the west (only due west on the equinoxes), and appears in the south at midday. So if you want a dramatic view from an overlook that faces north, go there in the early morning (light coming from eastern sunrise) or in the late afternoon (light coming from western sunset). If you want a nice sunset view, find an overlook that faces roughly west. Similarly, find one that looks east for a sunrise.

When using compass and map to locate a point of interest, note that all maps have an arrow indicating which way is north. By convention (almost) all are drawn with North at the top. Be sure to understand and be able to calculate the difference between True North and Magnetic North when using a map and compass. There are many types of maps, each with their strengths and weaknesses. Some, like the road atlas, are useful when you need to see an overview of the entire state on one page, for instance. They are great for cross-country travel because they offer a lot of information in one large, but manageable book. However, if you plan to visit a smaller section within a particular state, a more detailed road map would be more appropriate, as it provides enough information for the casual traveler to traverse an area from one town to the next. Maps that cover the Blue Ridge Parkway, for example, show towns located adjacent to its route, as well as major and minor thoroughfares that intersect, in case you need to exit for gas or a meal.

Topo maps—However, if you are more interested in seeing the contours and elevation changes of the mountains, along with trails, creeks, and rivers surrounding a particular overlook, choose a more detailed, topographic map. They provide a level of detail, scale, 3-dimensionality, and accuracy not offered by other types of maps, making them the most popular with hikers and backpackers. The tradeoff is that they are generally large and only show a limited area, requiring that numerous maps might be needed to cover a planned route of just a few miles. All of these kinds of maps were used in the making of this book, with the topographic being the most useful. The computer versions that allow you to zoom from one scale to another combine the best features of each type map, but require a computer, so are best for home use.

Note that signs on the Parkway only list locations as North or South, even though they may actually be east or west of you by compass heading, due to the circuitous routes of the

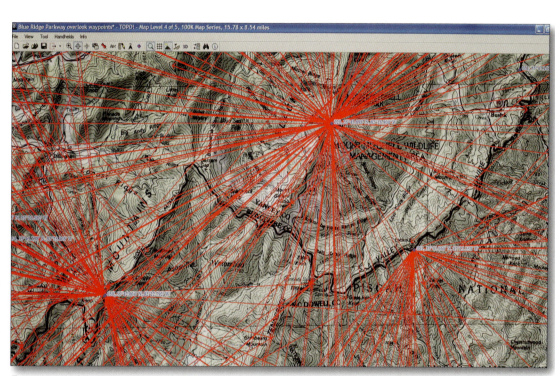

To generate the information used in the images, hundreds of points were plotted and connected. First an anchor point was placed on the map at the overlook or viewpoint, based on the GPS coordinates taken from there. Lines were then plotted, connecting it to the mountain peaks and points of interest visible from the location. Once created they provided distance and compass headings for the identifications used throughout the book.

roads. The north end of the Parkway is at Milepost 0, near Waynesboro, VA, while the south end is at Milepost 469.1, where it meets Highway 441 in the Great Smoky Mountains National Park. To keep things simple, these north-south directions are used in this book, so if the text mentions that something is south on the Parkway from an overlook, you are heading generally toward its terminus, even though you may actually be driving west if you were to take a compass heading. This is especially true on the section between Devil's Courthouse (about Milepost 422) and Highway 441, because the Parkway swings sharply to the west from its general north/south orientation.

When photographing, telephoto lenses bring objects closer and allow you to isolate and concentrate on elements within the overall environment, as with these details of dogwood trees in bloom.

... allow plenty of time to reach your destination so you can enjoy the drive and the spectacular views detailed in this book.

Understanding GPS—If you are using a GPS unit to calculate your location, it might be useful to understand a bit about how they work. GPS stands for Global Positioning System, an array of 24 satellites (plus spares), each orbiting the Earth twice a day, and set up in a pattern so that at least four are available in the sky overhead at any one time. Originally developed by the United States military, the satellites were placed in orbit by the United States Department of Defense. In the 1980s, they were made available for civilian use, and today receiver units are commonplace in many cars and even cell phones.

To produce useful information, these passive terrestrial GPS units receive signals sent by the solar-powered satellites. Orbiting the earth at about 12,000 miles, they are timed so that at least four are accessible overhead from any one spot at a time. By comparing the time the signal was transmitted from each of multiple satellites to the time it was received, the GPS unit can calculate longitude, latitude, and altitude (elevation) for its location and display that location on an electronic map. The receiver can also show these coordinates numerically, as longitude and latitude.

Longitude (think of parallel horizontal lines around the Earth, at an equal distance from each other) expresses how many degrees (°), minutes ('), and seconds (") north or south of the equator (0°) a place is located. Latitude (visualize vertical lines curving around the Earth) is the degrees east or west of Greenwich, England (0°). The latitude lines extend 180° east and 180° west of Greenwich, meeting in the Pacific Ocean to form the International Date Line. Each degree of longitude or latitude is roughly 69 miles apart. There are 60 minutes in a degree and 60 seconds in a minute. The readings for Asheville, NC, are 35° 36' 3" N (Latitude) and 82° 33' 15" W (Longitude). This means the city is located about 35 degrees, 36 minutes, and 3 seconds north of the equator and 82 degrees, 33 minutes, and 15 seconds west of the longitude line (also known as the prime meridian) running through Greenwich, England.

Conventions Used in This Book

FOR CONVENIENCE AND TO REDUCE REPEATING IT CONSTANTLY, the Blue Ridge Parkway is most often referred to simply as the "Parkway" throughout the book. Abbreviations used in the photographs include, "Mtn" for "mountain" (as in Black Mtn), "Mt." for "Mount" (as in Mt. Pisgah), and "Hwy" for "Highway." All compass headings, mileage distances, GPS coordinates, and mountain elevations used are close approximations. Compass headings and distances were generated from computer mapping software. The compass headings, therefore, are much more accurate than what can be shown on a compass dial, so are rounded to the nearest degree. Distances are rounded to the nearest mile, unless the feature is less than five miles from the viewpoint, in which case they are rounded to tenths of a mile. Multiply feet by .3048 to convert to meters (example 6,000 feet equals 1828.8 meters). A feet-to-meters conversion table is included in the Resources section in the back of the book (page 119) for those more comfortable with the metric system.

GPS coordinates for the viewpoints are close approximations, limited by the accuracy of the unit used for measurement—in this case a typical portable car-mounted one made by Garmin. Used in conjunction with the Parkway Milepost number, you should have no problem locating a featured overlook. Be aware that some of the wooden signs bearing the overlook name are missing due to theft.

One of the most vexing problems in collecting information for the book was to find a reliable, official, source for elevations. The elevations given for each overlook are from the Blue Ridge Parkways' own official list, used by the National Park Service in creating area signage and printed material, rather than from a GPS reading. Elevations for the actual peaks shown within the photograph were generated from a different source, the Geographical Names Information System (GNIS) website (see Resources page), administered by the United States Geological Survey. As it was not uncommon to find five different elevations listed for a particular peak depending on which map, computer program, website, sign, or book I referenced, I realized that I needed one source that had all the peaks in its database. As the point of showing such information is to be able to compare peaks relative to each other, I used the GNIS figures, even though these differed from other "official" signage, maps, and printed information.

As multiple entries would show up in this database if a name were fairly common, such as Big Bald, I made sure that the GPS coordinates and county matched up with the particular peak I was searching. A master list was also created so that I could keep track of the figures and be consistent in their use when a peak appeared in multiple images, such as Celo Knob in the Black Mountains.

Travel Tips—Although I designed this book to be used without other aids, I suggest you carry some additional items. For example, even though maps are included at the beginning of each segment in the book, others are also beneficial. There is a great series of three, Detailed Guidemap to the Blue Ridge Parkway and Surrounding Area, in which the Parkway is separated into the Northern Section—Milepost 0–123; Central Section—Milepost 106–269; and Southern Section—Milepost 269–469.1. Together they detail its route through the mountains of Virginia and North Carolina. These maps are commonly sold in outfitting stores and Parkway shops.

Be sure your maps have the level of detail needed to safely complete your journey. If your trip includes hiking plans, choose a more detailed trail map with topographic features. I also highly recommend using a GPS unit. However, they offer limited functionality along some sections of the Parkway, and there are many ways a GPS unit can lead you astray. But used in conjunction with a good local map, it can ensure that you arrive safely and on time at your planned destination. Keep in mind that the GPS coordinates listed with each viewpoint in the book may not be the exact reading your unit displays for that location, because all types of models vary in their accuracy.

Even if your plans do not include leaving the pavement of the Parkway overlooks, it's always prudent to carry bug spray, sunscreen, polarizing sunglasses, flashlight, and a broad brimmed hat for standing in the sun. You might take along a folding chair or a blanket to sit on to enjoy the view, watch a sunset, or eat a picnic lunch, if tables are not available (always pack out your trash). And don't forget your rain gear and a jacket. While it may be balmy and clear when you leave home, it can easily cloud over as storms pop up, especially in the warmer months, and it will get three degrees cooler, on average, for each 1,000 feet you gain in elevation.

Also pack a few of your favorite guidebooks for hiking, plant identification, and the like, along with pen and paper. A pair of binoculars, 7 x 35 or similar, would allow you to study distant features of the landscape, as well as enjoy a detailed view of a colorful bird, or wildflowers growing on a high ledge, and don't forget a camera to record your discoveries. A magnifying glass (with light) makes map reading much easier, and a small ruler can aid you in figuring distances using the maps legend. A waterproof map pouch is also handy when hiking the damp, rain-prone mountains of the area.

Be sure to fill your car's gas tank before hitting the road because there are no stations along the entire length of the Parkway; you must exit to neighboring towns to refill your tank. Don't forget some snacks, water bottle, and a small cooler; stores are few and far between, especially along the North Carolina section. The most important point is to allow plenty of time to reach your destination so you can enjoy the drive and the spectacular views detailed in this book. With a 45 mph maximum speed limit, and slow vehicles common (with few turnouts), the Parkway is not the quickest way to get from one town to the next, but it is certainly the most beautiful!

Note About Parkway Closures—It's a good idea to check the status of any facilities you will need before traveling the Parkway because visitor centers, campgrounds, and picnic areas may be temporarily closed due to government spending changes each year, as well as changes in vendors who operate other facilities.

TOP: *Trees frame this view of the fog-laden valley as seen from the Chestnut Cove overlook, located on the Parkway between Asheville, NC, and Mt. Pisgah.*

BOTTOM: *Late afternoon light reveals the textures of the landscape, including the signature fences along the Doughton Park section of the Parkway.*

TOP: *The Blue Ridge Parkway runs 469 miles along the crest of the mountains from Waynesboro, Virginia, to Highway 441 near Cherokee in the Great Smoky Mountains of North Carolina.*

BOTTOM: *Construction began in 1935 at Cumberland Knob near the NC/VA line, with the idea of connecting the Skyline Drive in the Shenandoah National Park (Virginia) to the Great Smoky Mountains National Park. While private contractors did much of the construction, a variety of New Deal public works programs were also employed, including the Works Progress Administration (WPA), the Civilian Conservation Corps (CCC), and the Emergency Relief Administration (ERA). (Historical photos provided by the NC Division of Archives and History).*

The Blue Ridge Parkway

The Blue Ridge Parkway is a spectacular skyline road, 469 miles long, most of it located along the crest of the Blue Ridge, a mountain chain that is part of the Appalachian Mountains. The Parkway winds its way through 17 North Carolina and 12 Virginia counties, numerous communities, and countless different southern Appalachian landscapes. It links the Shenandoah National Park in Virginia and the Great Smoky Mountains National Park in North Carolina and Tennessee, averaging about 3,000 feet in elevation, and occasionally descending into the coves and hollows. From Milepost 0 at Rockfish Gap, Virginia, the road travels to Milepost 355 near Mt. Mitchell State Park in North Carolina. The summit of Mt. Mitchell, at an elevation of 6,684 feet, is the highest point east of the Mississippi. From there, the Parkway travels westward through the Black Mountains, and into the Craggies, before dropping down to Asheville. The Parkway then climbs to elevations over 6,000 feet in the Balsam Mountains, crossing Richland Balsam—the highest point on the Parkway at 6,047 feet—before entering the Great Smoky Mountains National Park near Cherokee.

Often referred to as "America's most scenic highway," the Parkway offers motorized travelers unparalleled access to the southern Appalachians, inviting them to ride for a while, pull off onto one of the hundreds of overlooks to take in the view, stop to picnic or hike, and visit area attractions.

The Parkway, although not a "national park," is the most visited unit of the National Park System, welcoming more than 20 million visitors in 2012. The manicured, noncommercial land on both sides of the road is owned and maintained by the National Park Service and, in many places Parkway land is bordered by United States Forest Service property.

Conceived and executed in the 1930s, the Parkway's construction provided much needed work during the Great Depression. The road was built in sections, took decades, and employed thousands. By World War II, about half of the Parkway was completed, and by the 1960s, all but one section was opened to the public. The Linn Cove Viaduct, a 1,243-foot concrete segmental bridge that winds around the slopes of Grandfather Mountain in North Carolina, was the last section of the Parkway to be finished in 1987. The recent completion of the Parkway's main visitor center in Asheville, North Carolina, and the Blue Ridge Music Center near the Virginia/North Carolina state line is evidence that the Parkway experience continues to expand.

The Origins of the Parkway

The "seeds" of the Blue Ridge Parkway were planted in North Carolina as early as 1919 by farmers, state politicians, and resort developers, who shared the common goal of building reliable, hard-surface roads to boost the economy through the expansion of markets, new business opportunities, and tourism. Advocating for good roads was in fact a national pastime, spurred by the impressive sales of cars and the growth of tourism. The expansion of the national park system between 1916 and World War II was fueled by the desire of Americans to "see the U.S.A. in their Chevrolet."

By the 1930s, when the green light was given to begin building the Parkway, planners benefitted from the example and experience of municipal, regional, and state park development, along with a decade of road building in national parks, including neighboring Great Smoky Mountains National Park. As a result of these endeavors, a clearly American "rustic" design sensibility was defined and brilliantly executed in the Blue Ridge Parkway.

Who Built It?

Originally called the Appalachian Scenic Highway, Parkway construction began on September 11, 1935, during the administration of U.S. President Franklin D. Roosevelt. In 1936, Congress formally called the project the Blue Ridge Parkway and placed it under the jurisdiction of the National Park Service. Private contractors did most of the construction under federal contracts. Italian and Spanish immigrant stonemasons contributed their skills. The Works Progress Administration (WPA) built some of the roadways. Crews from the Emergency Relief Administration handled landscape work and the development of parkway recreation areas. Personnel from several Civilian Conservation Corps (CCC) camps

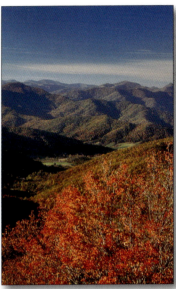

TOP: *The Parkway offers many spectacular views, like this one looking over Hominy Valley near Mt. Pisgah*

BOTTOM: *Late afternoon light adds to the warm fall colors in the Doughton Park area along the Parkway.*

Often referred to as "America's most scenic highway"

The ridgeline, dressed in fall foliage, drops from the Parkway to the valley floor along the section of road between Asheville and Mt. Pisgah.

Construction began on September 11, 1935, during the administration of U.S. President Franklin D. Roosevelt.

worked on roadside cleanup and plantings, grading slopes, and improving adjacent fields and forest lands.

The WPA and the CCC were programs under the New Deal of President Roosevelt, which from 1933 to 1943, employed millions of unemployed people in manual labor jobs related to public works, and to the conservation and development of natural resources in rural lands owned by federal, state, and local governments. The CCC hired unemployed and unmarried men, ages 18 to 25, for no longer than 18 months. His family had to be receiving some form of government financial assistance. Each enrollee earned a monthly salary of $30, of which $25 was sent home to his family to help buy food, clothing, and fuel. The enrollee kept the remaining $5 to use as he chose. In each camp, about 150 men, called enrollees, lived in barracks, and received food, clothing, medical care, and educational and recreational opportunities.

Impact on Local Communities

IN GENERAL, THE PARKWAY IMPROVED THE LIVES OF THE people who lived near the scenic highway, either by directly offering employment in the building of the road, or by attracting visitors to new local businesses that cropped up in the 29 counties through which the Parkway passes. However, some farmers and other landowners were negatively affected. Then as now, politics favored some; others felt slighted. There are a number of excellent books that explore the complicated and fascinating history of the early days of the Parkway and how its conception and construction impacted local people and communities. The story of how North Carolina won out over Tennessee is filled with intrigue!

Making Mountains

THE APPALACHIAN MOUNTAINS ARE VERY OLD: MOST OF the rocks that form the Blue Ridge are ancient granitic charnockites, metamorphosed volcanic formations, and sedimentary limestone, some of which are over one billion years in age. Recent studies suggest that the Blue Ridge basement is a composite orogenic crust that was created during several episodes from a crustal magma source.

The Blue Ridge Mountains began forming during the Silurian Period over 400 million years ago, when the motion of the crustal plates changed, and the continents began to move toward each other. Then, about 270 million years ago, the continents ancestral to North America and Africa collided. Huge masses of rock were pushed westward along the margin of North America and piled up to form the Appalachians. In their prime, the Appalachians were as high as the present-day Rocky Mountains, but over millions of years, erosion has carved them down, and only their cores are standing. Erosion is ongoing, and continues to change the landscape of the Southern Appalachians.

Geology, Ecology & History

THE FLORA AND FAUNA ALONG THE PARKWAY HAVE BEEN determined, in large part, by the geological history of the Appalachians. With an elevation range of 5,700 feet, the Parkway provides a home for both southern species at the lower elevations and northern species on the mountaintops. In fact, the 469-mile road features an amazing diversity of climate, vegetation, and physiographic zones. For instance, the eastern edge of the Blue Ridge is consistently more rugged and steep than the western edge due to the direction of uplift during the creation of the mountains. Because of this, the eastern slopes of the Blue Ridge have more rugged river drainage, examples of which are Linville Gorge (Milepost 316) and Rockcastle Gorge (Milepost 169).

Among the features of the more than 81,000 acres of Parkway lands are 600 streams (150 headwaters), 47 Natural Heritage Areas (protected as national, regional, or state examples of exemplary natural communities), a variety of slopes and exposures, and possibly 100 different soil types. As a result of this diversity, the Parkway supports 14 major vegetation types, about 1,600 vascular plant species (50 threatened or endangered), and nearly 100 species of non-native plants. More than 130 species of trees grow along the Parkway, about as many as are found in all of Europe. In fact, The Blue Ridge Mountains are blue because of all the trees: they release isoprene, a common organic compound in plant life, which contributes to the characteristic haze on the mountains and their distinctive color. In addition to the trees, about 400 species of mosses and nearly 2,000 species of fungi thrive in the varied eco-zones the Parkway offers.

Many types of animals live along the Parkway, too, including 74 different mammals, more than 50 salamanders, and 35 reptiles. Experts have identified 159 species of birds that nest here, and dozens of others that pass through during fall and spring migrations.

The Parkway's vast range of vegetative life, gorgeous seasonal floral displays, colorful autumn foliage, geological features, and wildlife are the main attractions of this popular scenic highway.

This amazing road also provides a cross-section of Appalachian mountain life, and features some of the oldest settlements of both pre-historic and early European settlement. See Resources on page 118 for a listing of the Parkway's historic and cultural attractions, including sites where you can enjoy the music and handcrafts of the regions you want to visit. This information and much more is available at *www.blueridgeparkway.org*.

Traveling the Parkway

YOU WILL NEED TO GAS UP YOUR CAR OR MOTORCYCLE BEFORE you get on the Parkway because you won't be able to "fill-er up" once you begin your journey. If you plan your trip with this in mind, you can build in gas stops at local communities off the Parkway, and shop or dine out there—all part of the Blue Ridge Mountains experience. Enjoying this scenic road includes visiting the towns and cities of the region.

At 45 miles an hour, the Parkway's maximun posted and enforced speed limit, you could drive the entire road in 11 hours. However, Parkway planners graced the route with countless overlooks to encourage travelers to stop often to enjoy the mountain views. Whether you're driving a car or a motorcycle, don't exceed the speed limit, and don't expect to average more than 35 mph; surprising changes in weather, sudden and remarkable curves, people riding bicycles, as well as hikers, deer, and wild turkeys crossing the road require you to pay attention and drive carefully. With so much beauty everywhere, don't forget to watch the road if you're behind the wheel. Many folks ride motorcycles on the Parkway, so be particularly attentive to their safety. There aren't very many straightaways that allow safe passing of slower vehicles—and the Parkway is a magnet for large and slow-moving RVs. You will need to be patient. And if you fall into the slow-moving category, follow good Parkway etiquette and pull over at one of the overlooks or other pullouts to permit others to pass you. The only vehicles not allowed on the Parkway are commercial ones.

The Parkway is the slowest way to get from point A to point B—that's the whole point! If you're in a hurry to

The 469-mile road features an amazing diversity of climate, vegetation, and physiographic zones.

ABOVE: *A car rounds a bend in the Parkway near Graveyard Fields. Clouds fill the valleys between mountain ridges in the distance beyond.*

LEFT: *The upper waterfall at Graveyard Fields, accessed from a trailhead at the parking overlook, is a popular hiking destination.*

Catawba Rhododendron bloom profusely along sections of the Parkway starting in mid-June.

... the route feels timeless... blessed with the beauty and abundance of the natural world.

reach a desired destination that is 50 miles away as the crow flies, you're better off on an interstate. There are entrances and exits to the Parkway at all major federal and state highways. Asheville and Boone, North Carolina, and Roanoke, Virginia, are the largest cities on the route. The Parkway can be accessed in Virginia from Interstates 64, 81, and 77. In general, the Parkway runs northeast to southwest. The same is true for Interstate 81 in Virginia. In the U.S., east-west highways are even-numbered, while the north-south ones are odd-numbered.

When the spectacular autumn leaf season comes to an end and winter arrives, most Parkway facilities close—especially in high elevations—and reopen in the spring. In general, the road is open for travel unless snow and ice make conditions dangerous. You can check out road closures on the Parkway's website (*www.nps.gov/blri/planyourvisit/roadclosures.htm*).

Because of changes in elevation, you can't know for sure what the temperature and weather is going to be when you leave town and head up into the mountains. It becomes 3 degrees cooler for every 1,000 feet gain in elevation. It's smart to pack an extra jacket, raincoat, a blanket, tissues, water, and a few emergency supplies in the car.

Parkway Facilities

THERE IS NO FEE TO TRAVEL ON THE BLUE RIDGE PARKWAY. There are several developed sites along the route that offer food, lodging, information, restrooms, hiking, and interpretation from May to October. Only three Parkway facilities are open year round: Museum of North Carolina Minerals, near Spruce Pine, NC (Milepost 331), Folk Art Center, near Asheville, NC (Milepost 382), and Parkway Visitor Center, near Asheville, NC (Milepost 384).

Campgrounds charge a per night fee, and include access to drinking water, RV dump stations, and restrooms. For a listing of Parkway lodging, restaurants, and camping sites, visit *www.blueridgeparkway.org*.

The Parkway features more than a dozen formal picnic areas and lots of tables at overlooks. Take advantage of these areas to enjoy a picnic lunch, but please pick up after yourself. Dispose of your trash in the animal-proof receptacles available on site, or keep your trash in the car until you can dispose of it appropriately.

How This Section Is Organized

THIS SECTION OFFERS PANORAMIC VIEWS FROM MORE THAN 40 of the overlooks along the Parkway.

For ease of reference, the overlooks are divided into four sections. Section One begins with the Afton overlook at Milepost 0.2 near Waynesboro, VA, and runs to the North Carolina-Virginia state line. Section Two starts with the Fox Hunter's Paradise overlook at Milepost 218.6 near the state line, and runs to Three Knobs overlook at Milepost 338.8. Section Three picks up at the Crabtree Falls area, located at Milepost 339.5, and ends at Shining Rock near Log Hollow overlook at Milepost 416.3, a 77-mile stretch that includes Mt. Mitchell, the highest point in eastern America. While Mt. Mitchell State Park is not part of the Parkway, it can only be accessed by car from it, so is included in this part of the book. Section Four resumes at the Looking Glass Rock overlook, Milepost 417, and travels about 50 miles to the southern terminus of the Parkway, its intersection with Highway 441 in the Great Smoky Mountains National Park. A separate section (page 105) located after the four Parkway segments, features viewpoints throughout western North Carolina that are a short drive from the Parkway or offer views of the mountains through which the Parkway traverses.

Featured overlooks—those with photographs and accompanying identifications and descriptions—are shown in red type in each index. And while many Parkway overlooks offer limited or no views, most of the named overlooks are listed in black type for reference. Many times you can use the identified views to locate points of interest at nearby locations that are not featured; for instance, the vista from the top of Devil's Courthouse is similar to that from the Wolf Mountain overlook, located just to its north.

The Future of the Parkway

AS AMERICA'S SCENIC HIGHWAY LOOKS FORWARD TO ITS 80th birthday in 2015, this national treasure faces challenges. The National Park Service has experienced considerable staff cutbacks and government spending cuts since 2001, leaving some Parkway facilities temporarily closed. The more than 300 overlooks, 100 historical and cultural sites, and 350 miles of trails all require maintenance and upkeep. Some of the scenic vistas are being compromised by encroaching development. In fact, as you travel the Parkway, you'll see real estate developments here and there because the road does not provide a visual buffer, especially in Virginia. But, in general, the route feels timeless and untouched by contemporary life... blessed with the beauty and abundance of the natural world. And this is no accident: many, many volunteers work hard to protect the road and its gifts. Their help is vital to ensure a healthy and sustainable future. Two organizations welcome your participation: FRIENDS of the Blue Ridge Parkway and the Blue Ridge Parkway Foundation.

FRIENDS is a non-profit membership organization founded in 1988. The group provides major support to the park's Volunteers in Parks program, who assist with a wide variety of Parkway projects. Visit *www.blueridgefriends.org* for more information.

The non-profit FOUNDATION, founded in 1997, is the primary fundraising organization for the Blue Ridge Parkway, providing private funding to the Parkway. The FOUNDATION solicits donations and bequests from individuals, as well as grants and corporate support for a broad range of programs and activities. However, the funds don't support maintenance, but focus on projects and programs that add a margin of excellence to the park's mission, enhance the visitor's experience, and have a lasting value. See *www.brpfoundation.org* for details.

ABOVE: *A couple enjoys the view from an overlook near Mt. Pisgah.*

LEFT: *Fog shrouds a roadside waterfall. There are many such falls a short drive from the Parkway especially in Transylvania, Haywood, and Jackson Counties in North Carolina.*

Parkway planners graced the route with countless overlooks to encourage travelers to stop often to enjoy the mountain views.

Blue Ridge Parkway overlooks

Afton parking overlook—Milepost 0.2 | Elev. 2054

Rockfish Valley overlook—Milepost 1.5 | Elev. 2148 18

    Shenandoah Valley overlook—Milepost 2.9 | Elev. 2354

    Humpback Gap—Milepost 5.8 | Elev. 2353

    Greenstone overlook—Milepost 8.8 | Elev. 3007

    Rock Point parking overlook—Milepost 10.4 | Elev. 3113

Raven's Roost parking overlook—Milepost 10.7 | Elev. 3200 20

    The Priest overlook—Milepost 17.6 | Elev. 2695

    20-Minute Cliff overlook—Milepost 19 | Elev. 2715

    Fork Mountain overlook—Milepost 23 | Elev. 3294

    Big Spy overlook—Milepost 26.4 | Elev. 3185

    Chimney Rock widening—Milepost 44.9 | Elev. 2485

    Buena Vista overlook—Milepost 45.7

    House Mountain overlook—Milepost 49.3 | Elev. 2498

    Bluff Mountain overlook—Milepost 52.8 | Elev. 1850

    Upper Otter Creek overlook—Milepost 57.6 | Elev. 1085

    Otter Creek overlook—Milepost 59.7 | Elev. 885

    Terrapin Hill overlook—Milepost 61.4

    Otter Lake overlook—Milepost 63.1 | Elev. 655

    James River overlook & Visitor Center—Milepost 63.6 | Elev. 668

    Terrapin Mountain—Milepost 72.6 | Elev. 2885

    Arnold Valley (north)—Milepost 75.2 | Elev. 3510

    Arnold Valley (south)—Milepost 75.3 | Elev. 3700

    Sunset Field overlook—Milepost 78.4 | Elev. 3472

    Onion Mountain overlook—Milepost 79.7 | Elev. 3145

    Falling Cascades—Milepost 83.1 | Elev. 2557

    Peaks of Otter Visitor Center—Milepost 86

    Upper Goose Creek overlook—Milepost 89.4 | Elev. 1925

    Mills Gap—Milepost 91.8 | Elev. 2435

Purgatory Mountain overlook—Milepost 92.1 | Elev. 2400 22

    Sharp Top—Milepost 92.5 | Elev. 2415

SECTION ONE
Milepost 0 in Virginia to the NC/VA State Line, Milepost 216.9

    Pine Tree overlook—Milepost 95.2 | Elev. 2490
    Harvey's Knob overlook—Milepost 95.3 | Elev. 2524
    Montvale overlook—Milepost 95.9 | Elev. 2441
    Iron Mine Hollow (north)—Milepost 96.2 | Elev. 2364
    The Quarry overlook—Milepost 100.9 | Elev. 2170
    Stewart's Knob overlook—Milepost 110.6 | Elev. 1365
    Roanoke River parking area—Milepost 114.9 | Elev. 985
    Virginia's Explore Park & Visitor Center—Milepost 115
    Pine Mountain—Milepost 115.1 | Elev. 1002

Mill Mountain Spur Road off Parkway—Milepost 120.5
    (includes View from Roanoke Mtn. and Mill Mtn. overlooks) 24
    Buck Mountain overlook—Milepost 123.2 | Elev. 1465
    Poages Mill overlook—Milepost 129.3 | Elev. 2035
    Lost Mountain overlook—Milepost 129.9 | Elev. 2200
    Slings Gap overlook—Milepost 132.9 | Elev. 2817
    Poor Mountain overlook—Milepost 134.9 | Elev. 2975

Cahas Knob overlook—Milepost 139 | Elev. 3013 26
    Devils Backbone overlook—Milepost 143.9 | Elev. 2687
    Pine Spur overlook—Milepost 144.8 | Elev. 2703
    Smart View—Milepost 154.5
    Rakes Mill Pond overlook—Milepost 162.4 | Elev. 2477

Saddle parking overlook—Milepost 168 | Elev. 3351 27
    Rocky Knob—Milepost 168.2 | Elev. 3572
    Rock Castle Gorge overlook—Milepost 168.8 | Elev. 3195
    Rocky Knob Visitor Center—Milepost 169
    Mabry Mill—Milepost 176.2 | Elev. 2855
    Groundhog Mountain picnic area—Milepost 188.8 | Elev. 3025
    Puckett Cabin—Milepost 189.9 | Elev. 2848
    Fancy Gap—Milepost 199.4 | Elev. 2925
    Blue Ridge Music Center—Milepost 213.3
    North Carolina/Virginia State Line—Milepost 216.9

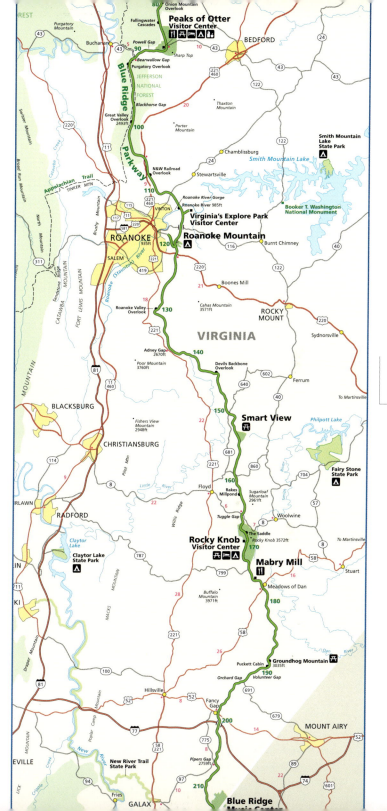

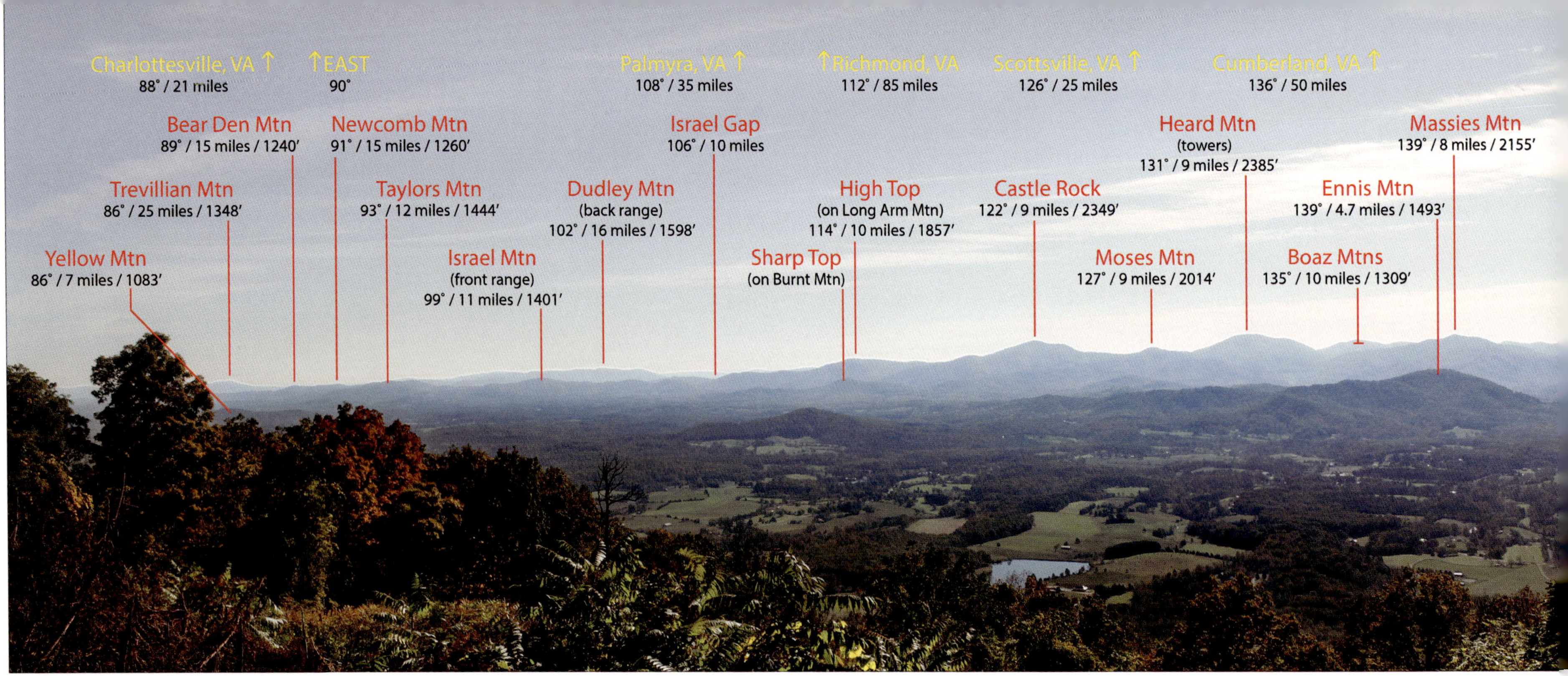

Panorama labels (left to right):

- Charlottesville, VA ↑ — 88° / 21 miles
- ↑EAST — 90°
- Palmyra, VA ↑ — 108° / 35 miles
- ↑Richmond, VA — 112° / 85 miles
- Scottsville, VA ↑ — 126° / 25 miles
- Cumberland, VA ↑ — 136° / 50 miles
- Bear Den Mtn — 89° / 15 miles / 1240'
- Newcomb Mtn — 91° / 15 miles / 1260'
- Israel Gap — 106° / 10 miles
- Heard Mtn (towers) — 131° / 9 miles / 2385'
- Massies Mtn — 139° / 8 miles / 2155'
- Trevillian Mtn — 86° / 25 miles / 1348'
- Taylors Mtn — 93° / 12 miles / 1444'
- Dudley Mtn (back range) — 102° / 16 miles / 1598'
- High Top (on Long Arm Mtn) — 114° / 10 miles / 1857'
- Castle Rock — 122° / 9 miles / 2349'
- Ennis Mtn — 139° / 4.7 miles / 1493'
- Yellow Mtn — 86° / 7 miles / 1083'
- Israel Mtn (front range) — 99° / 11 miles / 1401'
- Sharp Top (on Burnt Mtn)
- Moses Mtn — 127° / 9 miles / 2014'
- Boaz Mtns — 135° / 10 miles / 1309'

MILEPOST 1.5 — Rockfish Valley overlook

County, State: Nelson County, VA
GPS Coordinates: N 38° 01.159 x W 078° 52.195
Elevation at Viewpoint: 2,148 ft
Location: Located at Milepost 1.5 on the Blue Ridge Parkway, just south of its juncture with the Skyline Drive, near Waynesboro, VA.

THE BLUE RIDGE PARKWAY STARTS JUST OUTSIDE Waynesboro, VA, at the intersection of Highways 64, 250, and the Skyline Drive. There are milepost markers along the entire length of the Parkway, located on the west (right) side as you drive south toward its terminus at Highway 441 in the Great Smoky Mountains National Park (Milepost 469.1) near Cherokee, NC.

Highways 64 and 250 run parallel from Staunton, VA, to the northwest, through Waynesboro (behind overlook), to meet the Parkway at its beginnings at Rockfish Gap, then continue east (passing just left of Bear Den Mountain), to Charlottesville (located at the foreground base of Trevillian Mountain), and on to Richmond.

The Skyline Drive, also delineated by milepost markers, runs 105 miles north/south along the crest of the Blue Ridge Mountains, through the Shenandoah National Park, from Front Royal, VA, (Milepost 0) to end at Rockfish Gap (Milepost 105), located just north of this overlook, where the Parkway begins. Its 75 overlooks are similar to the Parkway's, and offer views of the Shenandoah Valley to the west and the Piedmont to the east.

The Appalachian Trail (AT) is intertwined with the Skyline Drive from Rockfish Gap to Front Royal, separating just south of town before continuing north. This renowned hiking trail stretches from Springer Mountain in north Georgia to Mount Katahdin, Maine, crossing 14 states and five national parks, mostly through wilderness areas, on its 2,181-mile path. From Rockfish Gap, the AT passes just below this overlook and across Humpback Mountain, paralleling the Parkway south to Roanoke, VA, where it bears away to the southwest.

Interstate 81, the main north-south thoroughfare through western Virginia, parallels both, but runs further to the west, from Abingdon, near the North Carolina border, to Marion, Wytheville, Radford, Roanoke, Lexington, Staunton, Harrisonburg, and Winchester, before entering West Virginia.

At this, the second Parkway overlook, you are viewing southeast over Nelson and Albemarle Counties. Highway 29 travels behind Heard Mountain and Castle Rock, running from Lynchburg to Charlottesville. Highway 6 from Richmond runs from Highway 29 through the valley to the right of Pilot Mountain and into Rockfish Valley in the foreground. Highway 6 is intersected by Highway 151 (running from the south), in front of Pilot Mountain.

The headwaters of the North Fork of the

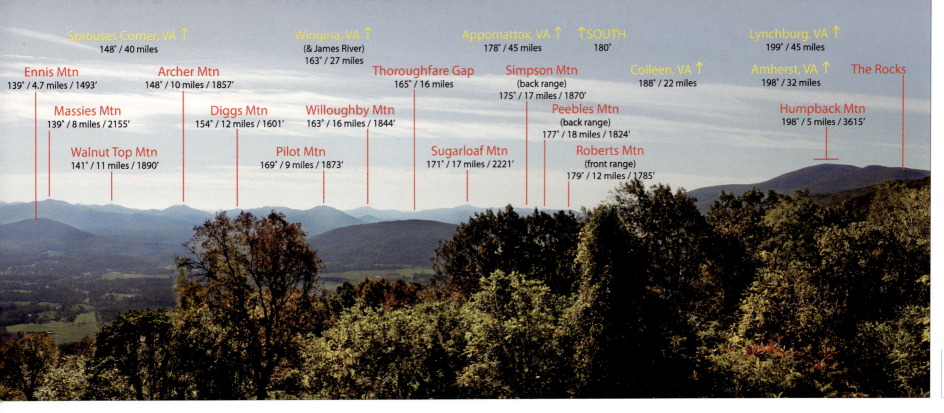

Rockfish River start near the Parkway a few miles south of this overlook and flow along the foreground base of Humpback Mountain. The South Fork, which also forms along the Parkway (but beyond Humpback), joins the North Fork in the valley between Humpback and Pilot Mountain.

From their junction, the Rockfish flows southeast to join the James River. This major waterway forms in the mountains of Virginia further to the west, and crosses under the Parkway to the south, at the James River Visitor Center, before continuing through Richmond to the coast, where it empties into the Chesapeake Bay near Norfolk.

Just south of the overlook is the Humpback Rocks Visitor Center (Milepost 5.8), which has restrooms, a ranger-staffed information desk, a gift shop, interpretive exhibits, a small museum, and a collection of 19th-century farm buildings. A picnic area is located just south of the visitor center on the Parkway.

ABOVE: *Monticello, located in nearby Charlottesville, VA, was the home of Thomas Jefferson, who drafted the Declaration of Independence and was the third president of the United States. It is open to visitors year round, except for Christmas day.*

RIGHT: *The William Carter farm at the Humpback Rocks Visitor Center, includes an authentic replacement cabin, along with numerous outbuildings, situated along a path from the parking lot near the stone visitor center.*

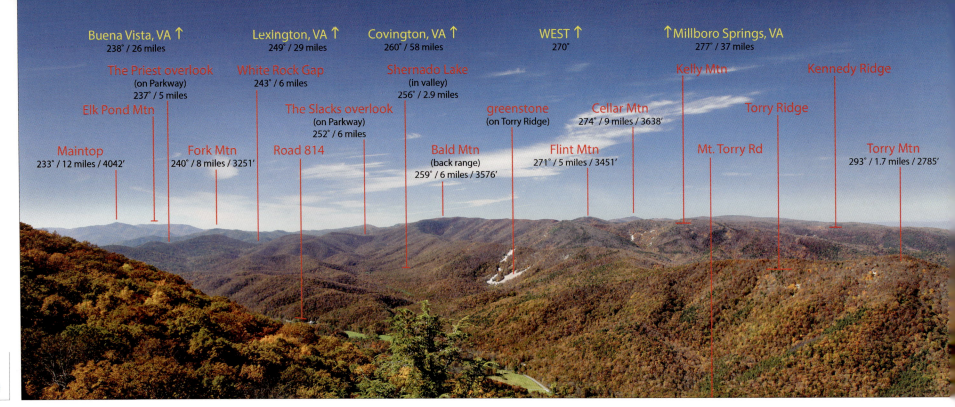

MILEPOST 10.7 Raven's Roost overlook

County, State: On the Augusta/Nelson County line, VA
GPS Coordinates: N 37° 56.021 x W 078° 57.137
Elevation at Viewpoint: 3,200 ft
Location: Located at Milepost 10.7 on the Blue Ridge Parkway, just south of the Humpback Rocks Visitor Center.

THIS VIEW LOOKS WEST AND NORTHWEST over much of Augusta County and the Shenandoah Valley between the Blue Ridge Mountains, here, and the Alleghany Mountains (part of the larger Appalachian Mountain Range) to the west. The George Washington National Forest surrounds the Parkway through this northern section and also includes many lands in the distance. Together with the adjoining Jefferson National Forest further to the southwest, the two national forests form one of the largest areas of public land in the eastern United States, covering more than 1.8 million acres.

For much of the drive south on the Parkway, the overlooks provide views over the wide Shenandoah Valley, which ranges west of the Blue Ridge Mountains through which the Parkway travels, south to the James River, and north to the Potomac River. The Shenandoah Valley is part of the larger Great Valley or Great Appalachian Valley, an approximately 1,200-mile trough that extends from Quebec, Canada, to Alabama. The Great Valley was a major travel, migration, and commerce route for early white settlers, many of whom moved south from Pennsylvania on the Great Wagon Road, also called the Valley Pike, through the Shenandoah Valley. Earlier, Native Americans followed a series of footpaths, known as the Great Indian Warpath or Seneca Trail, through the Great Valley.

Modern day hikers follow the Appalachian Trail up the eastern side of the Shenandoah Valley. It parallels the Parkway along this section, traveling in the woods just below this overlook.

The city of Staunton, county seat of Augusta

Great views of Fork Mountain (center) can be seen from 20-Minute Cliff at Milepost 19. The North Fork of the Tye River flows in the right valley and around the foreground base of Fork Mountain. The sharp Pinnacle Ridge is further left, with The Priest further still on the far range.

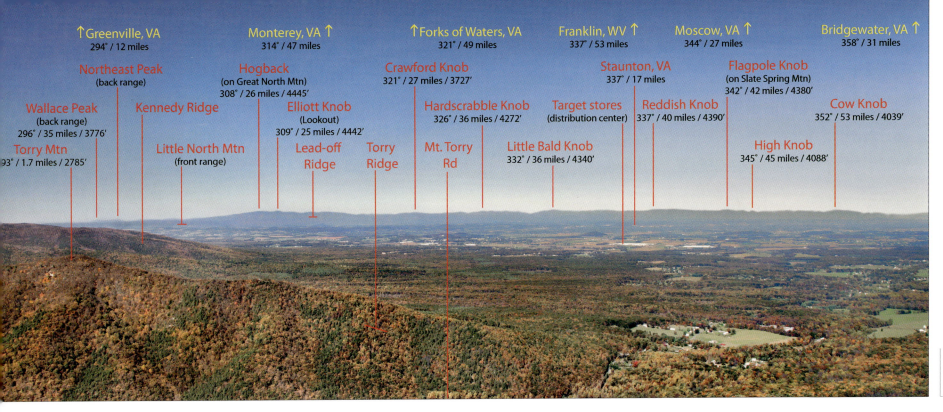

County, is located in the foreground valley, right, mostly hidden behind a low hill. Birthplace of Woodrow Wilson, the 28th U.S. president, the city is home to his Presidential Library, as well as the historic Stonewall Jackson Hotel, and the Museum of American Frontier Culture.

Shenandoah Mountain rises up behind the town, and runs along the horizon at the far end of the valley. Highway 81 travels through from Lexington (out of frame, left), to Staunton and Harrisonburg (out of frame, right). Highways 64 and 250 parallel each other from Staunton to Waynesboro (just out of frame, right), to the beginning point of the Parkway north of here. From there, these highways continue east to Charlottesville.

The area around the peaks, left, including Cellar Mountain, are part of the St. Mary's Wilderness, the largest wilderness in Virginia located on national forest land. It consists of 35,000 acres, with many miles of hiking trails within its boundaries. The St. Mary's River runs through the wilderness in the valley behind Flint Mountain and flows between Bald and Cellar Mountains to join the South River. This larger waterway continues to Buena Vista, VA, and eventually into the James River.

The bare rocks on the foreground hills are referred to as greenstone and are lava flow remnants formed about 570 million years ago, when tectonic plates began to separate, and molten lava rose to the surface east of the Shenandoah, and flowed through the area. These flows occurred over several million years, and were originally made of basalt, a black volcanic rock like those found in Hawaii and Iceland. The rocks in the Shenandoah, however, were metamorphosed, meaning their minerals and textures were changed through heating and pressure, in this instance during the formation of the Appalachian Mountains. New minerals grew within the basalt, giving the rocks a lighter gray or green color, thus the greenstone rocks.

Southern Virginia University, founded in 1867, is located on a tree-lined hilltop in Buena Vista, VA. It is a private liberal arts college that embraces the values of The Church of Jesus Christ of Latter-day Saints. The town can be accessed near Milepost 45.6 using Highway 60.

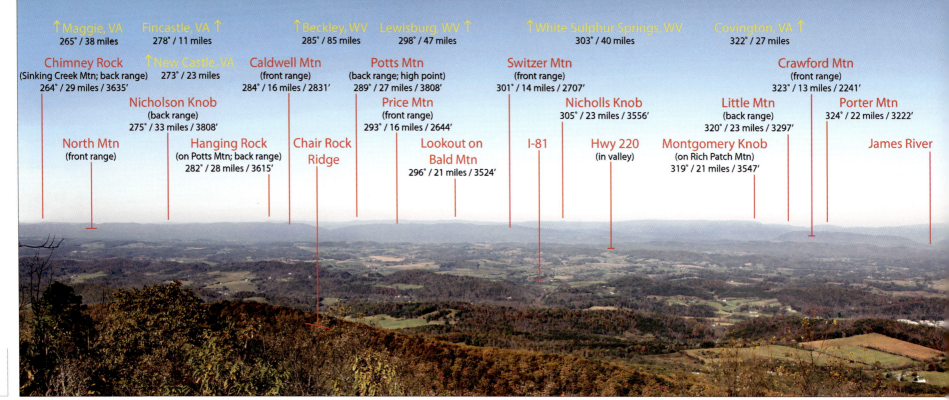

MILEPOST 92.1 Purgatory Mountain overlook

County, State: On the Botetourt/Bedford County line, VA
GPS Coordinates: N 37° 28.662 x W 079° 41.284
Elevation at Viewpoint: 2,400 ft
Location: Located at Milepost 92.1 on the Blue Ridge Parkway, just south of Peaks of Otter and north of Roanoke, VA.

Much of the Virginia section of the Parkway travels through rural farmland, skirting towns and suburbs. In some areas, new homes dot the roadside, and many roads and driveways access the Parkway. Most of the overlooks on the western side of the road, between Waynesboro and Roanoke, offer similar views over the Shenandoah Valley. Many others are wooded pull offs, or offer limited or obstructed views, especially through the flatter areas around Peaks of Otter. However, in addition to the ones included here, there are many stops worth a look, especially those at Irish Creek Valley overlook (Milepost 42.2), Thunder Ridge overlook (Milepost 74.7), and Pine Tree overlook (Milepost 95.2).

Looking north and northwest from Purgatory Mountain overlook across Botetourt County, toward West Virginia, much of the land you see is part of Jefferson and George Washington National Forest. Interstate 81 and Highway 11 run through the foreground valley, crossing the James River at the southern base of Purgatory Mountain. These roads connect Roanoke (out of frame, left), to the south, with Lexington (out of frame, right), to the north. The town of Buchannan lies along Highway 11, just east of where it crosses the James River in the foreground, right. The Appalachian Trail skirts north of Roanoke to join the Parkway a few miles south of this overlook, and passes behind it headed north.

The James River flows along the southern base of Purgatory Mountain, passing between Rathole and Crawford Mountains. The community of Eagle Rock lies along the James River, in front of Rathole. Highway 220 crosses the river near

The James River passes under the Parkway at the James River Visitor Center, Milepost 63.6, where travelers can get information on the area, picnic by the river, or take a short hike from one of the two trailheads.

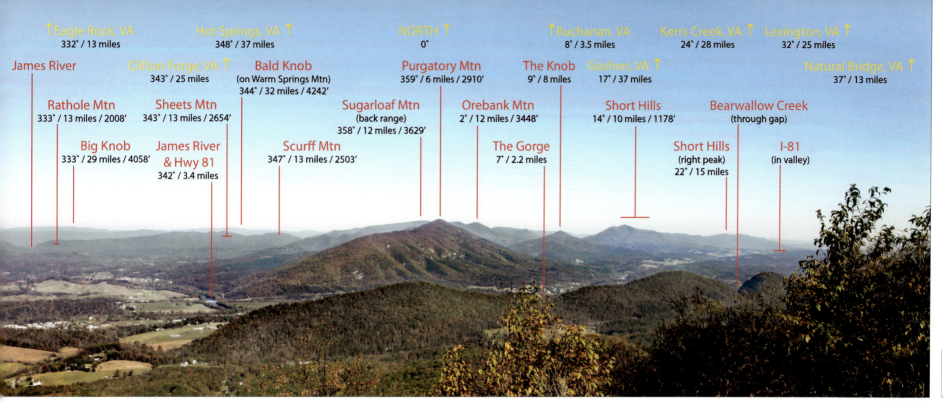

Eagle Rock on its way from Roanoke to Fincastle (in the foreground valley between Highway 81 and Caldwell Mountain), to Clifton Forge and Covington. Highway 43 descends from the Parkway just north of this overlook, down to Buchannan, and then along the James River to Eagle Rock.

The large Craig Creek runs along in the valley behind North, Caldwell, Switzer, and Patterson Mountains and in front of Bald and Rich Patch Mountains from Newcastle to Eagle Rock where it joins the James River. The Cowpasture and Jackson Rivers converge in northern Botetourt County to form the James, near Clifton Forge. The 16-mile stretch between Eagle Rock and Springwood (at the base of Purgatory Mountain) is the only part of the James to be declared a Virginia Scenic River and is a popular spot for canoeing and fishing (notably for the muskie). The James continues east to Lynchburg and on through Virginia to the Atlantic Ocean.

Just north of the overlook is Peaks of Otter, one of the most popular spots on this leg of the Parkway. It is a wonderful stopover that offers a visitor center, restaurant (serving three meals a day), lodge (open even in the winter on a limited basis), gift shop, country store, campground, and 24-acre Abbott Lake, all within sight of the impressive Sharp Top Mountain (elevation 3,829 feet). This pointed peak was once thought to be the highest point in Virginia, but it was later determined that it was far short of Mt. Rogers (5,728 feet), now known to be the state's highest elevation.

In fact, even nearby Flat Top Mountain in the Peaks of Otter group is taller, at 3,973 feet. Rock from the craggy knoll of Sharp Top was included in the Washington Monument and inscribed: "From Otter's Summit, Virginia's Loftiest Peak, To Crown a Monument to Virginia's Noblest Son." The third mountain that makes up The Peaks is Harkening Hill. Nearby is the Johnson Farm, a restored farmstead representing life in the 1930s.

Sharp Top rises up behind Abbott Lake, as seen from the Peaks of Otter Lodge and Restaurant. A flat one-mile loop trail encircles the lake, offering visitors a chance to stretch their legs.

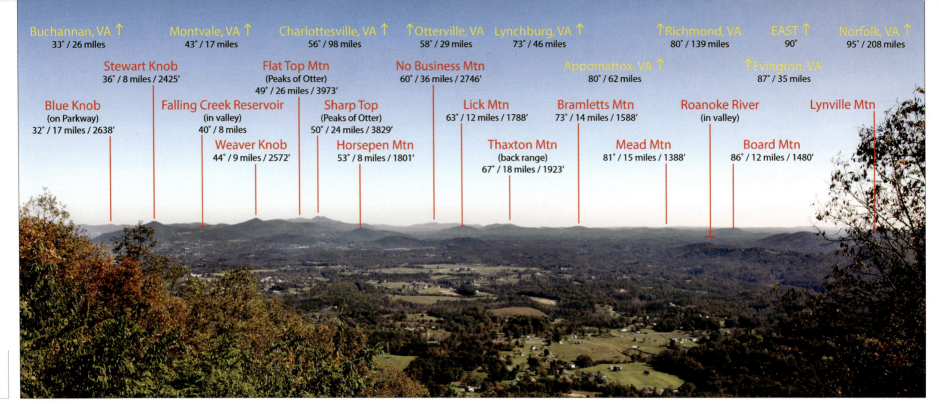

MILEPOST 120.5 Roanoke Mountain overlook

County, State: Roanoke County, VA
GPS Coordinates: N 37° 12.673 x W 079° 56.132
Elevation at Viewpoint: 2,161 ft
Location: As the Blue Ridge Parkway swings east of downtown Roanoke, turn off the Parkway onto the Mill Mountain Spur Road at about Milepost 120.5, and drive to the end of the loop. The Roanoke Mountain overlook (above) and View Mill Mountain overlook (right page) are on opposite sides of the ridge at the top of Roanoke Mountain.

ROANOKE COUNTY, FORMED IN 1838, WAS SEPARATED from the huge Botetourt County (created in 1769 with Fincastle as its seat), which once encompassed land from what is now western Virginia to the Mississippi River. The town of Salem (just out of frame, left) was established as its seat, and today the population of the county is around 92,000. The larger city of Roanoke is located about midway between New York City and Atlanta, GA, along I-81, 168 miles west of the Virginia state capitol in Richmond. I-81, and the earlier Highway 11, whose path it followed, largely trace the northeast/southwest route taken along the Appalachian Mountains by migrating game, American Indians, and early settlers.

Looking northeast you will notice the prominent shapes of the Peaks of Otter, which include Sharp Top and Flat Top Mountains. The Parkway runs north from Roanoke around Stewart Knob and across Blue Knob to the Peaks of Otter.

Between Stewart and Weaver Knobs are the small Falling Creek and Beaverdam reservoirs, located in Bedford County, just east of Vinton (out of frame, left). In the distance, the Parkway swings west (left) of No Business Knob before crossing the James River, which flows behind the knob. The North and South Forks, the headwaters of the Roanoke River, merge just west of Roanoke in Lafayette, then flow through the city and into

Many sections of the Parkway run through urban areas such as Roanoke, as well as rural farmland, providing visitors with a wide variety of beautiful landscapes.

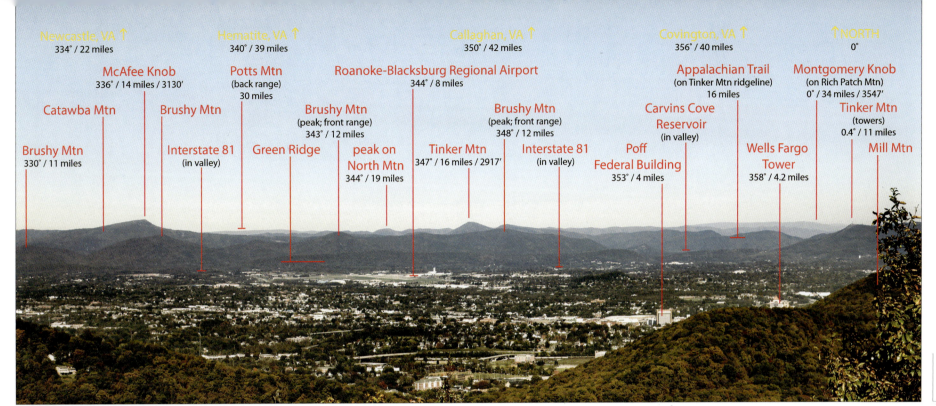

MILEPOST 120.5 Mill Mountain overlook

the foreground valley, exiting between Lynville and Board Mountains, to its impound at Smith Mountain Lake to the southeast. The river then continues through many such impounds across Virinia and into North Carolina, where it empties into the Albemarle Sound, which is separated from the Atlantic Ocean by the Outer Banks.

The Mill Mountain overlook offers a view over the city of Roanoke, the largest populated area along the Blue Ridge Parkway. Located about midway along the 217-mile stretch, from Waynesboro in the north to the NC state line to the south, the city is a perfect base from which to explore its many attractions. Downtown Roanoke is partially obscured from here by Mill Mountain, but the Wells Fargo Tower, the tallest building in the city (at 320 feet), and the Poff Federal Building, the second tallest, are visible. A major transportation hub, Roanoke is served by the Norfolk Southern railroad, Interstate 81, the Roanoke River, and the Roanoke-Blacksburg Regional Airport.

Looking northwest over the city from Roanoke Mountain, you can see the airport, which sits at the base of the long, low Green Ridge. I-81 and Highway 220 run along the foreground base of Green Ridge between it and the airport. The undulating Brushy Mountain rises up behind, with Catawba and Tinker Mountains further back. The Appalachian Trail (AT) travels along the ridgeline from Catawba Mountain, across the sharp peak of McAfee Knob, then along the horseshoe shape of Tinker Mountain, before paralleling the Parkway north of town.

In the bowl formed by Tinker is the Carvins Cove Reservoir (a water source for the city of Roanoke), a 640-acre body of water surrounded by Carvins Cove Nature Reserve, the country's second largest municipal park, with almost 12,700 acres. Popular activities there include hiking, fishing, mountain biking, horseback riding, and boating. One of the most visited and photographed points along the AT is McAfee Knob, which overlooks the park.

Downtown Roanoke as seen from the Stewart Knob overlook at Milepost 110.6 on the Parkway. Wells Fargo Tower, with its copper-colored roof, anchors the city skyline. Fort Lewis Mountain (with towers) rises up behind.

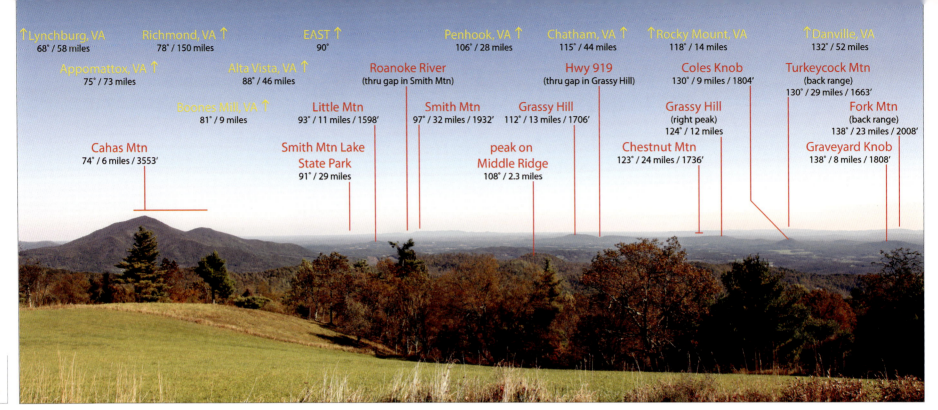

MILEPOST 139 Cahas Knob overlook

County, State: On the Franklin/Floyd County line, VA
GPS Coordinates: N 37° 05.664 x W 080° 06.712
Elevation at Viewpoint: 3,013 ft
Location: Located at Milepost 139 on the Blue Ridge Parkway, about 17 miles south of Roanoke, VA, between Mill Spring Spur Road and the Saddle overlook.

FROM HERE YOU ARE VIEWING EAST OVER FRANKLIN County. The largest road traversing the county is Highway 220, which runs in front of Fork Mountain, through the town of Rocky Mount (behind Grassy Hill), to Boones Mill (behind Cahas Mountain), and on to Roanoke. Highway 221 runs through Floyd County, behind the overlook, from Hillsville through Floyd to Roanoke.

The North and South Forks of Blackwater River run in the foreground valley, flowing just north of Rocky Mount, the seat of Franklin County, and into Smith Mountain Lake (foreground base of Smith Mountain), a major recreation area on the northeastern edge of the county. The lake is also fed by the much larger Roanoke River, which runs southeast from Roanoke. The river was impounded to form the lake in 1963 with the construction of the Smith Mountain Dam.

Franklin County was formed in 1785 and named by early settlers in honor of Benjamin Franklin. In the 20th Century, it became known as the "Moonshine Capitol of the World" because it was said that for every 100 families living in the county in the 1920s, 99 were in some way involved in the illegal liquor business. Even today, abandoned stills can be found along many of the creeks. In 1935, the federal government indicted 34 people as part of the "Great Moonshine Conspiracy," which drew national attention.

Later, the county was known for its tobacco production. It remains rural today, with most of the growth happening around Smith Mountain Lake.

Reverend Daniel Shaver (1860-1949), his two wives and several children, are buried in this stone-walled roadside cemetery, located at Milepost 135.7 just north of the overlook.

MILEPOST 168 Saddle overlook

County, State: On the Floyd/Patrick County line, VA
GPS Coordinates: N 36° 49.387 x W 080° 20.495
Elevation at Viewpoint: 3,351 ft
Location: Located at Milepost 168 on the Blue Ridge Parkway, about 8 miles north of Mabry Mill.

FROM THIS OVERLOOK, YOU ARE VIEWING NORTHEAST toward Cahas Mountain. Just south of this overlook is the Rocky Knob Visitor Center, featuring a gift shop, restrooms, picnic tables, a shelter, and a beautiful campground adjacent to the Parkway.

Virginia's Highway 8 runs in the immediate foreground between the overlook and Sugarloaf Mountain, and crosses the Parkway just north of here, connecting Stuart to the south, with Floyd and Christiansburg to the north. Highway 40 passes through the valley behind Pocket Ridge and the Haycocks to skirt just east (right) of Cooks Knob to Rocky Mount. Highway 221 travels behind the overlook through the town of Floyd, and parallels the Parkway north to Roanoke.

The topography flattens out to the right of Sugarloaf as you view the Smith River Valley (out of frame, right). The many creeks that drain the east side of the Parkway flow into the Smith River, which is impounded in Lake Philpott in the valley below. Fairy Stone State Park adjoins the popular 168-acre lake, and features camping, cabins, hiking trails, picnic areas, and canoeing. Another popular draw is the "fairy stones," geological rock Staurolite crystals that form in the shape of crosses. Legend and superstition have it that these crystals protect the wearer from sickness, accidents, and witchcraft.

Mabry Mill, one of the Parkway's most popular spots, is located south on the Parkway at Milepost 176.2. Built by Ed Mabry (1867–1936) in the early 1900s, this water-powered gristmill operated until he died, providing a service to the surrounding area for over 25 years.

The tens of thousands of images of Mabry Mill have made it an iconic representation of the Parkway. Visitors can tour the restored working gristmill and related exhibits on rural life in Appalachia, shop for souvenirs in the gift shop, and have a great meal at the Mabry Mill Restaurant.

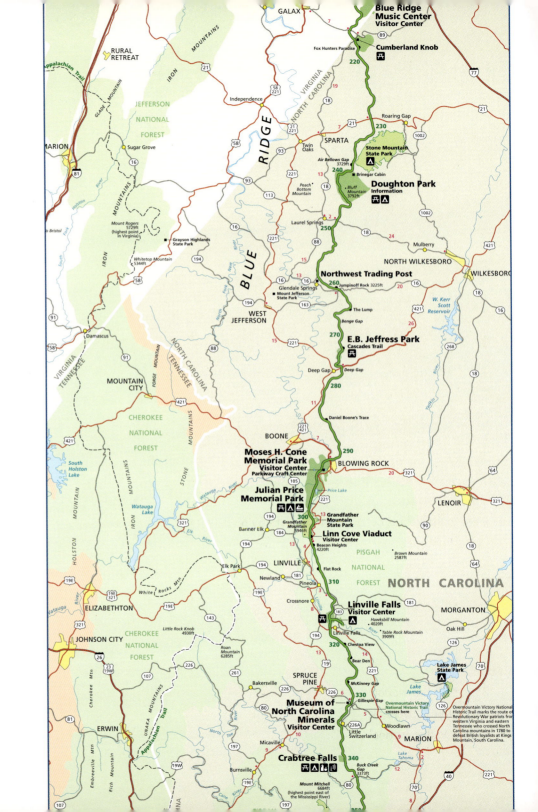

Blue Ridge Parkway overlooks

SECTION TWO
From the NC/VA line to Three Knobs overlook

Fox Hunter's Paradise overlook—Milepost 218.6 | Elev. 2805 30
    Little Glade Mill Pond overlook—Milepost 230.1 | Elev. 2709
    Stone Mountain overlook—Milepost 232.5 | Elev. 3200
    Bullhead Mountain overlook—Milepost 233.7 | Elev. 3200
    Mahogany Rock overlook—Milepost 235 | Elev. 3420
    Devils Garden overlook—Milepost 235.7 | Elev. 3428
Air Bellows Gap overlook—Milepost 236.9 | Elev. 3729 32
    Brinegar Cabin overlook—Milepost 238.5 | Elev. 3508
    Wildcat Rocks overlook—Milepost 241.1
    Doughton Park Concessions—Milepost 241.1
    Alligator Back overlook—Milepost 242.4 | Elev. 3388
Bluff Mountain overlook—Milepost 243.4 | Elev. 3421 34
    Basin Cove overlook—Milepost 244.7 | Elev. 3312
    Sheets Gap overlook—Milepost 252.8 | Elev. 3342
    Northwest Trading Post/Sallie Mae's on the Parkway—Milepost 259
    The Lump overlook—Milepost 264.4 | Elev. 3465
Mt. Jefferson overlook—Milepost 266.8 | Elev. 3699 36
    Betseys Rock Falls overlook—Milepost 267.8 | Elev. 3400
    Lewis Fork overlook—Milepost 270.2 | Elev. 3290
    Cascades overlook—Milepost 271.9 | Elev. 3570
Elk Mountain overlook—Milepost 274.3 | Elev. 3795 40
    Stoney Fork Valley overlook—Milepost 277.3 | Elev. 3405
    Osborne Mountain View overlook—Milepost 277.9 | Elev. 3500
    Carroll Gap overlook—Milepost 278.3 | Elev. 3430
Grandview overlook—Milepost 281.4 | Elev. 3240 44
    Boone's Trace overlook—Milepost 285.1
    Raven Rocks overlook—Milepost 289.5 | Elev. 3810
    Yadkin Valley overlook—Milepost 289.9 | Elev. 3830
Thunder Hill overlook—Milepost 290.4 | Elev. 3795 46

    Moses Cone overlook—Milepost 293.5 | Elev. 3888
    Moses H. Cone Visitor Center—Milepost 294.1
    Sims Creek overlook—Milepost 295.3 | Elev. 3608
    Sims Pond overlook—Milepost 295.9 | Elev. 3447
    Price Lake overlook—Milepost 296.7 | Elev. 3380
    Boone Fork overlook—Milepost 297.2 | Elev. 3410
    Cold Prong Pond overlook—Milepost 299 | Elev. 3580
    View of Calloway Peak overlook—Milepost 299.7 | Elev. 3798
    Green Mountain overlook—Milepost 300.6 | Elev. 4134
    Pilot Ridge overlook—Milepost 301.8 | Elev. 4400
View of Wilson Creek Valley overlook—Milepost 302.1 | Elev. 4356 48
    Raven Rocks overlook—Milepost 302.4 | Elev. 4335
    Wilson Creek overlook—Milepost 303.6 | Elev. 4357
    Yonahlossee overlook—Milepost 303.9 | Elev. 4412
    Linn Cove Viaduct Visitor Center—Milepost 304.4
    Grandfather Mountain overlook—Milepost 306.6 | Elev. 4154
    Lost Cove Cliffs overlook—Milepost 310 | Elev. 3812
    Camp Creek overlook—Milepost 315.6 | Elev. 3443
    Linville Falls Visitor Center—Milepost 316.4
    North Toe Valley overlook—Milepost 318.4 | Elev. 3540
Chestoa View overlook—Milepost 320.8 | Elev. 4090 50
Bear Den overlook..Milepost 323 | Elev. 3359 52
    Heffner Gap overlook—Milepost 325.9 | Elev. 3067
    North Cove overlook—Milepost 327.3 | Elev. 2815
    The Loops overlook—Milepost 328.6 | Elev. 2980
    Table Rock overlook—Milepost 329.8 | Elev. 2870
    Museum of NC Minerals Visitor Center—exit near Milepost 331
    Deer Lick Gap overlook—Milepost 337.2 | Elev. 3452
Three Knobs overlook—Milepost 338.8 | Elev. 3875 54

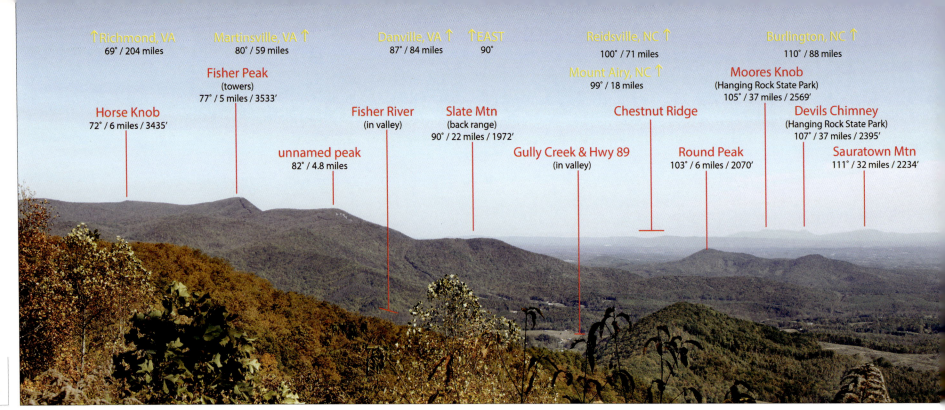

MILEPOST 218.6 Fox Hunters Paradise overlook

County, State: Alleghany County, NC
GPS Coordinates: N 36° 32.523 x W 080° 55.109
Elevation at Viewpoint: 2,805 ft
Location: Located at Milepost 218.6 near Cumberland Knob on the Blue Ridge Parkway, between Fancy Gap, VA, and the Air Bellows overlook, less than 2 miles south of the NC/VA state line.

In this view the Blue Ridge Mountains drop quickly to the Piedmont, an area of low hills and valleys. Located along the Alleghany and Surry County lines, the overlook offers views east and southeast over Surry County. Pilot Mountain, at the eastern edge of the county, is the most prominent and distinctive shape on the horizon. There are actually more than eight Pilot Mountains in North Carolina, and even though it is not the highest, this one is the best known, due to its unique shape.

Pilot Mountain is a metamorphic quartzite dome-shaped form known as a monadnock, which is a lone dome or small mountain set apart from nearby mountains. Rising abruptly from the valley floor to a height of 2,398 feet, it is a remnant of the ancient chain of the Sauratown Mountains, one of the most easterly ranges in the state. The highest peak in that range is Moore's Knob in the 6,921-acre Hanging Rock State Park to the east of Pilot. Once a part of a much larger layer of rock, the softer rock has been affected by erosion and other natural forces, leaving only the harder quartzite under the peaks of Moore's, Pilot, and Hanging Rock.

Pilot Mountain is made up of two distinct features, Big Pinnacle, defined by its larger mass and bare rock walls, and Little Pinnacle. Together they form the central feature of the larger Mt. Pilot State Park, a 3,700-acre expanse. Utilized for its unique appearance and prominence, Pilot Mountain served as a guidepost to travelers, from early American Indian inhabitants to later European settlers.

The tallest point in the county is Fisher Peak.

The Blue Ridge Music Center, located at Milepost 213 on the Parkway, features live music performances most days, along with special concerts, an outdoor amphitheater, indoor interpretive center, and gift shop.

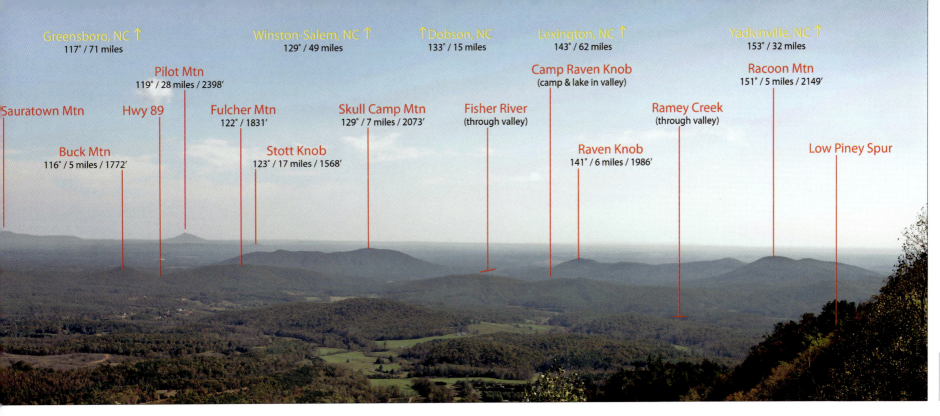

The Surry County, NC/Grayson County, VA, line runs across its peak. The Fisher River forms on its southern slopes, and flows along the foreground base, across the valley, in front of Fulcher Mountain, then passes between Skull Camp Mountain and Ravens Knob. The Fisher River continues south to join the Yadkin River just east of Elkin. Two other tributary rivers in the county—the Ararat and Mitchell—feed the Yadkin, which flows along the southern border of Surry County.

Interstate 77 runs north/south through the county in the distance, behind Skull Camp Mountain and Round Peak, from Elkin (to the south) to Hillsville, VA, and points north. Highway 52 runs north/south beyond I-77, from Winston-Salem to Mount Airy and on to Hillsville as well. Highway 21 runs north/south, paralleling I-77 from Statesville (in the south), before turning more northwest as it passes through Elkin to Sparta, NC. Dozens of wineries dot the path these routes take through the Yadkin Valley, many of which offer daily tours.

To the north of Pilot Mountain lies the town of Mount Airy, birthplace of actor Andy Griffith (1926–2012). The town is located in the valley on the foreground side of Chestnut Ridge, along the Ararat River, about five miles south of the NC/VA state line. Originally incorporated in 1885 near what was soon a large granite quarry, Mount Airy once boasted numerous industries, including furniture manufacturing and tobacco facilities. Today it is a popular tourist destination, in large part due to its association with the classic TV series. For more than 50 years, the town has celebrated an annual "Mayberry Days" festival the last week in September.

Mount Airy also has a long association with traditional music, being the home of old-time musician Tommy Jarrell (1901–1985) and fiddle great Benton Flippen (1920–2011). A local radio station, WPAQ, has been hosting a live broadcast of old-time and bluegrass music in town since 1948.

Wally's Service is one of many Andy Griffith Show–themed businesses in Mount Airy, NC. Others include the popular restaurant the Snappy Lunch, as well as Floyd's City Barbershop a few doors down on Main Street.

MILEPOST 236.9 Air Bellows overlook

County, State: Alleghany County, NC
GPS Coordinates: N 36° 25.827 x W 081° 07.378
Elevation at Viewpoint: 3,729 ft
Location: Located at Milepost 236.9 on the Blue Ridge Parkway, between Fox Hunters Paradise overlook and Brinegar Cabin, just south of the Parkway junction with Highway 21.

From this overlook along the southern edge of Alleghany County (bordered by Virginia on the north) you are looking northwest to the Peach Bottom Mountains that run through its center. Highway 221 traverses the valley on the back side of this range on its way from Boone and West Jefferson, NC, to the west. It continues behind Cheek and Fender Mountains, before intersecting Highway 21, just north of Sparta. From there, 221/21 moves on to Independence, VA, where it splits, and 21 continues north to Wytheville, while 221 turns east to Galax.

Looking northwest over Peach Bottom Mountain, you can see Mt. Rogers, located in the far southwestern part of Virginia. It is the state's highest point and a part of the larger Mt. Rogers National Recreation Area, some 200,000 acres of national forest. This area is a mixture of mountain balds, rock formations, spruce-fir forest, and has a small population of wild ponies. It is also home to Virginia's highest elevated road, which runs to Whitetop (located west/left of Mt. Rogers), the state's second highest peak at 5,525 feet. From there, the Iron Mountains run west to east above Troutdale, VA, to include Comers Rock and Jones Knob in the Jefferson National Forest.

In the valley between Peach Bottom and Mt. Rogers, the North and South Forks of the New River flow, before joining near the Mouth of Wilson community. From there, the New River continues east, passing between Sparta and Independence and north of Galax, around the end of Round Top,

Brinegar Cabin, built in the 1880s, is located just south on the Parkway at Milepost 238.5 near Doughton Park. Craft and weaving demonstrations by park rangers offer visitors a glimpse of life in the early 20th century.

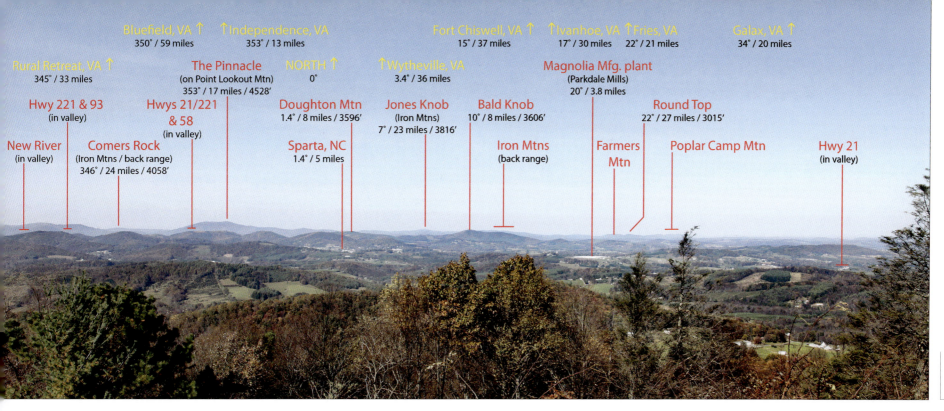

before crossing Interstate 77 and Highway 52. In the valley in front of Peach Bottom Mountain, runs Highway 18, which comes from Wilkesboro, NC, to the south, to downtown Sparta. There it intersects with Highway 21 which runs from Elkin, NC, also to the south. Highway 21 crosses under the Parkway a few miles north of this overlook and through the foreground valley, right. Immediately south of the overlook, the dirt Air Bellows Road cuts off, passing back under the Parkway through a narrow underpass and continues across the ridges in the foreground, left, eventually intersecting Highway 18, which leads to Sparta.

Sparta, the Alleghany County seat, sits near the county's center, and is its only municipality. Named for the ancient city-state of Greece, it has a population of about 1,800, and sits at an elevation of 2,927 feet. It has been home to Sparta Industries/Dr. Grabow International Pipes since 1943. They produce more than 200,000 smoking pipes annually at this facility, the largest number produced in one place anywhere in the world. The large white building in the center of the image is the Parkdale Mills-Magnolia Manufacturing plant, a yarn-spinning mill, located on Pine Swamp Road.

Alleghany County is North Carolina's fifth smallest county by area, encompassing only 233 square miles, and the sixth smallest in number of people, with a population of about 10,000. The average elevation is 2,500 to 3,000 feet, with the highest peaks of 4,000 feet or more located in the Peach Bottom Mountains. The county has been home to many notable North Carolinians, including Robert Doughton, a powerful politician who was influential in promoting the construction of the Blue Ridge Parkway. A few miles south on the Parkway is Doughton Park, named in his honor. Also in Alleghany County lies Cumberland Knob, near the NC/VA state line, where construction of the Blue Ridge Parkway began on September 11, 1935.

The Northwest Trading Post/Sallie Mae's on the Parkway is located at Milepost 259 near Glendale Springs. Open seven days a week, it offers visitors crafts, drinks, and snacks.

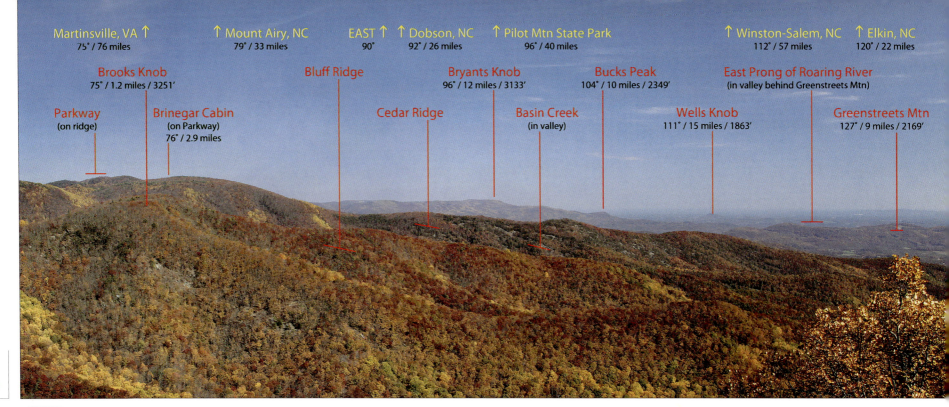

MILEPOST 243.4 Bluff Mountain overlook

County, State: Alleghany County, NC
GPS Coordinates: N 36° 24.518 x W 081° 11.734
Elevation at Viewpoint: 3,421 ft
Location: Located at Milepost 243.4 on the Blue Ridge Parkway in Doughton Park, near Laurel Springs, NC, and the junction of Alleghany, Wilkes, and Ashe counties, about 26 miles south of the NC/VA state line.

THIS OVERLOOK OFFERS VIEWS TO THE SOUTHEAST, with Wilkes County and Doughton Park in the foreground. It is located on the north end of the 7,000-acre park, an area originally known as the Bluffs, but renamed for Congressman Robert L. Doughton (1863–1954), who was instrumental in the creation of the Blue Ridge Parkway and its routing through this part of North Carolina. He spent 42 years in the United States House of Representatives serving North Carolina, including 18 as chairman of the powerful U.S. House Committee on Ways and Means, and he was a key sponsor of the Social Security Act of 1935.

Doughton Park is bordered on the southwest by the Thurman Chatham Wildlife Management Area and on the east by Stone Mountain State Park, located in the valley between Greenstreets Mountain and Bucks Peak. Established in 1969, this 14,000-acre park features the signature Stone Mountain—a 600-foot granite dome—the Hutchinson Homestead, trout waters, hiking trails, camping, and picnicking.

The Yadkin River runs west to east in the Yadkin Valley along the front side of the Brushy Mountains, through Wilkesboro, North Wilkesboro, and Elkin. It is one of the longest rivers in the state, flowing more than 200 miles from its headwaters near the Thunder Hill overlook on the Parkway, to Badin Lake near Albemarle, where it becomes the Pee Dee River, which continues to the South Carolina coast. The East, Middle, and West Prongs of the Roaring River, which drain much of the foreground valley, converge behind Greenstreets Mountain, flowing to join the Yadkin River just west of Elkin.

The Kerr Scott Reservoir (just out of frame, right, below Pores Knob), located just west of Wilkesboro, is one of seven reservoirs formed by damming the Yadkin, and the only one not used to generate hydroelectric power. Alcoa, who owns more than 36,000 acres along the river, operates the numerous power plants.

Built by the Army Corps of Engineers in 1962, the Kerr Scott Reservoir was named for William Kerr Scott ((1896–1958), 62nd Governor (1949–53) of the state, and a U.S. Senator, who was instrumental in gaining approval for the construction of the dam and reservoirs. Encompassing 1,475-acres with five miles of shoreline, its facilities include three campgrounds, public beaches, and boat docks.

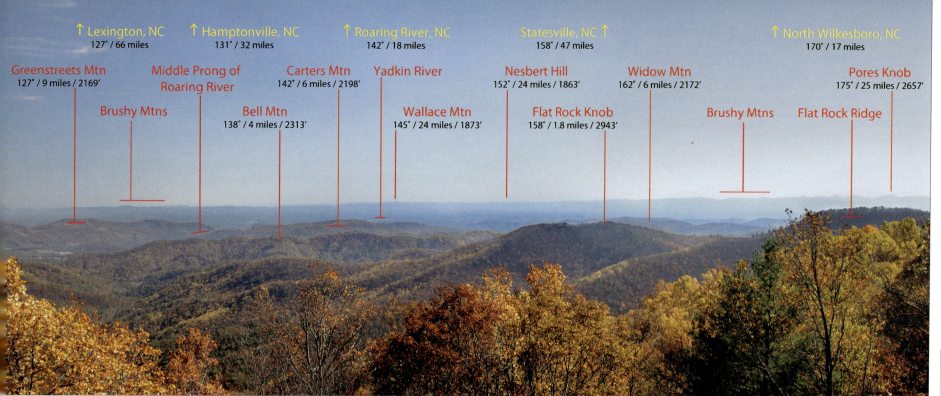

There are numerous roads serving the area. Just east of the reservoir, Highway 421 runs from Wilkesboro, passing on this side of the lake. It crosses the Parkway south of here near the Elk Mountain overlook before reaching Boone. Highway 18 heads north from North Wilkesboro, running behind Widow Mountain, to cross the Parkway just south at Milepost 248, before continuing to Laurel Springs where it turns east, running behind this overlook to Sparta (out of frame, left).

I-77 runs north/south from South Carolina, through Statesville, and behind the Brushy Mountains to pass just east of Elkin, then west of Dobson and on to Virginia. Highway 21 parallels I-77 from South Carolina, through Charlotte and Statesville to Elkin. From there it bears northwest to pass behind Wells Knob, around this side of Bryants Knob, crossing the Parkway north of here, before continuing on to Sparta (where it intersects Highway 18), and into Virginia.

ABOVE: *Beautiful rolling hills lined by split rail fencing are characteristic features of the Parkway along the Doughton Park section (Mileposts 238.5–244.7). This Park is the largest recreation area on the Parkway.*

RIGHT: *The beautiful Bluffs Lodge at Doughton Park (Milepost 421) has 24 rustic rooms. It is closed as of winter 2014, while the National Park Service finds a concessioner to operate it and the nearby coffee shop.*

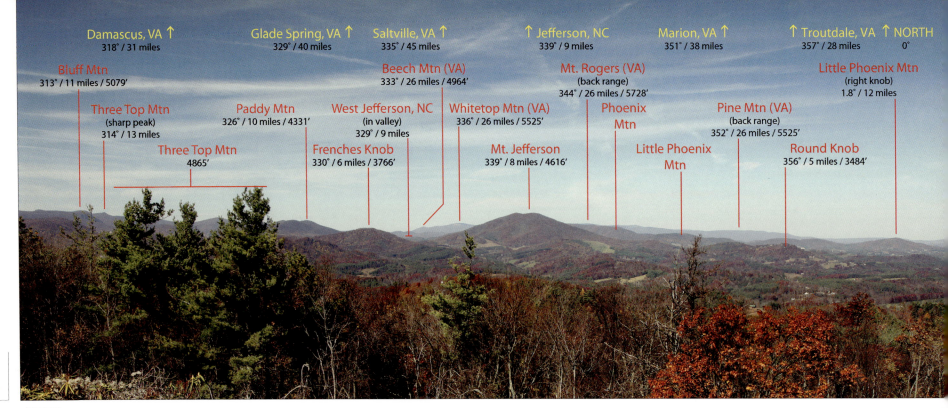

Milepost 266.8 — Mt. Jefferson overlook (looking north)

County, State: On the Wilkes/Ashe County line, NC
GPS Coordinates: N 36° 17.700 x W 081° 24.782
Elevation at Viewpoint: 3,699 ft
Location: Located at Milepost 266.8 on the Blue Ridge Parkway between Bluff Mountain and Elk Mountain overlooks, near West Jefferson, NC. This view to the north is from the parking lot; the view to the west (pages 38–39) is from just south of the overlook.

LOOKING NORTH, MT. JEFFERSON RISES MORE THAN 1,600 feet from the surrounding landscape. An oak/chestnut forest covers the highest elevations on the south, east, and west faces, making this mountain one of the best examples of this type of forest in the southeast. The windswept northern face is covered with low, gnarled trees and shrubs, their growth stunted by strong winds and winter ice. Due to the diverse array of trees, shrubs, and wildflowers on its forested slopes, Mt. Jefferson was designated a national natural landmark by the National Park Service in 1974.

Once part of a much taller mountainous region, Mt. Jefferson is the result of millions of years of erosion that weathered away the softer rock, leaving the harder portions beneath. It lies between the North and South Forks of the New River, which come together in Ashe County to flow north to West Virginia. The New River is one of the oldest in the world, actually predating the uplift that created the Appalachian Mountains, and one of the few in the country, along with the French Broad (also in North Carolina), to flow north.

Known by a variety of names, including Negro Mountain (because runaway slaves were thought to have hidden there while fleeing north) and Panther Mountain, Mt. Jefferson was renamed in 1952 after the town of Jefferson and its namesake, Thomas Jefferson. He and his father, Peter, owned land in the area and surveyed the nearby NC/VA border in 1749. A state park since 1956, Mt. Jefferson is a popular spot for hiking and picnicking. The town of West Jefferson is in the valley just to its left, behind Frenches Knob. Jefferson, the seat of Ashe County, is hidden behind Mt. Jefferson, between it and Phoenix Mountain. Located in the extreme northwestern part of the state, Ashe is bordered by two other states—Virginia to the north and Tennessee to the west.

The town of West Jefferson, established in 1915, was built around the Virginia-Carolina Railroad depot and was served by the Northwestern Railroad, better known as the "Virginia Creeper," nicknamed for its slow crawl up the steep mountains. After railroad traffic ceased in 1977, local efforts coalesced to repurpose a 34-mile-long section of the rail bed, from Abingdon, VA, to Whitetop Station on Whitetop Mountain in the Mt. Rogers National Recreation Area (in the distance behind Mt. Jefferson). Today this segment is a shared-use trail, open to hikers, horseback riders, and bicyclists.

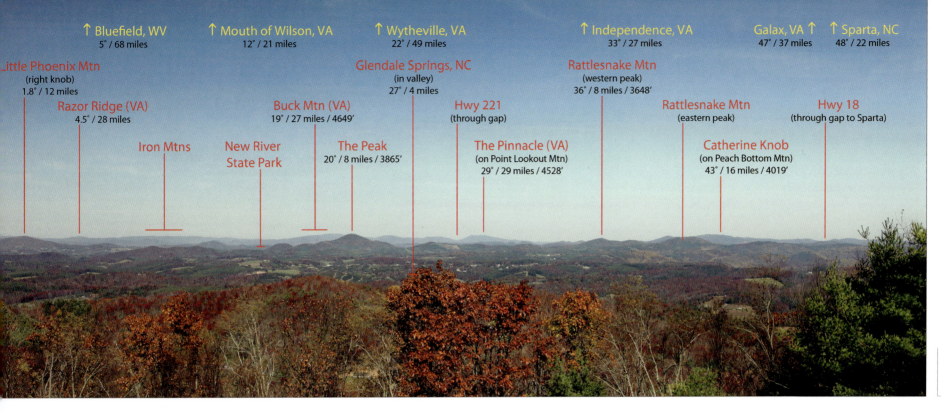

Each year thousands of visitors bike the especially popular 17-mile segment from Whitetop to Damacus, VA. Many outfitters in Damascus offer shuttle service to the mountaintop for visitors and their bikes. The Appalachian Trail passes through the town before climbing to cross Beech, Whitetop, Mt. Rogers, and Pine Mountain on its way north.

Highway 16 from Wilkesboro, to the south, crosses the Parkway at Horse Gap, just north of this overlook, before dropping to the town of Glendale Springs, through the foreground valley, behind Round Knob and along the northeastern (right) base of Mt. Jefferson to Jefferson. There it turns north along this side of Little Phoenix Mountain to Mouth of Wilson, just across the state line in Grayson County, VA. Highway 163 starts at Horse Gap and travels further south in the valley to pass between Frenches Knob and Mt. Jefferson to West Jefferson, where it meets Highway 221, the county's main north/south road.

Many of the roads that traverse Ashe County, NC, converge at West Jefferson, including Highways 221, 163, 88, 194, and 16. The quaint downtown, above, is a mix of old farm supply stores and modern art galleries.

One of more than a dozen murals on the walls of buildings in downtown West Jefferson, this one commemorates the Virginia Creeper, a train in use until 1977.

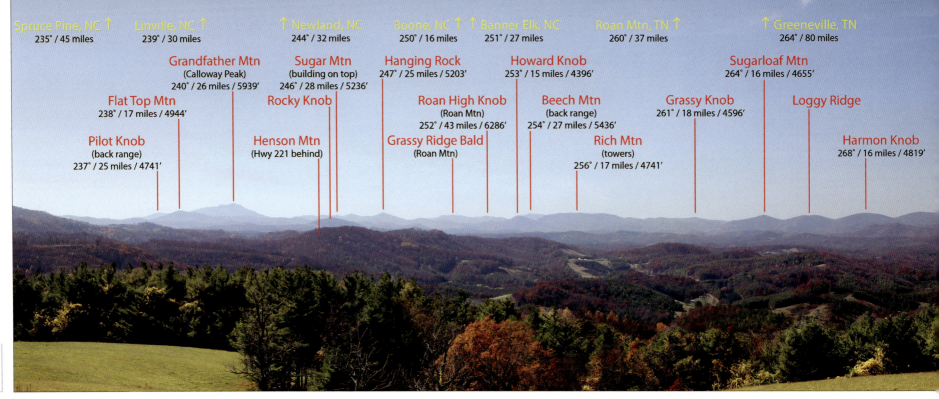

Mt. Jefferson overlook (looking west)

MILEPOST 266.8

County, State: On the Wilkes/Ashe County line, NC
GPS Coordinates: N 36° 17.700 x W 081° 24.782
Elevation at Viewpoint: 3,699 ft
Location: Located at Milepost 266.8 on the Blue Ridge Parkway between Bluff Mountain and Elk Mountain overlooks, near West Jefferson, NC. This view to the west is from just south of the overlook; the view to the north is from the parking lot (pages 36–37).

Looking southwest from the Mt. Jefferson overlook, you can see profiles of many of the area's most popular peaks that line the horizon. To the southwest, Grandfather Mountain dominates the ranges at 5,939 feet. One of the region's biggest attractions, it draws visitors year round to its cool, windy peaks to enjoy natural beauty, a plentitude of hiking trails, and the famous Mile High Swinging Bridge. Grandfather Mountain also hosts the Highland Games, a gathering of Scottish clans. Held annually each July and open to the public, 2014 marked the 59th anniversary of these events.

West of Grandfather Mountain are Sugar and Beech Mountains, resort communities tied to popular skiing resorts. In summer and fall, visitors and vacationers from lower climes come here to savor cooler weather and the spectacular fall color. In the distance, between Hanging Rock (not to be confused with the Hanging Rock State Park in Stokes County) and Beech Mountain, is the undulating shape of Roan Mountain, known for the rhododendrons that bloom on its grassy bald ridges in the summer. Its numerous rounded peaks include Roan High Bluff and Roan High Knob on the western (right) end, and Grassy Ridge Bald on the eastern, with Carvers Gap between. The NC/VA state line and Appalachian Trail run along its crest.

The area's largest town, Boone, is located on the far base of Howard Knob. It is the seat of Watauga County, NC. The Moses Cone and Julian Price Memorial Parks are located just south of town, along the Parkway near Blowing Rock. The region's major highways pass through Boone, including Highways 221, 321, 421, and 194.

Highway 321 comes through Lenoir in the south to Blowing Rock and Boone, where it turns west through the valley, between Rich and Beech Mountains (where the Watauga River flows) to Johnson City, TN. Highway 221 enters North Carolina from South Carolina and continues to track north through Marion (along I-40), Linville Falls, and Linville (located behind Grandfather Mountain from this viewpoint) to Boone. There Highway 221 jogs northwest to pass behind Henson Mountain and through the foreground valley before passing between Mulato Mountain and Bald Knob to West Jefferson (out of frame, right). From there it continues to Independence, VA, and points north.

Highway 421 travels east from North Wilkesboro in Wilkes County, NC, to Boone, where

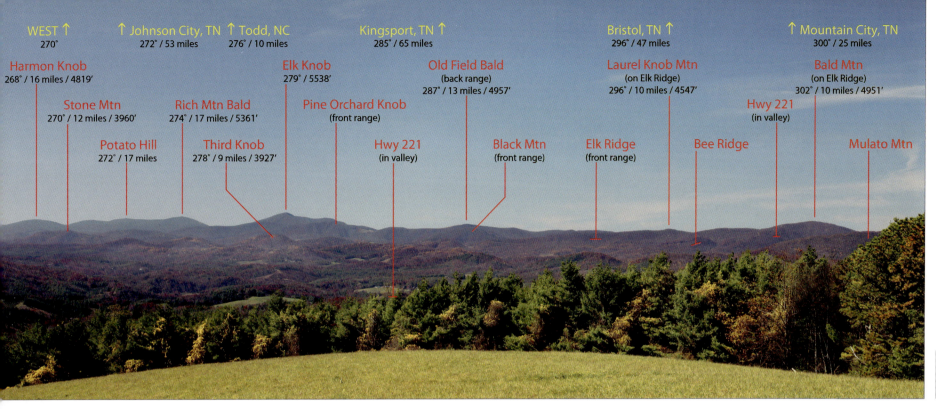

it turns north, passing behind Howard Knob, Rich Mountain (towers visible with binoculars), Grassy Knob, Rich Mountain Bald, and Elk Knob to Mountain City, TN, where it turns west to Bristol. Highway 194 treks north from Linville Falls through the Avery County, NC, communities of Newland, Elk Park, and Banner Elk (located at the southern base of Beech Mountain), to Valle Crucis (behind Grassy Knob) and Boone. From there it heads northeast in this direction, passing in front of Elk Knob, through Todd (located just behind Third Knob), along the foreground base of Laurel Knob and Bald Mountains on Elk Ridge, to Baldwin (located behind Mulato Mountain), where it joins Highway 221 to West Jefferson.

The South Fork of the New River begins near Blowing Rock and the Eastern Continental Divide and travels north through Boone, passing in front of Stone Mountain, to Todd, through the valley to the right of Henson Mountain, and snakes between the hills immediately below this overlook to West Jefferson and Jefferson. The North Fork of the New River forms in the valley on the far side of Elk Knob and flows north to join the South Fork near the NC/VA state line.

From there the New River continues into Virginia, passing near Galax and on to West Virginia, where it joins the Gauley to form the Kanawha, which flows into the Ohio River. The Ohio becomes part of the Mississippi River, which means that water from the New River eventually flows into the Gulf of Mexico. Although it is older than the mountains it traverses, the course of the New River has remained relatively unchanged over millions of years. Peter Jefferson, father of U.S. President Thomas Jefferson, named the river when he surveyed the area, a largely unexplored frontier at that time. A skilled cartographer, he produced the first accurate map of the Province of Virginia.

Roan Mountain, one of the many ridges visible from here, is covered by rhododendrons that bloom each June, drawing visitors from hundreds of miles to its grassy balds.

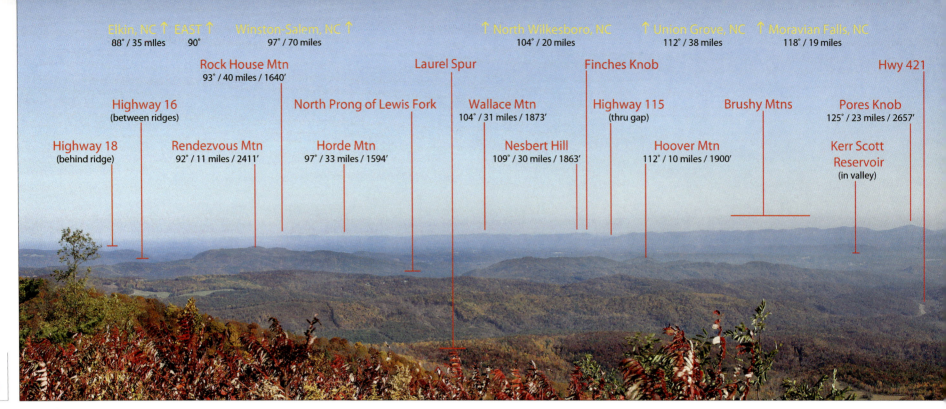

MILEPOST 274.3 Elk Mountain overlook (1 of 4)

County, State: Watauga County, NC
GPS Coordinates: N 36° 13.967 x W 081° 29.195
Elevation at Viewpoint: 3,795 ft
Location: Located at Milepost 274.3 on the Blue Ridge Parkway, between Fire Scale Mountain and Tompkins Knob, near the community of Deep Gap.

FROM THIS OVERLOOK, LOCATED NEAR THE JUNCTURE of Ashe, Wilkes, and Watauga Counties, you are looking east over much of Wilkes County, to the Yadkin Valley and the Brushy Mountains, an isolated spur of the Blue Ridge Mountains that run along the southern border of the county. Their range of relatively low peaks includes Horde and Wallace Mountains, and Finches, Pores, Walnut, and Cox Knobs.

Wilkes County was formed in 1777, and named after John Wilkes, an English political figure, who championed American rights around the time of the Revolution. His support cost him his position as mayor of London. The county's largest town, North Wilkesboro, can be seen in the valley on this side of the Brushy Mountains, in line with Wallace Mountain. Many of the key roads servicing the Yadkin Valley pass through, or near, the town, and nearby Wilkesboro, including Highways 18, 268, 16, and 421.

Highway 18 runs roughly north-south along the base of the Brushy Mountains, on this side of the ridgeline, between Jerry Mountain and Cox Knob, from Lenoir to Moravian Falls, Wilkesboro, and North Wilkesboro. From there it turns northwest, crossing the Parkway near Doughton Park, and continues on to Laurel Springs, where it turns northeast to Sparta, NC, and on to Cumberland Knob near the Virginia state line, where it intersects the Parkway once again.

Highway 268 runs parallel to Highway 18, but closer in this direction, following the Yadkin River from Happy Valley, crossing the Kerr Scott Reservoir (which lies in line with Moravian Falls) and on to Wilkesboro, running between Licklog and Green Mountains. Highway 16 travels from Newton and Conover, north through Taylorsville, and crosses to this side of the Brushy Mountains between Bald Rock and Pores Knob, entering the Yadkin River Valley. It passes through Wilkesboro and tracks northeast passing behind Rendezvous Mountain to cross the Parkway north of this overlook at Horse Gap near Glendale Springs.

The Rendezvous Mountain State Park and Forest (3,316 acres) at Rendezvous Mountain offers visitors a variety of experiences, with an extensive trail system, a working sawmill, picnic facilities, and educational exhibits including "talking trees," where recordings along the wooded trail explain features about the particular hardwoods. The Park has seasonal hours so call ahead for details and visiting times (336-667-5072).

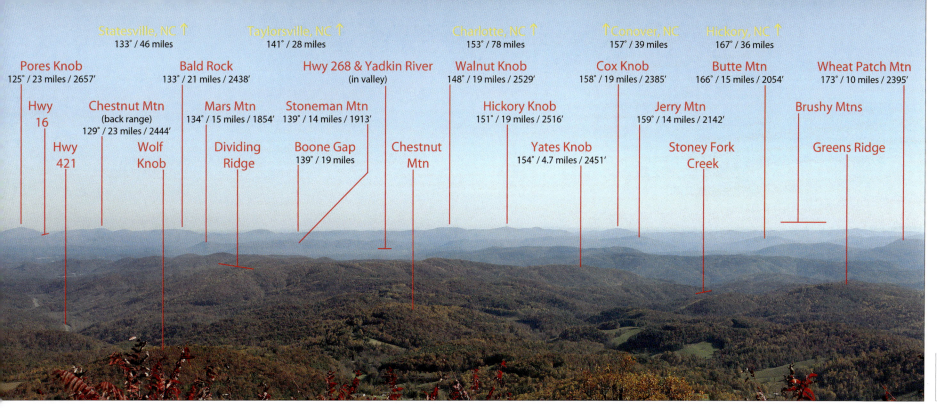

(2 of 4)

Just off the Parkway north of this overlook is Glendale Springs, home of the Holy Trinity Church of the Frescoes. The frescoes, made by painting on wet plaster, were done by Asheville, NC, artist Ben Long and his students between 1974 and 1980. Long learned the technique in Italy and created the frescoes in the Holy Trinity Episcopal Church (built in 1901), and in the St. Mary's Episcopal Church, twelve miles away in West Jefferson. The churches are open to visitors daily.

The charming mountain town of West Jefferson also boasts over a dozen murals painted on the walls of downtown buildings. Begun in 1996 when local artist Jack Young was commissioned to create a mural entitled, *History of Ashe Through the Ages,* additional images were created every few years by other painters, in many cases with the cooperation and participation of local Ashe County students. Subjects include wildflowers, mountain vistas, rural farm scenes, musicians playing

ABOVE: *Tweetsie Railroad, located nearby in Blowing Rock, is one of many popular tourist attractions that are located in mountain towns along the route of the Blue Ridge Parkway through western North Carolina.*

RIGHT: *The Last Supper fresco, created by artist Ben Long and students, was finished in 1980. It is located on the wall in the chapel of the Holy Trinity Episcopal Church in Glendale Springs, NC.*

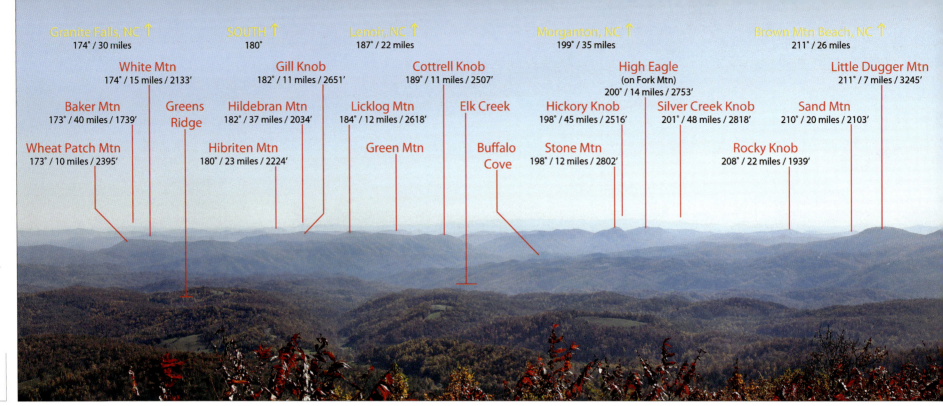

MILEPOST 274.3 Elk Mountain overlook (3 of 4)

traditional instruments, the Virginia Creeper train, and local history.

Highway 421 from Winston-Salem tracks east, crossing the north-south path of Interstate 77, just north of the small town of Union Grove in Iredell County. The Fiddler's Grove music festival is held there every year on Memorial Day weekend and is the oldest continuous fiddler's contest in the country, having been started almost a century ago. It is a family event held at the campground there and is limited to 5,000 attendees, making it a great venue for jamming with other musicians, and watching bands perform and fiddlers compete.

Highway 421 continues west toward the overlook, passing between Horde and Wallace Mountains into the foreground valley, to North Wilkesboro, along the South Prong of the Lewis River and passing just under the overlook before crossing the Parkway immediately south of here near Deep Gap. US 421 is a spur route from US 21, beginning at Fort Fisher on the North Carolina coast, and running west through the state and traversing Tennessee, Virginia, Kentucky, before ending in Indiana.

North Wilkesboro, the hub of all these roads, is the largest town in Wilkes County with a population of just over 4,000. It is the home of Merlefest, an annual music festival, started in 1988 by renowned musician Arthel "Doc" Watson and friends to honor Merle, Doc's son, who died in an accident. Each year, the last week in April, as many as 85,000 people congregate around more than a dozen stages set up on the campus of Wilkes Community College to listen to masters of traditional music as well as some of the top contemporary artists. The festival is the primary fundraiser for the college, and continues, despite the passing, in 2012, of Doc and his wife, Rosa Lee, who made their home in nearby Deep Gap.

Located between North Wilkesboro and Moravian Falls, Wilkesboro is the second largest municipality in Wilkes County and the county seat. It can be seen in the valley beyond, and to the left of, Hoover Mountain, in line with Nesbert Hill in the Brushy Mountains. Nearby Pores Knob, the highest peak in the Brushy Mountains, is located in the township of Moravian Falls, a community originally settled in 1753 by members of the Moravian Church, a protestant group from Moravia in central Europe. The town and nearby waterfall were named after their church. Today the falls are privately owned and operated as a tourist attraction along with an accompanying campground.

About three miles southwest of Wilkesboro is the Kerr Scott Reservoir, formed in 1962 by damming the Yadkin River to prevent devastating floods like those that hit the area in 1916 and 1940. Two of the major tributaries of the Yadkin, the Reddies and Roaring Rivers, form, and run their entire lengths, in Wilkes County. Stoney Fork

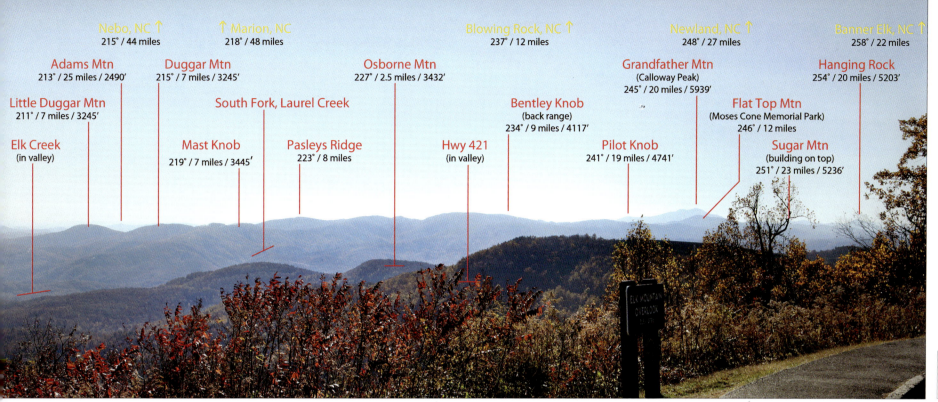

(4 of 4)

Creek and Elk Creek drain the valley just below the overlook, running south to the Yadkin River, located in the valley behind the ridges connecting Wheat Patch Mountain, Gill Knob, Cottrell Knob, and Spring Mountain.

Further south are Hibriten Mountain (near Lenoir) and Hildebran Mountain, on that line-of-sight between Valdese and Hickory, along I-40. Further east along the back range is Baker Mountain near Hickory. To the west, below Morganton, are the South Mountains which include Hickory Knob and Silver Creek Knob, near the Rutherford, Burke, and McDowell county lines.

Behind Duggar and Little Duggar Mountains, in the distance, is Nebo, at Lake James, with the town of Marion just to the west. Behind Bentley Knob are the Thunder Hill overlook (Milepost 290.4) near Blowing Rock, and the Wilson Creek Valley overlook beyond (Milepost 302.1) on the Blue Ridge Parkway, which offer additional, closer views of these areas.

Along the line of sight with Blowing Rock, but 40 miles further in the distance, lies the town of Spruce Pine in Mitchell County. On the far right, in the west, located at the junction of the Avery, Watauga, and Caldwell counties, lies Grandfather Mountain. Its crest dominates the horizon with Calloway Peak its highest point and Pilot Knob lower on its eastern slope. In front, at Flat Top Mountain, is the Moses H. Cone Memorial Park, near Blowing Rock on the Parkway (Milepost 293.5).

To the west of Grandfather Mountain are Sugar Mountain, with its distinctive building on Sugar Top visible through the trees, and the pointed Hanging Rock. Banner Elk is located in the valley between Sugar Mountain and Beech Mountain (out of frame, right), both popular winter skiing destinations.

As tourism has grown over the years, more and more hotels and motels have been constructed in towns along the Parkway. One of the oldest and most spectacular is the Green Park Inn in Blowing Rock, built in 1891.

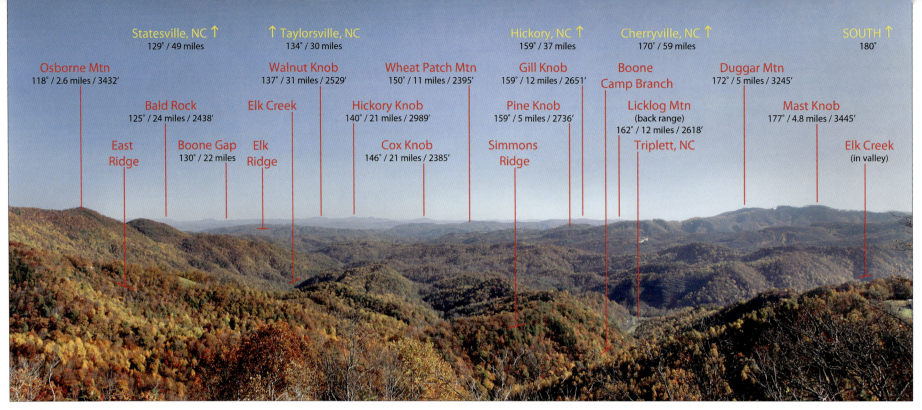

MILEPOST 281.4 Grandview overlook

County, State: Watauga County, NC
GPS Coordinates: N 36° 13.642 x W 081° 34.023
Elevation at Viewpoint: 3,240 ft
Location: Located at Milepost 281.4 on the Blue Ridge Parkway near Boone, NC.

Looking southeast from this overlook you are viewing from Watauga County into Wilkes County and toward Taylorsville, NC, in Alexander County. The Brushy Mountains, on the horizon, run along the border of Wilkes and Alexander Counties, and include Cox, Hickory, and Walnut Knobs.

The Yadkin River flows through the valley in front of the Brushy Mountains, and behind Licklog, Gill, and Wheat Patch Mountains, into the Kerr Scott Reservoir near North Wilkesboro (out of frame, left). Elk Creek drains the valley below the overlook, flowing into the Yadkin River at the east end of Wheat Patch Mountain.

The Boones Camp Branch area, just below the overlook, was a favorite hunting spot of legendary frontiersman, Daniel Boone (1734–1820). He and his wife, Rebecca, lived in the Yadkin Valley around 1769. The commemorative Daniel Boone Trail, marked out in 1915, begins at the Yadkin River and ends in Boonesborough, KY, site of a fort he built in 1775. Constructed on the Kentucky River, it was one of the first American settlements west of the Appalachian Mountains.

Nearby Boone, which bears his name, is the county seat of Watauga County. It is home to Appalachian State University, the town's largest employer. One of 16 schools in the University of North Carolina system, it offers more than 150 graduate and undergraduate majors. Boone's high elevation makes for cold and wet winters great for the area's ski resorts, and mild summers that draw tourists and retirees.

Glenn Causey, right, in buckskin attire, portrayed the rugged frontiersman, Daniel Boone, for 41 years in the popular summer outdoor drama, Horn in the West, *presented in nearby Boone, NC.*

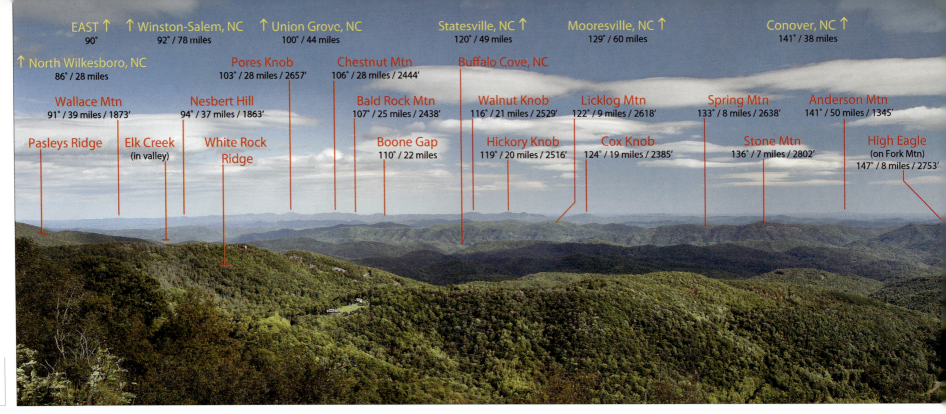

MILEPOST 290.4 — Thunder Hill overlook

County, State: Watuaga County, NC
GPS Coordinates: N 36° 08.173 x W 081° 38.601
Elevation at Viewpoint: 3,795 ft
Location: Located at Milepost 290.4 on the Blue Ridge Parkway just east of Blowing Rock, NC, and Moses Cone Memorial Park.

THIS OVERLOOK VIEWS SOUTHEAST FROM THE southern edge of Watuaga County over Caldwell and Wilkes Counties to the Brushy Mountains. The long low hills that make up the span of this range run southwest from about Lenoir, northeast to around Elkin, NC, and include Cox, Hickory, and Walnut Knobs, Bald Rock and Chestnut Mountains, Pores Knob, Nesbert Hill, and Wallace Mountain. Highway 18 runs along their foreground base from Lenoir through Moravian Falls to North Wilkesboro where it turns north to cross the Parkway near Doughton Park. Highway 268, which begins at Highway 321 just north of Lenoir near Happy Valley, parallels the Yadkin River which flows on this side of the Brushy Mountains along that same track from Lenoir through North Wilkesboro to Elkin, through the Yadkin River Valley.

Highway 18 also runs southwest from Lenoir to Morganton, located along Interstate 40, with Silver Creek, Icy, Hickory, and Benn Knobs and the South Mountains further to the south. Highway 321 runs north from Lenoir and continues in this direction passing through the foreground valley between Johnnys Knob and Fork Mountain then behind Bailey Camp to Blowing Rock (due west of overlook) before crossing the Parkway on its way to Boone and on into Tennessee.

The town of Blowing Rock, incorporated in 1889, has been a popular tourist retreat for over a hundred years as people from further south came north to the mountains to escape the summer heat. The nationally renowned Green Park Inn was built there in 1891 as demand for visitor lodging outgrew the capacity of local boarding houses and farms. Its many guests over the years have included Eleanor Roosevelt, Calvin Coolidge, Herbert Hoover, John Rockefeller, Annie Oakley, Henry Fonda, and Margaret Mitchell (who wrote part of *Gone With the Wind* while a guest there). It was extensively remodeled in 2010 and continues to draw overnight visitors from across the country.

The local geologic attraction known as "Blowing Rock" derived its name from a legend about an Indian maiden and warrior who fell in love. They were from tribes hostile to each other, one from the Cherokee and the other from the Catawba. While meeting at the rock the brave was torn between his duty to return to his tribe and the maiden's pleas to stay with her. Distraught he jumped from the rock toward the cliffs below. The maiden entreated the Great Spirit to bring him back and the winds lifted him up and onto the rock

outcropping. Today's visitors to this unusual rock formation can often feel those strong updrafts.

Other attractions in the area include Tweetsie Railroad (a wild west theme park with narrow gauge railroad, open spring through fall), Julian Price Memorial Park, and Moses Cone Memorial Park. Julian Price, located at Milepost 297, is comprised of more than 4,300 acres, including a small lake, large beautiful campground, 100-site picnic area, and 300-seat amphitheater. Related activities include hiking, fishing, and canoeing (rentals available at Price Lake).

Moses Cone Memorial Park, at Milepost 293.5, centers around Flat Top Manor, a 20-room white mansion built by textile magnate Moses Cone in 1901. Housed within its over 13,000 square feet of space is the Parkway Craft Center, one of five shops operated by the Southern Highland Craft Guild to sell handmade crafts by regional artists.

The small town of Blowing Rock, near Boone, NC, offers a variety of art and craft galleries, festivals, and events that draw visitors from across the area, mainly in the summer and fall months.

Known as Flat Top Manor, the Moses Cone mansion sits overlooking the expansive Moses Cone Memorial Park and features the Southern Highland Craft Guild gift shop with work by area craftspeople. There are also 25 miles of carriage trails that cross the 3,500-acre estate available to horse-drawn carriages, horseback riders, and hikers.

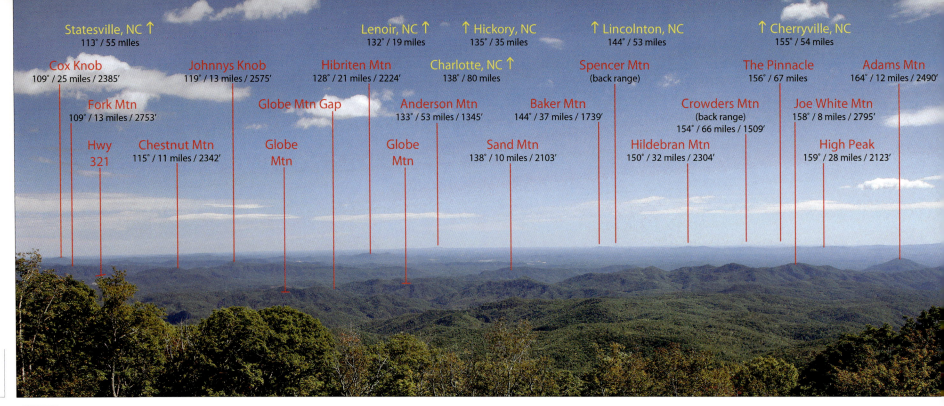

Wilson Creek Valley overlook
MILEPOST 302.1

County, State: Avery County, NC
GPS Coordinates: N 36° 05.816 x W 081° 47.074
Elevation at Viewpoint: 4,356 ft
Location: Located at Milepost 302.1 on the Blue Ridge Parkway near the Linn Cove Viaduct, just south of Julian Price Memorial Park, below Pilot Knob and Grandfather Mountain.

From the south end of the parking lot at this overlook you are looking south over Avery, Caldwell and Burke Counties (which all meet at Chestnut Mountain) toward Hickory and Charlotte. Grandfather Mountain is behind the overlook. A North Carolina State Park, its attractions include the Mile High Swinging Bridge, hiking trails, and animal exhibits. The entrance to Grandfather is located on nearby Highway 221.

The Linn Cove Viaduct adjacent to the overlook was built around Grandfather Mountain as the last section of the Blue Ridge Parkway. An engineering marvel, it is considered by many to be the most complicated bridge ever built. Officially dedicated in 1987, it celebrated its 25th Anniversary in 2012. The nearby Linn Cove Viaduct Visitor Center (with facilities), just south of the overlook, offers exhibits about the bridges construction.

Wilson Creek drains much of the area below the overlook and joins the Johns River behind Adams Mountain. The Johns forms near Globe, NC, and flows on this side of Globe and Sand Mountains, behind Adams, and south to join the Catawba River at Rhodhiss Lake just north of Morganton.

Interstate 40 runs east-west in the valley between Brown Mountain and Benn Knob, through Morganton and parallels Rhodhiss Lake from there to Hickory, where it intersects Highway 321. After crossing into North Carolina, 321 travels through Gastonia and Lincolnton to Hickory and Lenoir (located near Hibriten Mountain), before passing behind Johnnys Knob and Chestnut Mountain and in front of Fork Mountain, to Blowing Rock. From there it crosses the Parkway and continues to Boone and on to Johnson City, TN. In the distance on a line of sight between Hibriten and Sand Mountains lie Lenoir, Hickory, and Charlotte. Further right is Hildebran Mountain near Morganton. Much further beyond that are The Pinnacle and Crowders Mountain along Interstate 85 near Gastonia.

From the north end of the parking lot you are viewing toward the South Mountains on the horizon, which include Benn Knob at South Mountains State Park, Hickory Knob, Icy Knob, Silver Creek Knob, and Yellowtop Mountain. West of the South Mountains, Highway 64 passes between Camel Knob and Silver Creek Knob connecting Rutherfordton, to the south, with Morganton on this side of the range. Highway 221 also runs north through Rutherfordton passing just to the west of Conoway Knob to Marion, located near Lake James, in the valley between Chestnut Mountain and

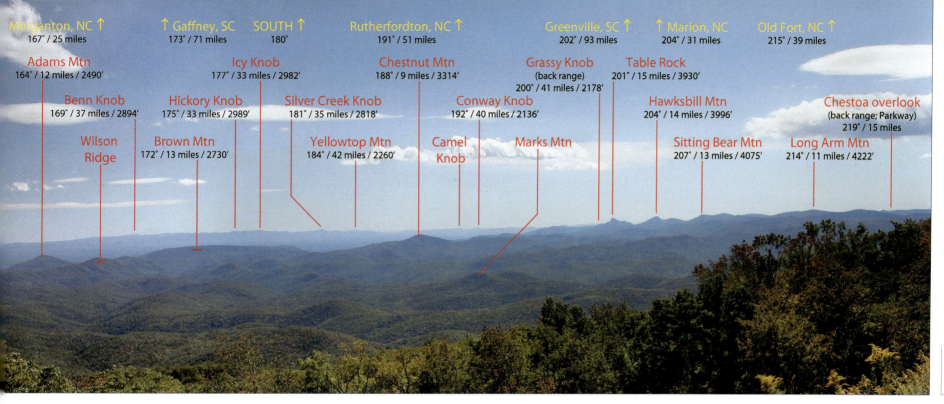

Conoway Knob. To the north of Lake James, in the Linville Gorge Wilderness, are the uniquely shaped Table Rock and Hawksbill Mountains, as well as Sitting Bear Mountain.

In the foreground is Brown Mountain, renowned for its Brown Mountain lights. These mysterious phenomenon have long baffled inhabitants and have been the subject of much lore and legend. Occasionally they appear over the mountain in the late evening hours and can be seen from several area vantage points including the Brown Mountain overlook on Highway 181 about 20 miles north of Morganton, from Wisemans View in the Linville Gorge Wilderness, and from the Lost Cove Cliffs overlook on the Parkway. Many scientific explanations have been advanced, from marsh gasses to reflections of city or railroad lights, but there are no marshes near the mountain and the lights were noted by Native Americans long prior to the advent of electricity or the railroads.

ABOVE: TThe Linn Cove Viaduct, built from 153 unique concrete segments, is an elevated 1,243-foot concrete bridge section of the Blue Ridge Parkway that winds 8 miles around Grandfather Mountain.

RIGHT: Julian Price Memorial Park, just north on the Parkway, offers visitors a variety of outdoor activities from camping and hiking to kayaking and canoeing on Price Lake (boat rentals available).

Panorama labels (left to right):

- Banner Elk, NC ↑ — 16° / 17 miles
- Linville, NC ↑ — 25° / 11 miles
- Boone, NC ↑ — 38° / 25 miles
- West Jefferson, NC ↑ — 38° / 42 miles
- Blowing Rock, NC ↑ — 48° / 21 miles
- North Wilkesboro, NC ↑ — 70° / 48 miles

- Beech Mtn — 13° / 18 miles / 5436′
- Sugar Top building
- Flattop Mtn — 21° / 14 miles
- Grandfather Mtn — 32° / 15 miles / 5939′
- Parkway
- Ball Ground Mtn — 44° / 4.2 miles / 4239′
- Long Arm Mtn — 53° / 3.8 miles / 4222′
- Jonas Ridge
- Sugar Mtn — 18° / 14 miles / 5236′
- Hanging Rock — 25° / 17 miles / 5203′
- Pilot Knob — 38° / 15 miles
- Linville Falls (waterfall in valley) — 45° / 2.2 miles

MILEPOST 320.8 — Chestoa View overlook

County, State: McDowell County, NC
GPS Coordinates: N 35° 55.604 x W 081° 57.194
Elevation at Viewpoint: 4,081 ft
Location: Located at Milepost 320.8 on the Blue Ridge Parkway. From the Chestoa View Parking Area, follow the short path down to the stone outcropping for this view.

THE DOMINANT PEAK IN THE DISTANCE IS Grandfather Mountain, one of North Carolina's premier tourist attractions. Developed by the late Hugh Morton, a well-known North Carolinian, it is now managed by the non-profit Grandfather Mountain Stewardship Foundation. Grandfather Mountain is open to the public year round, weather permitting (except Thanksgiving and Christmas).

The Parkway, which continues from this overlook, passes across the north end of the foreground valley and just to the left of Ball Ground Mountain where it crosses Highway 181 before reaching Grandfather. Highway 181 runs from Morganton through the valley behind Table Rock, Hawksbill, and Jonas Ridge before climbing along the back of Jonas Ridge to pass behind Ball Ground to the town of Linville.

Behind Grandfather Mountain lies the town of Boone, named for the famous frontiersman Daniel Boone, who was known to have camped there. Left of Grandfather are Sugar and Beech Mountains, popular skiing destinations. The town of Beech Mountain, at 5,506 feet, is the highest incorporated community in the eastern U.S. Sugar Mountain is easily identifiable by the ten-story condominium building at the Sugar Top development. While this building was being constructed in 1983, an outcry erupted regarding its prominent ridge top location leading to laws defining what could be built on the state's mountaintops, making Sugar Top the last development of its kind.

The renowned Linville Gorge, cut by the Linville River over millions of years, is located behind Linville Mountain in the valley below the peaks along Jonas Ridge. The river originates on Grandfather Mountain, flows through the gorge and over Linville Falls, a 90-foot multilevel waterfall, before emptying into Lake James (out of frame, right). The 12,000 acre Linville Gorge Wilderness is part of Pisgah National Forest, and is a rugged remote area so inaccessible that it was one of the few areas not logged in the early 20th century. Outward Bound, and even the United States military, uses the area to teach survival skills, and it is a popular spot for hikers.

Along the crest of Linville Mountain, on the McDowell/Burke County line, runs the rugged Kistler Memorial Highway, a gravel road that originates near the Linville Falls Visitor Center and runs across Laurel Knob to the Wiseman's View overlook. This viewpoint offers a spectacular look down into Linville Gorge and is a favorite place to see the "Brown Mountain lights," an unusual

atmospheric phenomenon where, occasionally, blobs of light seem to float and dance in the distance at night.

On the south end of the gorge is Table Rock, notable for its unusual shape. A popular spot for mountain climbing and hiking, the Mountains-to-Sea Trail runs across it before dropping to the valley behind Jonas Ridge and continuing along the Warrior Fork River. Beyond Table Rock in the distance is Rector Knob, located between Morganton and Valdese in Burke County.

Highway 221 runs through the foreground valley and connects Marion, to the south, with Boone, in the north. The North Fork of the Catawba River, which feeds into Lake James, runs along Highway 221, past Linville Caverns (below). This popular tourist attraction, open seasonally to the public, has a large cave system with geologic formations that extend into the mountain just below the overlook.

ABOVE: *The Sugar Top development on Sugar Mountain, seen from the Banner Elk side, sparked the enacting of ridge laws in North Carolina that limit how high a structure can rise above the ridgeline.*

RIGHT: *Linville Falls as seen from the Gorge View overlook on the Erwin's View Trail that runs along the western side of Linville Gorge. It is accessed from the Linville Falls Visitor Center just off the Parkway.*

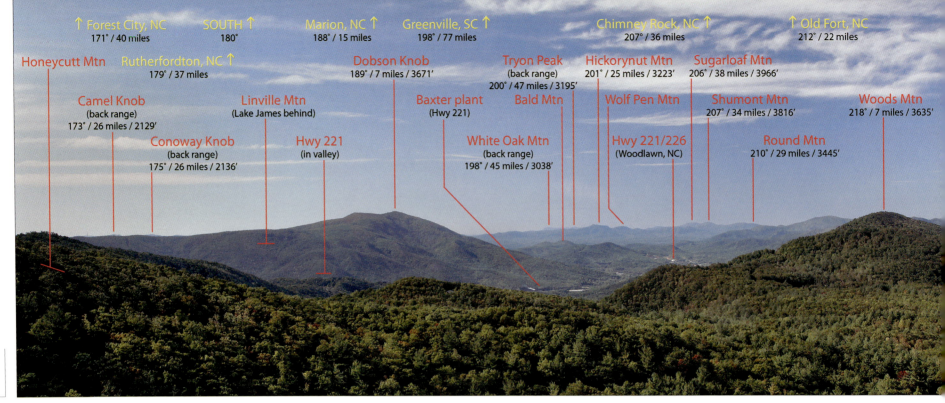

MILEPOST 323 Bear Den overlook

County, State: McDowell County, NC
GPS Coordinates: N 35° 54.212 x W 081° 58.143
Elevation at Viewpoint: 3,359 ft
Location: Located at Milepost 323 on the Blue Ridge Parkway, between Little Switzerland, NC, and the Chestoa overlook, near the junction of Mitchell, Avery, and McDowell counties.

From this overlook you are viewing much of McDowell County, with Marion, its county seat, to the south in the valley behind Dobson Knob, and Three Knobs to the southwest on its border with Yancey and Mitchell Counties. The popular Bear Den Campground is on the knoll in the immediate foreground with Woods Mountain behind.

The North Fork of the Catawba River forms just north of here and runs along the front base of Linville Mountain, between Dobson Knob and Bald Mountain, and into Lake James. A 6,510-acre recreational lake, Lake James, was formed by damming the Catawba River just north of Marion.

Following the North Fork of the Catawba River along the base of Linville Mountain is Highway 221. It runs from the Woodlawn community, visible at the eastern end of Woods Mountain, north to the small town of Linville Falls (out of frame, left), paralleling the Parkway around Grandfather Mountain, through Boone, NC, to end in Lynchburg, VA. Highway 226 splits off 221 at Woodlawn, near the Baxter Pharmaceutical plant, and passes through the valley below, in front of Woods Mountain, crossing the Parkway just west of here, before reaching Spruce Pine, NC.

Highway 221 also continues south from Woodlawn to Marion, where it crosses Interstate 40, then passes Conoway Knob at the Rutherford/McDowell County line, goes though Rutherfordton, into South Carolina and to its origins in Florida. While Highway 221 runs north/south, I-40 runs east/west from Asheville, through Black Mountain, Old Fort, and Marion, to Raleigh and points east.

The Blue Ridge Parkway runs from the Bear Den overlook, past the Orchard at Altapass (clearing visible on ridge in front of Three Knobs), to Three Knobs overlook, Mt. Mitchell, and Asheville. Built by the Clinchfield Railroad in 1904, the orchard shipped 125,000 bushels of apples a year by rail, and was the site of two resort hotels, a golf course, and railroad station, all of which disappeared after passenger service was discontinued. The last section built, known as the Loops, consisted of 18 tunnels and 13 miles of track near the orchard and was considered an engineering marvel of the time. In the 1930s the Parkway was built through the orchard splitting it in half. Today visitors can enjoy music, hayrides, a store, and much more offered by its current owners.

Just south of Altapass, Highway 226 crosses the Parkway at Gillespie Gap (along the line of sight to Pinnacle) on its way to Spruce Pine. The

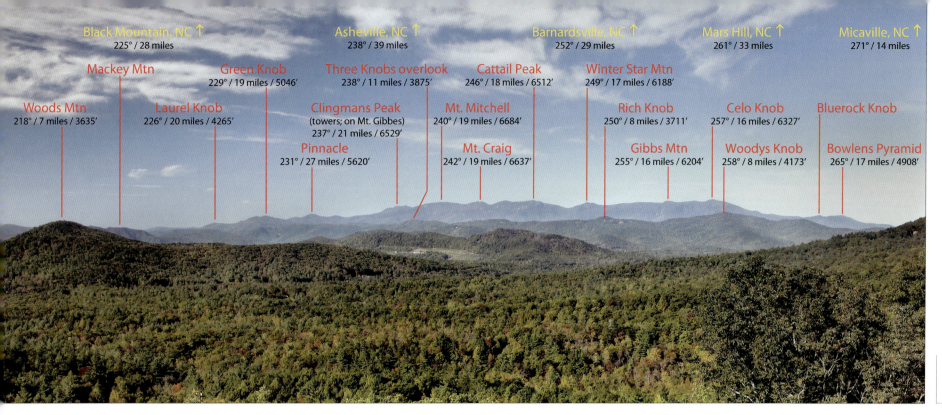

Museum of North Carolina Minerals, located just off the Parkway (Milepost 331) at that junction, houses mineral exhibits, a gift shop, and the visitor center for the Chamber of Commerce of Mitchell County. It is open to the public 9 am to 5 pm daily.

The dominating ridgeline of the Black Mountains in Yancey County, spans the southwestern horizon. Its many peaks include Mt. Gibbes on the south end, Mt. Mitchell, Mt. Craig, Cattail Peak, Winterstar and Gibbs Mountains, with Celo Knob on the north. From Celo Knob the ridge tapers down to Blue Rock Knob and Bowlens Pyramid before reaching the valley floor near Burnsville, NC, and Highway 19E. More than a dozen peaks in the range reach over 6,000 feet, including six of the 10 highest in the eastern United States—Mt. Mitchell being the highest, and Mt. Craig, second.

See page 61, "View from Mt. Mitchell (2 of 6)" for reverse view.

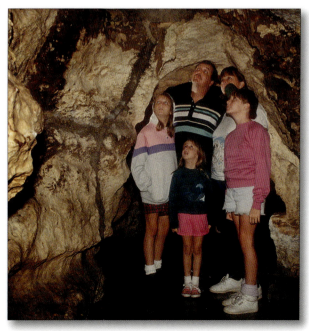

ABOVE: *The Museum of North Carolina Minerals, built in 1956 and renovated in 2002, is located just off the Blue Ridge Parkway (Milepost 311) at its junction with Highway 226 south of Spruce Pine, NC.*

LEFT: *Family exploring nearby Linville Caverns, a subterranean wonderland of formations located about 18 miles north of Marion, NC, along Highway 221, or 4 miles south of the Parkway exit at Milepost 317.*

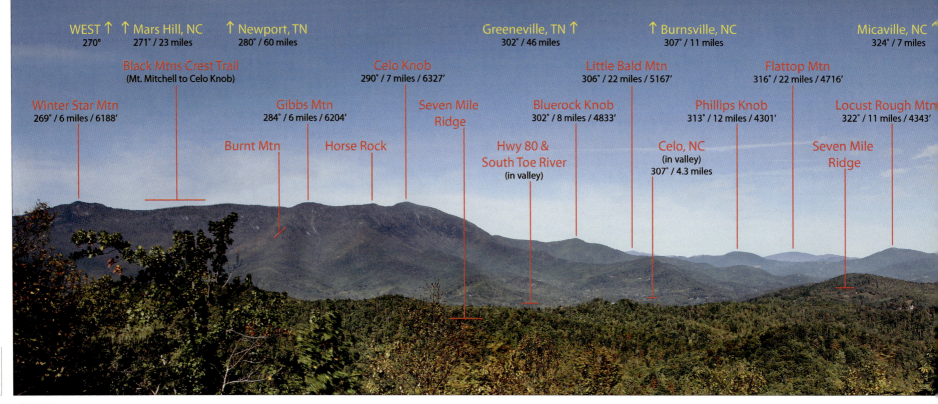

MILEPOST 338.8 Three Knobs overlook

County, State: Yancey County, NC
GPS Coordinates: N 35° 49.156 x W 082° 08.277
Elevation at Viewpoint: 3,875 ft
Location: Located at Milepost 338.8 on the Blue Ridge Parkway south of Little Switzerland, near the Crabtree Meadows Campground.

The Three Knobs overlook is located at the junction of Yancey, McDowell, and Mitchell Counties. The looming range to the west is the Black Mountains in Yancey County featuring five of the highest peaks east of the Mississippi. The tallest is Mt. Mitchell on the south end (out of frame, left), the highest point in eastern America at 6,684 feet.

The Black Mountains continue from Mt. Mitchell to include Winter Star and Gibbs Mountains, with Celo Knob on the north end. In the foreground valley, formed between the Black Mountains and Seven Mile Ridge, are Highway 80 and the South Toe River. Highway 80 crosses the Parkway just south of here near the Black Mountains overlook and continues through the valley below the Blacks, past Carolina Hemlocks, with its campground and popular summer wading area along the South Toe. It continues through the small artist community of Celo to Micaville where it intersects Highway 19E before continuing toward Bakersville, the county seat of Mitchell County.

Just behind Bluerock Knob, along Highway 19E, lies Burnsville, the Yancey County seat and the only incorporated town in the county. Highway 19E runs east/west from Burnsville, between Bluerock and Locust Rough, passing through Micaville, to Spruce Pine (just out of frame, right), where it turns north to Tennessee. It also continues west from Burnsville to its junction with Interstate 26 near Mars Hill. Along the far range beyond Phillips Knob are the Bald Mountains located on the NC/TN state line, which include Little Bald Mountain, with the Appalachian Trail (AT) running across its crest, its companion Big Bald to the south (hidden by Bluerock Knob), and Flattop Mountain to the north.

The AT follows the NC/TN state line across the crest of the Bald Mountains from Little Bald to the Unaka Mountains, and up the back side of Roan Mountain to its crest. The Roan High Knob Shelter is the highest backcountry shelter along the 2,181-mile trail. This main section of the larger Roan Highlands massif dominates the northern horizon and includes Yellow Spot, Roan High Bluff, Roan High Knob, and Grassy Ridge Bald. Renowned for the spectacular rhododendron bloom in mid to late June, it is said to be the world's largest rhododendron garden, and draws tens of thousands of visitors each year.

The main parking and picnic areas are between Roan High Bluff and Roan High Knob. This western section is covered with a dense spruce-fir forest, while east of Carver's Gap, along Grassy

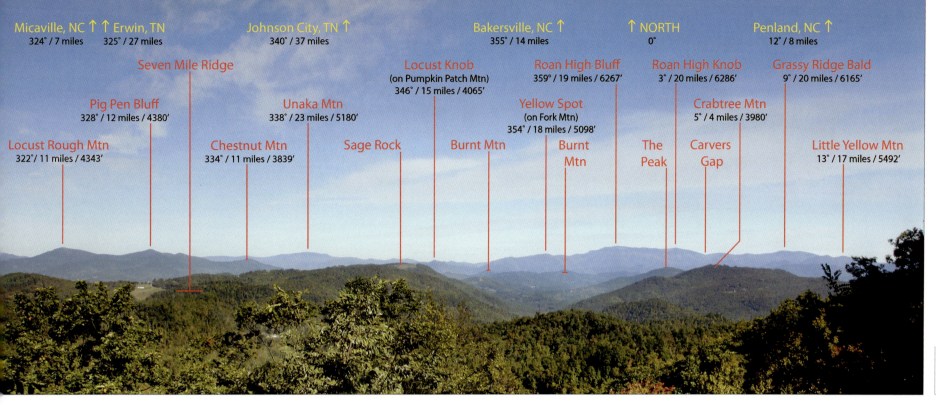

Ridge Bald, is the longest stretch (about 7 miles) of grassy bald in the Appalachian Mountains. To access Roan Mountain from the North Carolina side, many take Highway 197 (off 19E near Burnsville), which runs behind Locust Rough Mountain, Pig Pen Bluff, and Chestnut Mountain, to the community of Red Hill. From there one would follow Highway 226 east to Bakersville, located in the valley in front of Yellow Spot Mountain, then travel Highway 261, which heads north to Carvers Gap on Roan.

Seven Mile Ridge continues across the foreground before ending at Sage Rock. Behind Sage, Highway 19E runs in front of Locust Rough, Pig Pen Bluff, Chestnut Mountain, and The Peak, and behind Crabtree Mountain to Spruce Pine in Mitchell County. At the eastern base of The Peak is the artist community of Penland, home to the nationally recognized Penland School of Crafts, which offers workshops in a variety of mediums including glass, ceramics, metal, wood, and textiles.

Penland School of Crafts was founded by educator and weaver Lucy Morgan in the early 1920s, and today offers workshops on a variety of mediums, including glass, wood, ceramics, and weaving.

The southern end of the Black Mountain range, viewed from nearby Black Mountains overlook, includes Mt. Mitchell (the peak on the right end of a small shelf with towers, left of center) and Winter Star (the right peak).

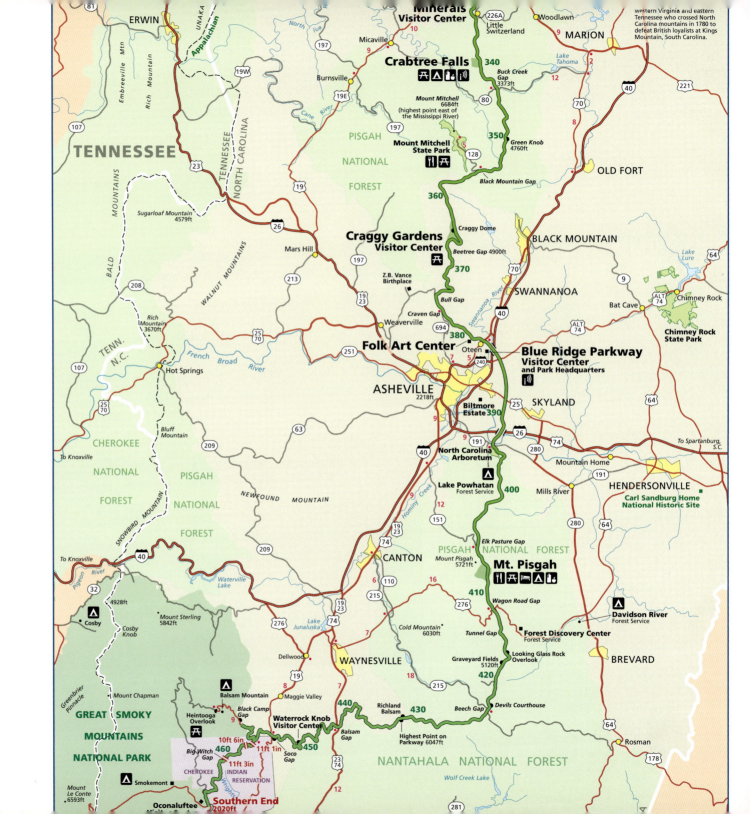

Blue Ridge Parkway overlooks

SECTION THREE
Crabtree Falls to View of Shining Rock Wilderness

Crabtree Falls Visitor Center—Milepost 339.5
Black Mountains overlook—Milepost 342.2 | Elev. 3892
Buck Creek Gap overlook—Milepost 344.1 | Elev. 3355
Singecat Ridge overlook—Milepost 345.3 | Elev. 3406
Curtis Valley overlook—Milepost 348.8 | Elev. 4460
Licklog Ridge overlook—Milepost 349.2 | Elev. 4602
Mt. Mitchell overlook—Milepost 349.9 | Elev. 4825
Green Knob overlook—Milepost 350.4 | Elev. 4761 58
Ridge Junction overlook—Milepost 355.3 | Elev. 5160
Mt. Mitchell observation platform—turn at Milepost 355.4 | Elev. 6689 . . . 60
Glassmine Falls overlook—Milepost 361.2 | Elev. 5200
Graybeard Mountain overlook—Milepost 363.4 | Elev. 5592
Craggy Dome overlook—Milepost 364.1 | Elev. 5640
Craggy Gardens Visitor Center—Milepost 364.5 | Elev. 5489 66
Lane Pinnacle overlook—Milepost 372.1 | Elev. 3890 71
Bull Creek Valley overlook—Milepost 373.8 | Elev. 3483
Tanbark Ridge overlook—Milepost 376.7 | Elev. 3175
Haw Creek Valley overlook—Milepost 380 | Elev. 2720 72
Folk Art Center—Milepost 382
Blue Ridge Parkway Visitor Center—Milepost 384
French Broad overlook—Milepost 393.8 | Elev. 2100

View of Biltmore Estate and Craggy Range—Milepost 394 | Elev. 2364 73
Walnut Cove overlook—Milepost 396.4 | Elev. 2920
Sleepy Gap overlook—Milepost 397.3 | Elev. 2930
View Chestnut Cove overlook—Milepost 398.3 | Elev. 3035 74
Bad Fork Valley overlook—Milepost 399.7 | Elev. 3350 75
Wash Creek Valley overlook—Milepost 401.1 | Elev. 3435
Beaver Dam Gap overlook—Milepost 401.7 | Elev. 3570
Stony Bald overlook—Milepost 402.6 | Elev. 3750
Big Ridge overlook—Milepost 403.6 | Elev. 3820
Hominy Valley overlook—Milepost 404.2 | Elev. 3980 76
Mills River Valley overlook—Milepost 404.5 | Elev. 4085
Buck Springs Gap overlook—Milepost 407.7 | Elev. 4980
Pisgah Inn—Milepost 408.6 | Elev. 4901 78
Funnel Top overlook—Milepost 409.3 | Elev. 4925
The Pink Beds overlook—Milepost 410.3 | Elev. 4822
The Cradle of Forestry overlook—Milepost 411 | Elev. 4710
Cold Mountain overlook—Milepost 411.9 | Elev. 4573 80
Pounding Mill overlook—Milepost 413.2 | Elev. 4700
Cherry Cove overlook—Milepost 415.7 | Elev. 4327
Log Hollow overlook—Milepost 416.3 | Elev. 4445 81
View of Shining Rock Wilderness—turn at Milepost 420.2 | Elev. 5809) . . . 83

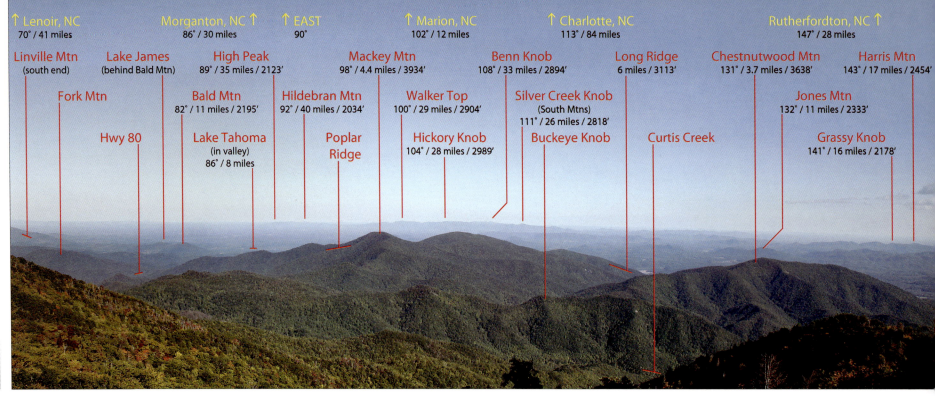

MILEPOST 350.4 Green Knob overlook

County, State: McDowell County, NC
GPS Coordinates: N 35° 43.060 x W 082° 13.358
Elevation at Viewpoint: 4,760 ft
Location: Located at Milepost 350.4 about 5 miles north of the entrance to Mt. Mitchell State Park.

This view, looking east toward the South Mountains and south toward Chimney Rock, NC, is similar to the views from Mt. Mitchell on page 62 and 63 (3 & 4 of 6). It is included in case your travels do not allow a visit to Mt. Mitchell (located directly behind you at this viewpoint), and because some features are obscured from there by Commissary Ridge.

Looking east, Curtis Creek flows through the immediate foreground valley. The paved Curtis Creek Road/SR1227 that turns off of Highway 70 just past Old Fort, NC, becomes Forest Service Road 482 once it enters Pisgah National Forest. From there this steep, winding, dirt and gravel track, runs along in front of Chestnutwood Mountain and Buckeye Knob to Big Laurel Gap, located a couple of miles north of this overlook on the Parkway. Curtis Creek Road closely parallels the creek, but was washed out by Hurricanes Frances and Ivan in 2004, and remained closed until 2008. There is a primitive campground (about 14 sites) operated by the US Forest Service about 5 miles up Curtis Creek from US 70; several nice waterfalls and hikes in the area make this a desirable destination.

Highway 70 continues from Old Fort, running in the valley behind Mackey Mountain, to Hickory and Morganton (located in front of High Peak), and continues east, paralleling I-40 to Statesville, NC. Lake James is north of I-40, covering much of the area between Marion and Morganton. Highway 80 cuts off from Highway 70 near Marion and heads north, passing behind Mackey Mountain to Lake Tahoma and up to the Parkway, before dropping down the other side, through the South Toe River Valley.

Just beyond where Highway 80 turns off Highway 70, and also tracking north, is Highway 221, which travels through Marion, crossing Highway 70, and passing between Lake Tahoma and the east end of Lake James. From there it continues in front of Bald and Linville Mountains, to Boone. In the distance beyond Mackey Mountain are the South Mountains, located below Morganton, in Burke County. Its peaks include Walker Top, Hickory Knob, Benn Knob, and Silver Creek Knob.

Looking south toward Chimney Rock, several creeks on the southern slopes (in the area just below the overlook) feed into the Catawba River, which flows between Youngs Ridge and Edmondson Mountain, and empties into Lake James to the east. I-40 and Highway 70 run parallel, west to east, through the same foreground valley, from Asheville (out of frame, right), through the Swannanoa Valley

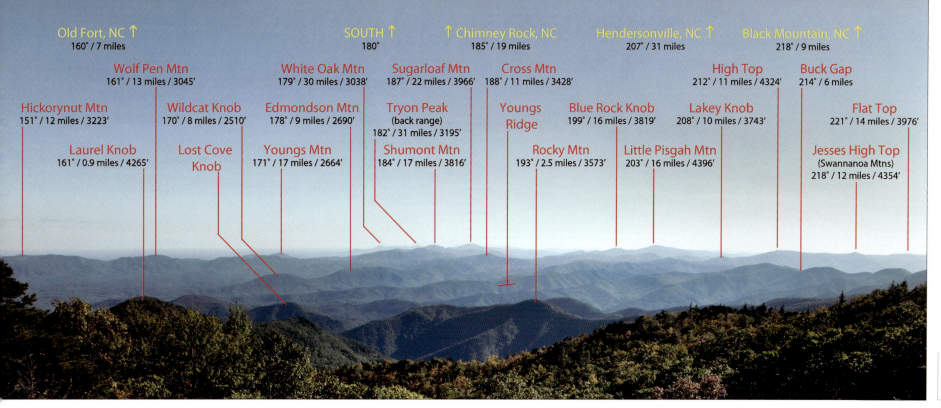

(located in front of Flat Top, Jesses High Top, and High Top in the Swannanoa Mountains), to Black Mountain (below Lakey Knob). The roads continue between Youngs Ridge and Edmondson Mountain, to Old Fort, Marion, and points east. Old Fort is located at the eastern end of Wildcat Knob (on a line of sight with Wolf Pen Mountain).

Highway 9 travels perpendicular to I-40 and Highway 70, south from Black Mountain, through the gap just east (left) of Lakey Knob, and follows the Broad River, past Shumont Mountain to Bat Cave (located between Shumont and Sugarloaf Mountains), near Chimney Rock, where it connects with Highway 64/74A. From there Highway 9 continues south, past Tryon Peak into South Carolina. Highway 74A travels east/west from Asheville through the Fairview community, before ascending to Hickory Nut Gap (behind Little Pisgah Mountain) on the eastern continental divide, then down to Bat Cave, Chimney Rock, and Lake Lure.

ABOVE: *Located on Curtis Creek Road, Curtis Creek Campground offers both roadside camping and campsites along a paved loop. The campground is located along the dirt section of Curtis Creek Road.*

LEFT: *Old Fort was named for the American Revolution-era Davidson Fort located there, which was once the westernmost outpost of Colonial civilization.*

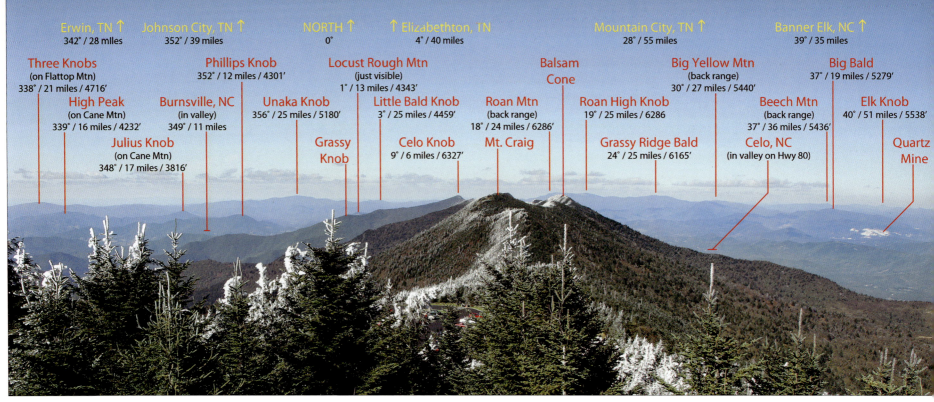

MILEPOST 355 View from Mt. Mitchell (1 of 6)

County, State: Yancey County, NC
GPS Coordinates: N 35° 45.897 x W 082° 15.908
Elevation at Viewpoint: 6,689 ft
Location: Mt. Mitchell State Park is located 33 miles north of Asheville, with the entrance at Milepost 355 on the Blue Ridge Parkway. Turn onto NC 128 and proceed 4.6 miles through entrance gate (no fees), to parking lot near the summit. Walk paved trail 5–10 minutes to observation ramp (handicap accessible). The Parkway can also be accessed from Burnsville or Marion, NC, using NC 80. There is a concession stand and gift shop at the parking lot, open 10 am–5:30 pm, May 1– October 31st. The park is open year-round weather permitting with limited access in winter months due to Parkway and weather closures. Check website for conditions and status at www.ncparks.gov/Visit/parks/momi/main.php.

FROM THE OBSERVATION RAMP LOOKING NORTH you see much of the 15-mile long spine of the Black Mountains, with its numerous peaks rising above 6,000 feet including Mt. Craig, Balsam Cone, Cattail Peak, Winterstar Mountain, and Celo Knob (at the north end). Six of the peaks in this range are among the ten highest in the eastern United States, but due to the even elevations along the ridgeline it was considered one mountain until the 1850s. Mt. Mitchell State Park was created in 1915 to protect this area, the first in a new state park system, and Mt. Craig was named after the governor of the time, who was instrumental in its creation.

The Blacks were formed over a billion years ago, but millions of years of erosion by nature's forces reduced the once-craggy pinnacles to the more rounded, undulating shapes seen today. The underlying harder igneous and metamorphic rocks that remain provide the base for this tall, but compact, range.

In the distance beyond Celo Knob is Roan Mountain on the NC/TN state line, with its long ridgeline that includes Roan High Bluff and Roan

From the parking lot you can walk the short paved trail, a moderate climb, to the stone observation platform, a popular spot for visitors to pose for photographs atop Mt. Mitchell.

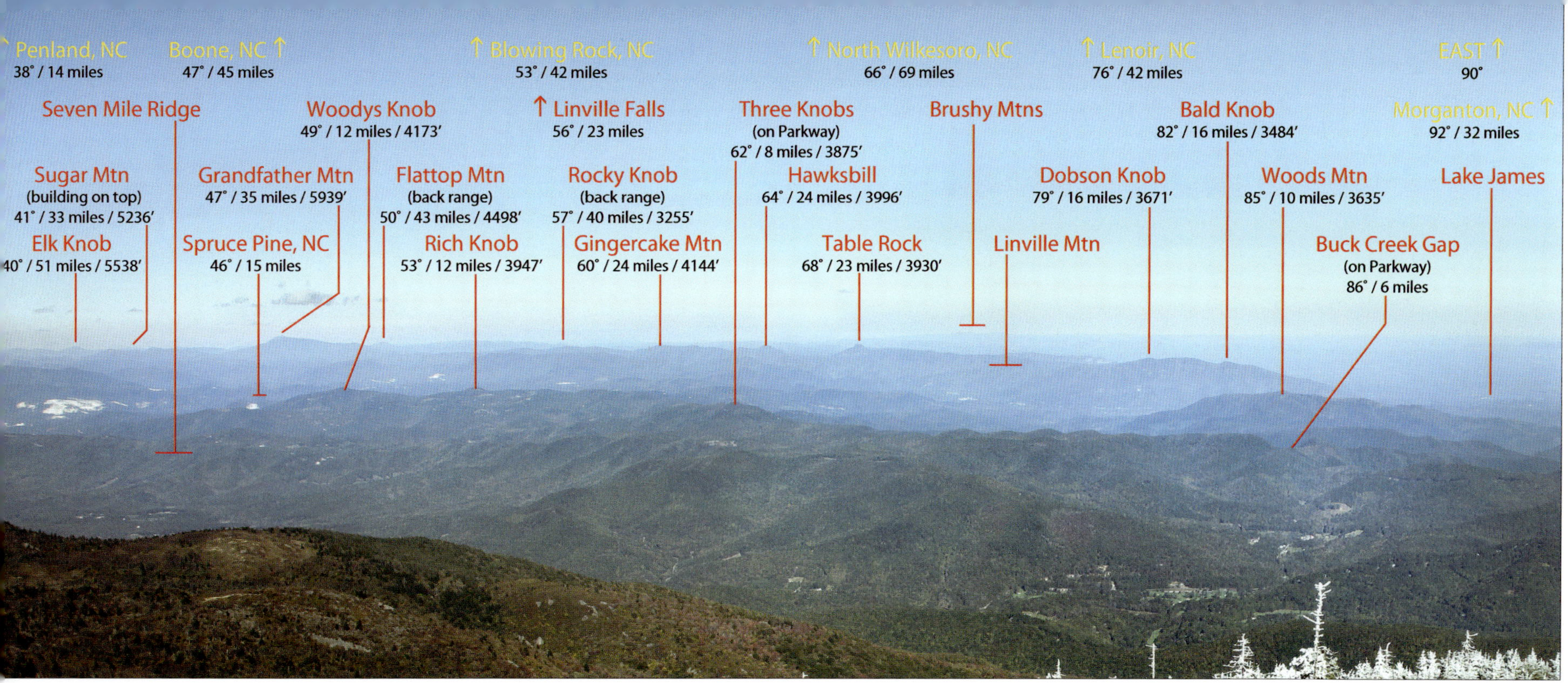

Panorama labels (left to right):

- Penland, NC — 38° / 14 miles
- Boone, NC ↑ — 47° / 45 miles
- ↑ Blowing Rock, NC — 53° / 42 miles
- ↑ North Wilkesboro, NC — 66° / 69 miles
- ↑ Lenoir, NC — 76° / 42 miles
- EAST ↑ — 90°
- Seven Mile Ridge
- Woodys Knob — 49° / 12 miles / 4173'
- ↑ Linville Falls — 56° / 23 miles
- Three Knobs (on Parkway) — 62° / 8 miles / 3875'
- Brushy Mtns
- Bald Knob — 82° / 16 miles / 3484'
- Morganton, NC ↑ — 92° / 32 miles
- Sugar Mtn (building on top) — 41° / 33 miles / 5236'
- Grandfather Mtn — 47° / 35 miles / 5939'
- Flattop Mtn (back range) — 50° / 43 miles / 4498'
- Rocky Knob (back range) — 57° / 40 miles / 3255'
- Hawksbill — 64° / 24 miles / 3996'
- Dobson Knob — 79° / 16 miles / 3671'
- Woods Mtn — 85° / 10 miles / 3635'
- Lake James
- Elk Knob — 40° / 51 miles / 5538'
- Spruce Pine, NC — 46° / 15 miles
- Rich Knob — 53° / 12 miles / 3947'
- Gingercake Mtn — 60° / 24 miles / 4144'
- Table Rock — 68° / 23 miles / 3930'
- Linville Mtn
- Buck Creek Gap (on Parkway) — 86° / 6 miles

(2 of 6)

High Knob on its western end and Grassy Ridge Bald on the eastern portion, separated by Carvers Gap where the main access road, Highway 261 from Bakersville, NC, crosses its crest and becomes Tennessee Highway 143 before dropping down the other side to the town of Roan Mountain.

Roan Mountain is a popular spot for summer visitors, especially during its spectacular rhododendron bloom which typically happens between mid-June to early July. Beech and Sugar Mountains, home of popular winter ski resorts, lie to the east of Roan with Sugar Mountain being easily identifiable by the large structure on its eastern ridgeline.

Northwest of Celo Knob are the Unaka Mountains on the Mitchell Co., NC/Unicoi Co., TN line. Highway 197 running north from Burnsville, passes across their western end, while Highway 226, which goes north from Spruce Pine through Bakersville, crosses on their eastern end between them and Roan. The Appalachian Trail (AT) tracks along the entire ridgeline connecting the Unakas to Roan Mountain before turning north and switching back behind them to follow the ridge of the Iron and Holston Mountains in the extreme northeast corner of Tennessee, and then arriving at Damascus, VA.

Burnsville, located in the valley below High Peak and Julius Knob, is the seat of Yancey County. Highway 19 passes through town and east-west in the valley at the far end of Celo Knob, to Spruce Pine, the largest town in Mitchell County. Known as the "Mineral City of the World," Spruce Pine is home to dozens of mine operations. A large quartz/feldspar mine can be seen as an exposed white area in the photograph.

Highway 19 turns north from Spruce Pine, passing between Roan and Sugar Mountains, to Bristol, TN, and eventually to its terminus in Erie, PA. Mitchell County was formed in 1861 and named after Dr. Elisha Mitchell, the first man to argue that this peak in the Black Mountains was the tallest east of the Mississippi River.

The Blue Ridge Parkway continues past the entrance of Mt. Mitchell State Park and runs along the ridge on the far side of the South Toe River Valley, located in the foreground looking northeast. It passes Buck Creek Gap (where it intersects with Highway 80), Three Knobs, Bear Den overlook, Chestoa overlook (in line with Gingercake Mountain), and Linville Falls before reaching Grandfather Mountain.

Highway 221 coming from Rutherfordton, to the south, continues into this view winding between Woods Mountain and Bald Knob and along the base of Linville and Gingercake Mountains, to Linville. From there it parallels the Parkway swinging just south of Grandfather Mountain to Boone, West Jefferson, and north into Virginia.

Another beautiful route, the Mt. Mitchell Scenic Drive, is one of 54 scenic byways in North

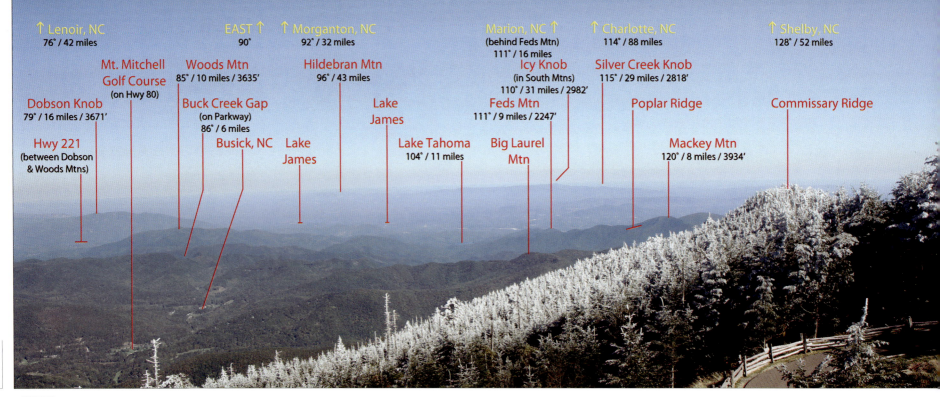

MILEPOST 355 View from Mt. Mitchell (3 of 6)

Carolina. Starting its 52-mile route atop Mt. Mitchell, it descends to the Parkway before dropping down Highway 80 at Buck Creek Gap into the South Toe River Valley. It passes the Mt. Mitchell Golf Course, Carolina Hemlocks campground, and the artist community of Celo, before intersecting Highway 19, which it follows through downtown Burnsville. It continues into adjoining Madison County passing through beautiful farmland and small communities to the intersection of Highway 19 and Interstate 26.

Looking east you are viewing across Lake James, which spans much of the area north of Interstate 40 between Marion and Morganton. This 6,510-acre lake, with over 150 miles of shoreline, is a popular boating and fishing destination. Created between 1916 and 1923 by damming the Catawba River and the tributaries of Paddys Creek and the Linville River, it was named for James Duke, founder of Duke Power Company, which built the dam and still uses the lake as a source of hydroelectric power.

The headwaters of the Linville River can be found on the slopes of Grandfather Mountain, and from there it flows south across Linville Falls and between Linville Mountain and Table Rock, before reaching Lake James. The Catawba River, named for the Catawba tribe of Native Americans, forms east of Black Mountain, and flows past Old Fort and Marion in McDowell County. The North Fork of the Catawba follows Highway 221 from near the town of Linville Falls to the north, south along this side of Linville Mountain and Dobson and Bald Knobs, to Lake James. The Catawba is a tributary of the Wateree River in South Carolina.

The range in the distance is the South Mountains, which include Icy Knob. Located south of Morganton, at the junction of Rutherford, Burke, and Cleveland Counties, they encompass over 100,000 acres, and the South Mountain State Park, which was formed in 1974. While a few peaks top 3,000 feet, most of its many sprawling low ridges average about 2,000. Prominent ones include Walker Top and Hickory, Silver Creek, Icy, and Benn Knobs. On very rare days when the air is especially clear, the tall buildings on the skyline of Charlotte are visible with binoculars on the far horizon, beyond.

From Morganton, I-40 runs east passing south of Lake James and Marion, through the valley on this side of Edmondson Mountain and Wildcat Knob in McDowell County, with the town of Old Fort just below their peaks. It continues through the towns of Black Mountain and Swannanoa, located at the far base of Graybeard Mountain, and through the Swannanoa Valley (located on this side of High Windy and Jesse High Top) to Asheville. See "Green Knob overlook" for a more detailed view of this area. Interstate 26 intersects I-40 near Asheville and connects Spartanburg, SC, and Hendersonville, NC,

with Asheville, before turning north to Weaverville, Mars Hill, and on to Johnson City, TN.

Due south from this overlook you are looking toward the popular tourist destination of Chimney Rock State Park and nearby Lake Lure, located in the valley immediately behind Shumont Mountain. To reach it from the north you can take Highway 9 from Black Mountain, located in the Swannanoa Valley between Graybeard Mountain and Jesse High Top. It passes along the western base of Shumont Mountain before joining Highways 64/74A.

From the east you can reach Chimney Rock from Asheville by traveling Highway 74A southwest through the Fairview community to pass between Little Pisgah and Bearwallow Mountains before dropping into Hickory Nut Gorge which opens out into Lake Lure just past the entrance to Chimney Rock State Park.

Further in the distance on that same line-of-sight with Shumont Mountain is Tryon Peak. Tryon and Columbus, are located in the valley just behind the ridge that runs from Tryon Peak to White Oak Mountain. To the west of the small tourist town of Tryon, located near the NC/SC state line, is Saluda with Hogback Mountain between and just beyond the two. I-26 from Spartanburg, SC, passes through Columbus and between Tryon Peak and Hogback Mountain to Hendersonville and Asheville.

In the immediate foreground you can see Mt. Gibbs and Clingmans Peak (with antenna towers) at the south end of the Black Mountain range. The Parkway is just beyond and is visible where it reappears just past the entrance to Mt. Mitchell State Park at the Ridge Junction overlook. It runs east-west on this side of the Pinnacle, and the Asheville Watershed, with its reservoir lake, is located in the valley to its right west of Graybeard Mountain.

The antennas on Clingmans Peak provide area radio stations, emergency responders, and others with a high altitude location to broadcast

Mt. Mitchell, right, as seen from the Ridge Junction overlook on the Blue Ridge Parkway. The communication towers often associated with Mt. Mitchell are actually located on Clingmans Peak, left.

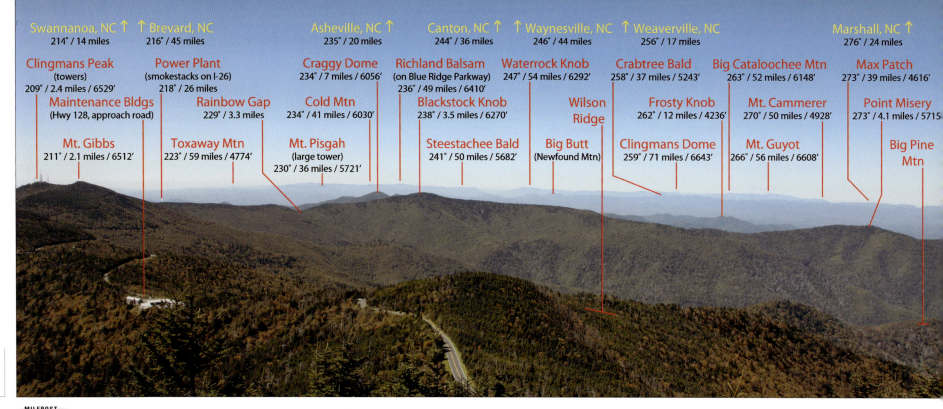

View from Mt. Mitchell (5 of 6)

MILEPOST 355

and relay their signals to the surrounding valleys of western North Carolina. The peak was named after Thomas Lanier Clingman (1812–1897), politician and surveyor, who was rivals with Dr. Elisha Mitchell in their views on the heights of the peaks along the Blacks. Mitchell, a professor at the University of North Carolina, came to this area on numerous trips between 1835 and 1844 to make elevation measurements. Until then Grandfather Mountain was assumed to be the highest in the area, but his readings, only 12 feet off from those done today, convinced him that the peak that now bears his name was higher.

Clingman, one of Elisha Mitchell's former students and later a U.S. Senator, contested the elevation reading prompting Dr. Mitchell to return in 1857 to verify his claim. While crossing the mountain he fell to his death from a cliff above a waterfall. A year later the prominence was named in his honor and his body was moved from its burial plot in Asheville to its current place near the observation platform on the mountain. The nearby peak to the south was named for Senator Clingman, as was the notable Clingmans Dome in the Great Smoky Mountains.

To the right of Mt. Gibbs, in the distance beyond, you can often see smoke rising from the stacks at the power plant along I-26 near the Skyland exit. Further west along the ridge that runs across to Blackstock Knob, is Rainbow Gap. The original railroad to Mt. Mitchell, built between 1911 and 1914, passed through the gap. This narrow-gauge line originated near the town of Black Mountain, and enabled the logging of Mt. Mitchell and surrounding Black Mountains. It ascended over 3,500 feet to Camp Alice, located just below the peak of Mt. Mitchell.

From this camp, constructed for tourists who started arriving in the summer of 1915, visitors could stay overnight in tent facilities on-site and hike to the summit about a mile above. Over 10,000 folks traveled the rail lines over the next four years, with the passenger cars sharing the tracks with the lumber extraction business. Due to government pressure for spruce lumber used in airplane construction during World War I, the passenger service was discontinued to maximize transport of timber.

The Mountains-to-the-Sea Trail parallels the Parkway from Asheville to Mt. Mitchell, passing Craggy Gardens and Craggy Dome before running behind Blackstock Knob to the entrance of Mt. Mitchell State Park where it follows Highway 128 and continues to the summit. From here it drops down Commissary Ridge on the eastern slope to Black Mountain Campground in the valley below, back up to the Parkway, and on to Buck Creek Gap.

South of Craggy Dome, the trail follows the Parkway across a succession of mountains ridges visible from here. After dropping to Asheville, it climbs back up to Mt. Pisgah, passes behind Cold

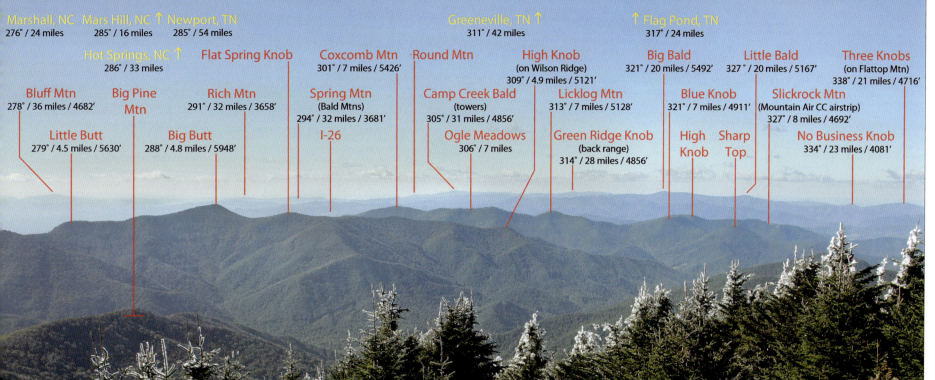

(6 of 6)

Mountain to Richland Balsam, the highest point on the Blue Ridge Parkway, on to Steestachee Bald, down through Balsam Gap and back up to Waterrock Knob. It follows the Parkway to its end point at Highway 441 near the Oconaluftee Visitor Center in the Great Smoky Mountains National Park, then climbs to its own origin point on Clingmans Dome in the Smokies. There it meets the Appalachian Trail, which continues along the spine of the Smokies from Clingmans Dome to Mt. Guyot and down to Mt. Cammerer before descending to Waterville Dam along I-40.

You can envision the path of the AT along the far range through Madison County, NC, as it crosses Max Patch and Bluff Mountain and follows the NC/TN state line to Rich Mountain, Spring Mountain, Camp Creek Bald, Green Ridge Knob, then to Big Bald and Little Bald in Yancey County. From there the trail tracks across the Unaka Mountains and Roan Mountain.

In the foreground valley the Cane River forms and flows along the base of Little and Big Butt Mountains, High Knob, Sharp Top, and Slickrock Mountains to Burnsville, located at the end of the valley. While there are no main roads in this valley, Highway 197 from Burnsville turns near Pensacola to pass between Blue Knob and High Knob (on Wilson Ridge) traveling through the valley on this side of the range that runs from Slickrock to Blue Knob, Licklog, and Coxcomb Mountains. Ogle Meadows, a large grassy area located along that same ridge, is a popular hiking destination. Highway 197 continues behind Big Butt to Barnardsville, located in the valley behind Little Butt, before intersecting with Interstate 26.

For reverse view of Mt. Mitchell, see Bear Den overlook, page 53.

Clouds fill the valley floor in this view, looking northwest toward High Knob, from Mt. Mitchell. The weather here can be extreme, with high winds and cold temperatures common year round.

MILEPOST 364.5 Craggy Gardens Visitor Center (looking east)

County, State: Buncombe County, NC
GPS Coordinates: N 35° 42.004 x W 082° 22.792
Elevation at Viewpoint: 5,489 ft
Location: Craggy Gardens Visitor Center is located at Milepost 364.5 on the Blue Ridge Parkway, between Asheville and Mt. Mitchell. These two photos were taken across the street from the visitor center looking east over the reservoir. Use caution when crossing the Parkway due to traffic congestion and limited sight distance for drivers. The two photos on pages 68–69 look west from the parking lot on the south side of the visitor center building.

From the sign opposite Craggy Gardens Visitor Center, you can look east from the Parkway over Burnett Reservoir, also known locally as the North Fork Reservoir, one of many man-made lakes in western North Carolina. You will notice an absence of houses, roads, or boat docks around this body of water, distinguishing it from all other lakes in the region; this is because the area is a protected watershed of 22,000 acres. Owned by the city of Asheville, the reservoir serves as a primary source of clean water, along with the nearby Bee Tree Lake.

Located 24 miles from downtown Asheville, Craggy Gardens is a popular destination for visitors, especially in mid and late June when the Catawba rhododendron are in bloom, blanketing the area with pink blossoms that grow in abundance on Craggy Dome, Craggy Pinnacle, and at the Craggy Gardens Picnic Area. From the upper parking lot, located just through the tunnel, a 1.4-mile round trip hiking trail leads through a canopy of rhododendron to the open bald of Craggy Pinnacle, which is covered by azaleas, rhododendron, and wild blueberry bushes.

The small wooden visitor center carries a selection of maps, books, postcards, and has restrooms below. Here, at the adjoining parking lot, you are standing on the ridgeline of the Great Craggy Mountains, which rise from the valley near Swannanoa (located to the south along Interstate 40) and run north to the Black Mountains, which include Mt. Mitchell and Celo Knob.

Burnett Reservoir is formed by damming the Swannanoa River, which is fed by creeks that drain the bowl-shaped valley formed between the Craggy Mountains on the west, the Black Mountains to the north, and the Pinnacle, Graybeard, and Middle Mountains to the east. Beyond Middle Mountain is Ditney Knob, located near the juncture of McDowell, Buncombe, and Rutherford counties. The small towns of Rutherfordton and Spindale lie in the "thermal belt" flatlands beyond, along that line of sight.

I-40 runs all along the Swannanoa Valley (foreground) from Asheville (out of frame right), through Black Mountain, in front of Ditney Knob, Hickorynut Mountain, and Wolf Pen Mountain, to Marion, and points east. Black Mountain is

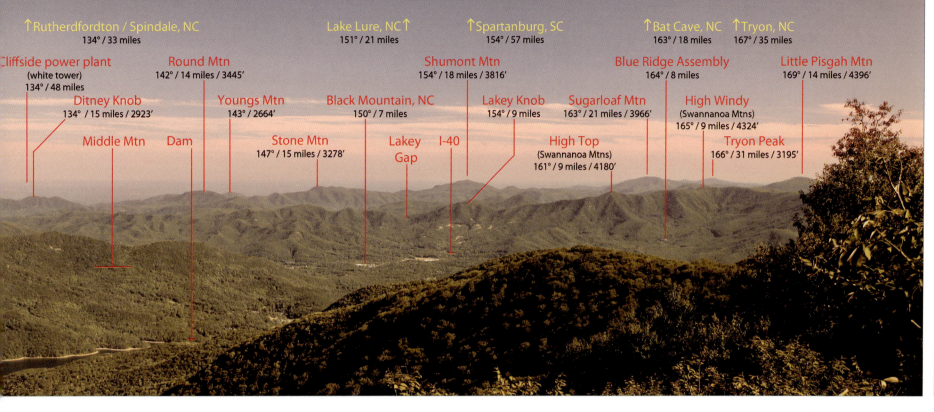

a popular tourist town, with many summer camps located in the surrounding area, including Ridgecrest and Camp Rockmont. Highway 9 travels south from there through Lakey Gap to Bat Cave (located near Chimney Rock State Park), passing on this side of Shumont, Stone, and Round Mountains. Farther right, in the valley below High Windy, is the Blue Ridge Assembly. You can see its buildings nestled among 1,200 acres of woodland. A YMCA student conference center, and listed in the National Register of Historic Places, the Assembly was founded in 1906 and serves 30,000 guests annually.

Tryon Peak, near the town of Tryon in Polk County, is behind High Windy. Little Pisgah Mountain is further south (right) along Highway 74A, which runs from Asheville to Bat Cave, passing just behind Little Pisgah through Hickory Nut Gap. Highways 9, 74A, and 64 intersect at Bat Cave, located in Hickory Nut Gorge just this side of, and in line with, Sugarloaf Mountain.

ABOVE: *Craggy Gardens Visitor Center at Pinnacle Gap along the Parkway offers great views to the east and west. Craggy Pinnacle, the third highest peak in the Great Craggy Mountains at 5,817 feet, rises up behind.*

RIGHT: *Lake Burnett, the reservoir of the Asheville watershed, as seen from the dam at the south end of the lake. Potato Knob near Mt. Mitchell is visible to the north (center of photo) along the Blue Ridge Parkway.*

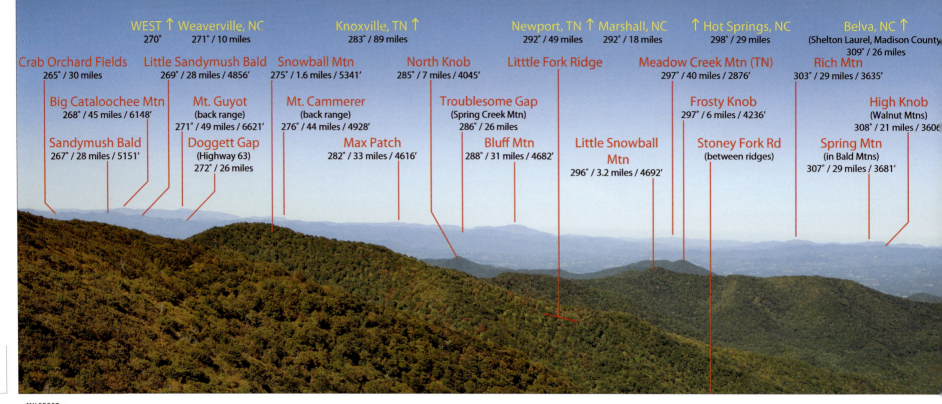

MILEPOST 364.5 Craggy Gardens Visitor Center (looking west)

This view is from the parking lot on the south side of the visitor center, looking west. An expansive one, it spans more than 100 degrees—from Big Cataloochee Mountain, Mt. Guyot, and Mt. Cammerer in the Great Smoky Mountains in the west, to Little Bald and the Bald Mountains on the NC/TN state line in the northwest. This parking area is one of the few that offers travelers a view of both sides of the Parkway. Located at Pinnacle Gap, it's also one of the windiest, because air from the west is funneled through the narrow pass.

In the foreground, you are looking over Buncombe County to Mars Hill (home of Mars Hill College) in Madison County, NC, and into Tennessee. On the slopes just below the overlook, Stoney Fork Road and FR63 (a dirt road) run from the Dillingham Community near Barnardsville, up the valley, below Little Fork Ridge, to Craggy Gardens Picnic Area. You can also drive to the main entrance of the picnic area off the Parkway by taking the marked turnoff just south of this overlook. You can even hike from here using the trail that leaves the south end of the parking lot. It climbs 0.3 miles up to the crest of the mountain, where there is a large wooden structure, originally built by the Civilian Conservation Corp in the mid-1930s as a picnic shelter (before this segment of Parkway was completed). From there, the trail descends about 0.5 miles to Craggy Gardens Picnic Area.

From their crest here, the Craggy Mountains descend west to the wide valley floor, where Highway 19/23/Interstate 26 passes from Asheville (out of frame, left), to Weaverville (behind Snowball Mountain), along the far side of North and Frosty Knobs, bypassing Mars Hill before splitting. I-26 can be seen as it snakes its way up the mountains to Sams Gap, where it crosses into Tennessee on its way to Johnson City. Highway 19 continues north (right) toward Burnsville, while Highway 23, the older, more winding narrow route over the mountains, parallels I-26 north to Sams Gap.

Due west, in the distance on the far side of the valley traversed by I-26, are Sandymush Bald and the Newfound Mountains, with the Spring Creek Mountains just to their north. Highway 63 (Leicester Highway) runs from Asheville through the Leicester community to Spring Creek, crossing between Little Sandymush Bald and the Spring Creek Mountains at Doggett Gap. From the gap, Highway 63 drops to the Spring Creek community where it intersects Highway 209, which runs from Lake Junaluska to Hot Springs, passing behind Crabtree Bald (just out of frame, left, south of Crab Orchard Fields), Sandymush Bald, and the Spring Creek Mountains.

I-40 also runs north from Lake Junaluska, paralleling Highway 209 through the valley behind Sandymush Bald before turning northwest to skirt the Great Smoky Mountains, passing just east of Cataloochee Valley (below Big Cataloochee Mountain), part of the Great Smoky Mountains

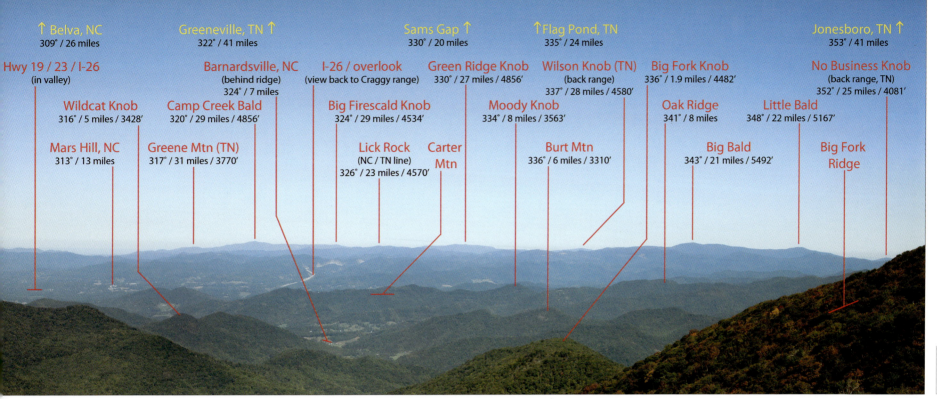

↑ Belva, NC	Greeneville, TN ↑		Sams Gap ↑	↑ Flag Pond, TN		Jonesboro, TN ↑
309° / 26 miles	322° / 41 miles		330° / 20 miles	335° / 24 miles		353° / 41 miles

Hwy 19 / 23 / I-26 (in valley)

Barnardsville, NC (behind ridge) 324° / 7 miles

I-26 / overlook (view back to Craggy range)

Green Ridge Knob 330° / 27 miles / 4856'

Wilson Knob (TN) (back range) 337° / 28 miles / 4580'

Big Fork Knob 336° / 1.9 miles / 4482'

No Business Knob (back range, TN) 352° / 25 miles / 4081'

Wildcat Knob 316° / 5 miles / 3428'

Camp Creek Bald 320° / 29 miles / 4856'

Big Firescald Knob 324° / 29 miles / 4534'

Moody Knob 334° / 8 miles / 3563'

Oak Ridge 341° / 8 miles

Little Bald 348° / 22 miles / 5167'

Mars Hill, NC 313° / 13 miles

Greene Mtn (TN) 317° / 31 miles / 3770'

Lick Rock (NC / TN line) 326° / 23 miles / 4570'

Carter Mtn

Burt Mtn 336° / 6 miles / 3310'

Big Bald 343° / 21 miles / 5492'

Big Fork Ridge

National Park. The NC/TN state line and Appalachian Trail (AT) travel along the crest of Mt. Guyot (on the northern end of the spine of the Smokies), to Mt. Cammerer, and to the valley floor at Waterville Dam on the Pigeon River and I-40, before climbing up to Max Patch and Bluff Mountain.

From there the AT descends to the town of Hot Springs along the French Broad River (which flows from Asheville through Marshall to Newport, TN), before continuing to Rich Mountain and following the NC/TN state line across Camp Creek Bald, Big Firescald Knob, Green Ridge Knob, Lick Rock, and Sams Gap (where it crosses I-26), and along the crest of Big and Little Balds to Roan Mountain (out of frame, right). On the far right, Big Fork Ridge descends from Craggy Pinnacle to Big Fork Knob, and then tapers to end at the Dillingham community on this side of Burt Mountain.

For the reverse view see, View from I-26 to Craggy Mountains, page 115.

ABOVE: *Catawba Rhododendron typically bloom in late June and early July along this section of the Parkway, drawing large numbers of visitors. This view is looking west from the top of Craggy Pinnacle.*

LEFT: *Craggy Gardens Visitor Center as seen from the top of Craggy Pinnacle. This viewpoint is accessed by a trail (0.7 mile one way) from the Craggy Dome Parking Area just north on the Parkway.*

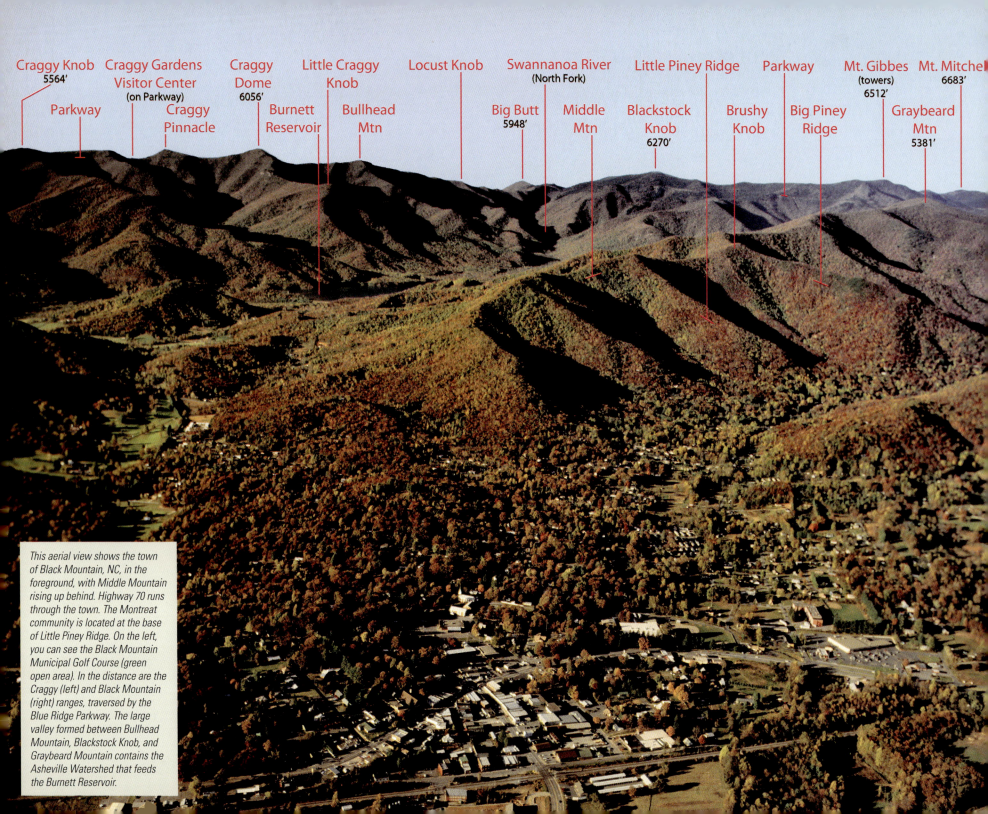

MILEPOST 372.1 Lane Pinnacle overlook

County, State: Buncombe County, NC
GPS Coordinates: N 35° 40.107 x W 082° 26.565
Elevation at Viewpoint: 3,890 ft
Location: Located just south of Lane Pinnacle at Milepost 372.1 on the Blue Ridge Parkway, between the Folk Art Center and Craggy Gardens.

FROM THIS OVERLOOK YOU ARE LOOKING SOUTHEAST toward the Swannanoa Mountains, whose peaks include High Top, High Windy, Jesse High Top, Flat Top, and Cedar Cliff. The Cliffs development, originally planned to include up to 1,200 homes, spans the mountain crest on Flat Top and continues on the other side into the Fairview community. It has struggled to stay viable since the economic downturn of 2008. Highway 70 and Interstate 40 run parallel through the Swannanoa Valley, located on the foreground side of the range, from Asheville (out of frame, right), through Swannanoa (located in line with Flat Top Mountain), to Black Mountain and points east.

On the far side of the range, Highway 74 travels from Asheville, through the Fairview community, passing between the Swannanoa Mountains and Busbee, Butler, and Bearwallow Mountains. It then crosses the eastern continental divide at Hickory Nut Gap on the back side of Little Pisgah Mountain, before dropping into Hickory Nut Gorge to Chimney Rock and Lake Lure. Highway 25 and Interstate 26 run southeast from Asheville, passing behind Busbee Mountain, to the power plant near the Skyland exit on I-26, and in front of Jump Off Rock, located near the town of Hendersonville.

Rock Knob is the tallest point on the ridgeline in the middle foreground, with Bee Tree Reservoir in the valley on the back side. The ridge tapers down from Rock Knob to Bartlett Mountain before ending along Bull Creek in the Riceville Community in east Asheville.

The sharp peak of Lane Pinnacle (center) rises to 5,230 feet and was named after Charles Lane, the original owner of the property, who had iron mining interests there. Just west (left) of the peak are Wolfden and Rich Knobs. Lane Pinnacle is visible from the overlook, to the north (left) of the main view (top photo).

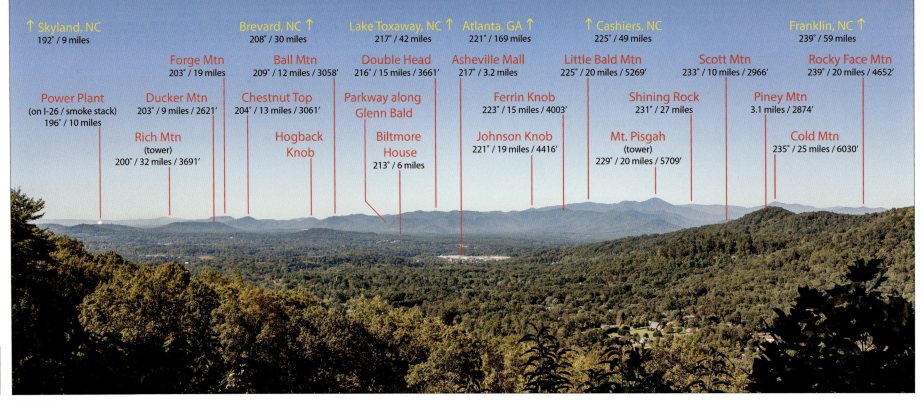

MILEPOST 380 Haw Creek Valley overlook

County, State: Buncombe County, NC
GPS Coordinates: N 35° 37.016 x W 082° 29.501
Elevation at Viewpoint: 2,720 ft
Location: Located at Milepost 380 on the Blue Ridge Parkway, between the Folk Art Center and the Tanbark Ridge overlook near Asheville, NC.

THIS OVERLOOK OFFERS A GREAT VIEW OF THE mountains near Asheville. The Haw Creek Valley, with its residential community, is in the foreground between the overlook and Piney Mountain. The large white complex in the middle of the view is the Asheville Mall. Highway 70 runs on the foreground side of the mall, from downtown Asheville (located just behind Piney) to the small Oteen community (just out of frame, left). The area's main tourist attraction, Biltmore Estate, is visible on the ridge just behind and to the left of the mall.

From the overlook, the Parkway continues through Oteen and south Asheville, crossing Hendersonville Road (Highway 25), which runs north/south between the mall and Ducker Mountain. A bit further on, it passes over Interstate 26, just to the right of Ducker Mountain, before climbing out of the valley to Glenn Bald. From there, the Parkway travels along the back side of the far mountains and ascends past Double Head to Ferrin Knob and Mt. Pisgah.

In front of Double Head is Ball Mountain, located on Brevard Road (Highway 191) near Avery Creek. Chestnut Top and Forge Mountain (on Highway 280 to Brevard) are south of Ball Mountain in the Mills River area. The long low shape of Ducker Mountain hides the Biltmore Park development at Long Shoals Road off I-26, behind. The French Broad River and I-26 run between Ducker and Ball Mountains through the main valley to Asheville.

For the reverse view from Glenn Bald, see Biltmore Estate and Craggy Mtn. Range on page 73.

The Folk Art Center, located at Milepost 382 on the Parkway near the Oteen/Highway 70 exit, is operated by the Southern Highland Craft Guild and showcases traditional and contemporary crafts of the Southern Appalachians.

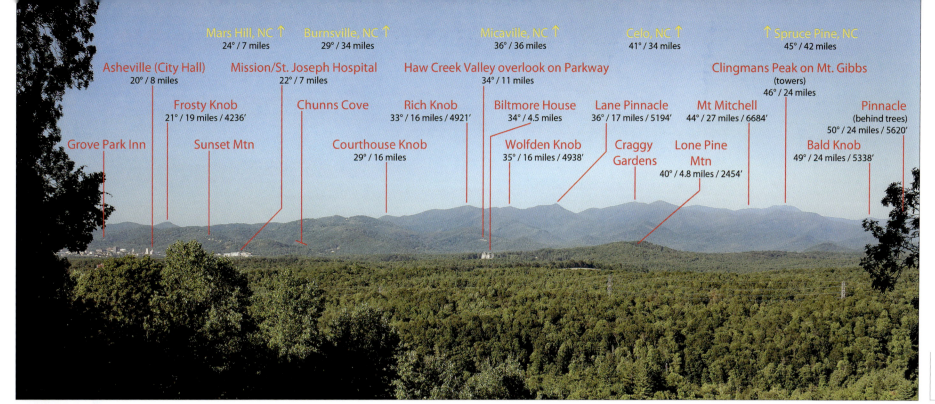

MILEPOST 394 — View of Biltmore Estate and Craggy Mtn. Range

County, State: Buncombe County, NC
GPS Coordinates: N 35° 29.215 x W 082° 35.818
Elevation at Viewpoint: 2,364 ft
Location: From the Brevard Road /NC Arboretum entrance to the Blue Ridge Parkway, travel south toward Mt. Pisgah a short distance to a clearing on the left at about Milepost 394. There is no overlook there (pull off on the grass shoulder), but this clearing offers a great view of the Biltmore Estate.

THE BILTMORE HOUSE (CENTER) IS SURROUNDED by about 8,000 acres of forest and fields that make up the estate grounds. To the left is downtown Asheville, with the City Hall and Buncombe County Courthouse buildings, and the historic red-roofed Grove Park Inn hotel behind the city. Nearer the estate the upscale Biltmore Forest residential community lies along Highway 25 (Hendersonville Highway), just behind Lone Pine Mountain.

The French Broad River runs along below this viewpoint, winding through the foreground valley, to pass just in front of the Biltmore House to Asheville, where in splits West Asheville from the main part of town. Brevard Road (Highway 191) is at the base of the foreground ridge on this side of the French Broad. On the far side, I-26 (mostly hidden by trees) travels in front of the Biltmore House through Asheville and north past Mars Hill. I-40 runs east from Asheville along the base of the far Craggy Mountain range, on its way to Black Mountain (out of frame, right), and points east.

The Parkway descends into the foreground valley crossing I-26 and the French Broad River, passing to the right of Lone Pine Mountain, to Oteen (far side of valley), before climbing up to become visible at the Haw Creek Valley overlook, and on to Rich and Wolfden Knobs, Lane Pinnacle, Craggy Gardens, and Mt. Mitchell.

See Haw Creek Valley overlook on page 72 for the reverse perspective.

Paddlers explore the French Broad River between Hendersonville and Asheville, passing the Biltmore Estate along their route. When the river level rises, the river becomes a popular canoeing destination.

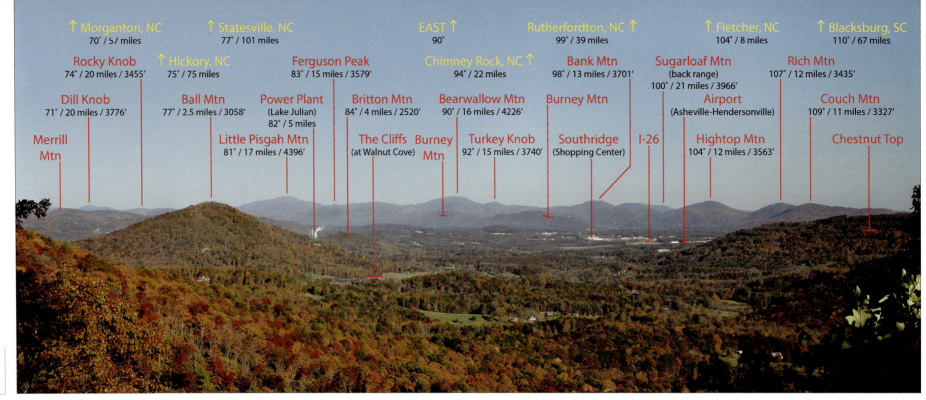

MILEPOST 398.3 View Chestnut Cove overlook

County, State: Buncombe County, NC
GPS Coordinates: N 35° 27.607 x W 082° 38.176
Elevation at Viewpoint: 3,035 ft
Location: Located at Milepost 398.3 on the Blue Ridge Parkway near Asheville, between the Walnut Cove and Bad Fork Valley overlooks.

FROM HERE YOU ARE LOOKING EAST ACROSS THE French Broad River valley. The Cliffs at Walnut Cove development with golf course spreads across much of the foreground below in the Avery Creek community. Four major roads, Interstate 26 and Highways 191, 25, and 74A, traverse this view west/east from Asheville (out of frame, left) through Buncombe and Henderson Counties, their paths running roughly parallel, at different distances.

The closest is Highway 191 (Brevard Road) which runs between Ball and Britton Mountains before passing behind Chestnut Top to Hendersonville (out of frame, right).

Next back is I-26 which runs between Britton Mountain and the power station with the French Broad River flowing between it and 191. The Asheville-Hendersonville Airport is on this side of I-26 with part of the runway and ancillary buildings visible. At the same exit, but on the far side of I-26, Airport Road heads north past Southridge Shopping Center (Lowes, Target, and more) to connect with Highway 25 (Hendersonville Highway) near Arden.

Highway 25 runs through Skyland and Fletcher (in the valley in front of Hightop) to Hendersonville. Highway 74, runs from Asheville to Fairview then climbs to pass through Hickory Nut Gap—located between Ferguson Peak and Little Pisgah Mountain, down Hickory Nut Gorge (behind Bearwallow and Sugarloaf Mountains) to Chimney Rock, Lake Lure, Rutherfordton, Charlotte, and points east.

The Quilt Garden at the North Carolina Arboretum is planted with a variety of flowering plants each season. The 434-acre complex is open year-round (small admission fee) and is located just north near the Parkway exit to Highway 191 at Milepost 393.

[Panoramic photo labels, left to right:]

↑ SOUTH
180°

↑ Brevard, NC
197° / 16 miles

Cashiers, NC ↑
228° / 34 miles

Franklin, NC ↑
246° / 43 miles

Sylva, NC ↑
261° / 33 miles

Waynesville, NC ↑
278° / 20 miles

Queen Creek Mtn
(back range)
194° / 4.5 miles / 3602'

Black Mtn
211° / 3.9 miles / 3907'

Kramers Vista

Little Bald Mtn
240° / 6 miles / 5269'

Buck Spring Gap
246° / 6 miles

↑ WEST
270°

Big Knob
175° / 4.4 miles / 2989'

North Mills River
(in valley)

Rich Gap Mtn
223° / 4.1 miles / 4049'

Laurel Mtn

Trace Ridge

Stoney Bald
258° / 4.2 miles / 4512'

Beaverdam Gap

Rich Mtn
(tower, back range)
185° / 19 miles / 3691'

Yellow Gap
199° / 4.1 miles

Trace Ridge

Laurel Ridge

Funnel Top
(back range)
216° / 7 miles / 4265'

Johnson Knob
231° / 4.7 miles / 4416'

Big Ridge

Mt Pisgah
(tower)
254° / 6 miles / 5709'

Mills River Valley overlook
(on Parkway)

MILEPOST 399.7 Bad Fork Valley overlook

County, State: On the Henderson/Buncombe County line, NC
GPS Coordinates: N 35° 27.044 x W 082° 39.106
Elevation at Viewpoint: 3,350 ft
Location: Located at Milepost 399.7 on the Blue Ridge Parkway, between Chestnut Cove and Wash Creek Valley overlooks.

THIS VIEW TO THE SOUTHWEST SHOWS MT. PISGAH dominating the far ridgeline. Its distinctive tower and conical shape make it easy to identify from any angle and is therefore a landmark that most area residents can recognize from wherever they are.

The Parkway continues from this overlook toward Mt. Pisgah, passing Ferrin Knob (just out of frame, right), Beaverdam Gap, Shell Knob, the Mills River Valley overlook (which offers spectacular views back in this direction), to Stoney Bald and Little Pisgah Mountain (the wide, flat shape located slightly in front and to the left of Mt. Pisgah from this angle). From there, the Parkway continues through Buck Spring Gap to the Pisgah Inn and restaurant, located behind Little Bald Mountain, past the Mt. Pisgah Campground; it then continues southwest, following the Haywood/Transylvania County line.

Laurel Mountain runs east/west from the Parkway at Little Bald Mountain, to include Johnson Knob, Rich Gap Mountain, Black Mountain (not to be confused with the larger Black Mountain near Funnel Top in the distance), to Yellow Gap, where Queens Creek Mountain picks up.

From Black Mountain, Laurel Ridge turns in this direction and tapers to the valley floor, where the North Mills River flows (behind the end of Trace Ridge). Fly fishermen, campers, hikers, mountain bikers, and outdoor enthusiasts of all types are drawn to these densely wooded environs. The North Mills River Recreation Area is accessed from Brevard Road/Highway 191 using the North Mills River Road.

Mountain bikers find many beautiful and challenging locations to explore in the mountains surrounding the Parkway, including the North Mills River area and DuPont State Forest (above), near Brevard.

Panorama labels (left to right):
- Big Cataloochee Mtn — 301° / 30 miles / 6155′
- Mt. Sterling ↑ (back range) — 308° / 28 miles / 5842′
- Pretty Hollow Gap — 305° / 29 miles
- Mt Sterling ridge — 28 miles
- Spring Mtn
- South Hominy Creek (in valley)
- ↑ Canton, NC — 311° / 9 miles
- White Rock Mtn
- Saw Mtn
- Doubletop Mtn — 317° / 6 miles / 4127′
- Warren Ridge
- Newport, TN ↑ — 323° / 44 miles
- Crabtree Bald — 322° / 18 miles / 5243′
- Sheep Top — 323° / 6 miles / 4003′
- Thompson Knob — 325° / 6 miles / 4150′
- Glade Mtn
- Max Patch ↑ — 331° / 28 miles
- Sandymush Bald — 329° / 18 miles / 5151′
- Standhill Mtn
- I-40 (in valley)
- Little Sandymush Bald — 333° / 19 miles / 4856′
- Holland Mtn

MILEPOST 404.2 Hominy Valley overlook

County, State: On the Buncombe/Henderson County line, NC
GPS Coordinates: N 35° 26.860 x W 082° 43.033
Elevation at Viewpoint: 3,980 ft
Location: Located at Milepost 404.2 on the Blue Ridge Parkway, between Big Ridge overlook and Mills River Valley overlook.

FROM HERE YOU ARE VIEWING NORTHWEST OVER THE Hominy Valley, a rural farming area located in Buncombe County. It is the only overlook, with views to the west, built on the western side of the ridgeline traversed by the Parkway, between Asheville and Wagon Road Gap, south of Mt. Pisgah.

Highway 151 and South Hominy Creek pass through the (foreground) valley. From its junction with Highway 19/23/74 near the small town of Candler (located at the eastern end of Peggy Peak), Highway 151 runs between Saw and Standhill Mountains, and climbs up to pass along the slope immediately beneath the overlook to its intersection with the Parkway just south of here.

South Hominy Creek, formed by the drainage from the hillsides surrounding Hominy Valley, starts where smaller creeks converge along the base of Warren Ridge. It follows Highway 151 to Candler, where it merges with Hominy Creek, which flows east through Enka to join the French Broad River in West Asheville (out of frame, right).

On the far wall of the valley are Doubletop Mountain, Sheep Top, and Thompson Knob, with the Buncombe/Haywood County line running along the ridgeline. Beyond are Big Cataloochee Mountain and Big Butt, peaks that rise on the far (western) side of Cataloochee Valley, part of the Great Smoky Mountains National Park. From Big Butt, the Mt. Sterling Ledge runs north to Mt. Sterling (hidden by the foreground ridgeline), and down to Big Creek and the Waterville Dam along Interstate 40.

I-40 runs west from Asheville, passing

An aerial view over Hominy Valley looking southeast back toward the Parkway and Ferrin Knob (high peak, center, right). The Pinnacle, located between Hendersonville and Brevard, is on the back range behind, with Hogback Mountain, near Saluda, on the horizon, left. The Hominy Valley overlook is out of frame, right.

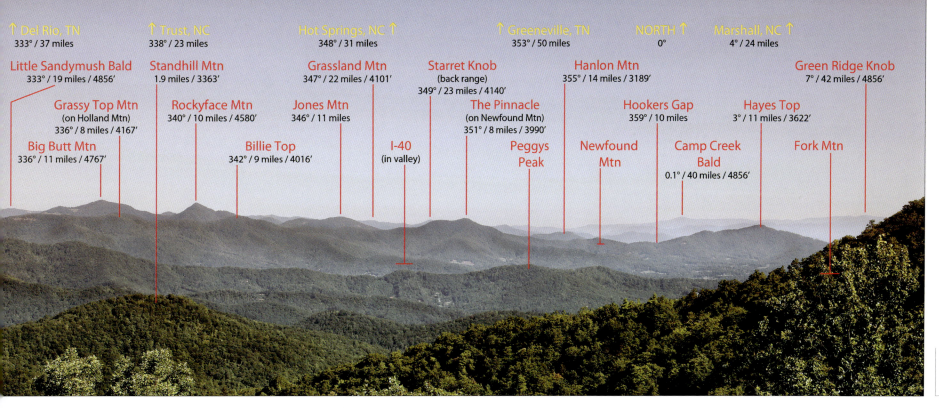

through the valley between Peggy Peak and The Pinnacle, along the foreground base of Hayes Top, Billie Top, and Grassy Top (on Holland Mountain). It continues through the gap between Thompson Knob and Holland Mountain to Canton, located on the far side of Doubletop Mountain and points west. It is paralleled along this route by Highway 19/23/74.

From Canton, I-40 and Highway 19/23/74 continue west to Clyde and Waynesville. Both towns are located in the valley between the foreground ridge and Big Cataloochee. Near Waynesville, I-40 turns northwest to follow the Pigeon River past Cataloochee Valley to Waterville Dam and into Tennessee, while Highway 19/23/74 splits. Highway 19 continues west from Clyde to Maggie Valley and Cherokee, while 23/74 turns southwest to Dillsboro.

Behind Thompson Knob and Holland Mountain are Crabtree Bald, Sandymush Bald, and Little Sandymush Bald. Highway 209 runs north from Lake Junaluska, passing along the far side of the ridgeline connecting these peaks. It continues through the tiny communities of Luck and Trust in the Spring Creek section of Madison County, to Hot Springs on the French Broad River.

Further north, in the valley behind Hayes Top, is the Leicester community of Buncombe County, with Highway 63 (Leicester Highway) running through from Highway 19/23 in Asheville to Spring Creek. After passing Leicester, Highway 63 climbs the mountains to cross the crest at Dogget Gap, just northeast of Little Sandymush Bald, before dropping down the far side to Trust, where it intersects Highway 209.

In the distance to the north, beyond Leicester, you'll find the town of Marshall, the Madison County seat, located along the French Broad River. Further along that line are Camp Creek Bald (traversed by the Appalachian Trail) and Green Ridge Knob, both situated on the Madison County, NC/Greene County, TN, line.

Heavy concentrations of Mountain Ash (not actually part of the ash tree family) can be found between here and Mt. Pisgah along the Parkway. Their defining clusters of red berries become prominent in the late summer and last into the fall.

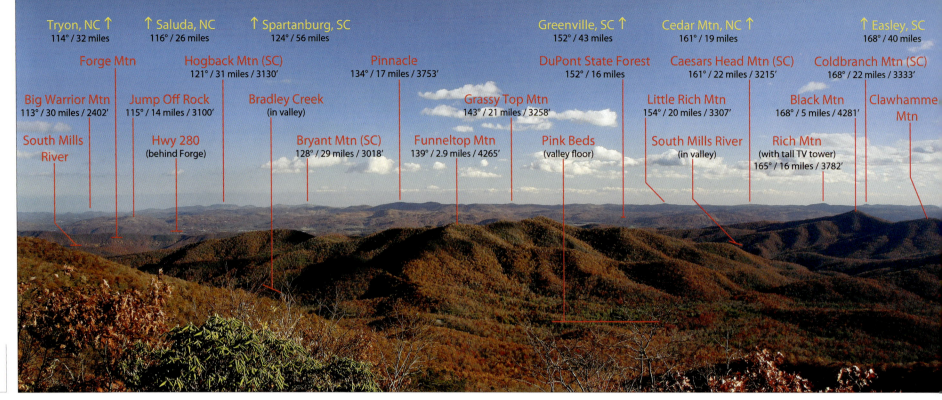

Pisgah Inn (observation deck)

MILEPOST 408.6

County, State: Haywood County, NC
GPS Coordinates: N 35° 24.152 x W 082° 45.283
Elevation at Viewpoint: 4,901 ft
Location: The Pisgah Inn is located just south of Mt. Pisgah at Milepost 408.6 on the Blue Ridge Parkway, about 20 miles south of Asheville. This view is from the observtion deck outside the restaurant.

THIS EXPANSIVE VIEW LOOKS SOUTHEAST TO SOUTH Carolina, with Transylvania County, NC, in the foreground. The present Pisgah Inn was built in 1964, and is operated as a concession through the National Park Service. Open March 30th to October 31st, it is part of a developed area which also includes a gift shop, restaurant, campground, and store.

Nearby Mt. Pisgah was once part of the Biltmore Estate, owned by George Vanderbilt, who purchased the land in 1897 from congressman and senator Thomas Clingman, for whom Clingmans Dome in the Great Smoky Mountains was named. Vanderbilt began purchasing land for his estate in 1888 and eventually owned 125,000 acres. In 1914, the Forest Service purchased nearly 80,000 acres of this tract, including Mt. Pisgah, from George's widow, Edith, to include in what is now the 479,000-acre Pisgah National Forest, which surrounds the Pisgah Inn today.

Three main highways traverse the area: 280, 64, and 276. They intersect behind Black Mountain near the entrance to Pisgah National Forest. From its junction with Highway 191 (Brevard Road) at the Mills River community (out of frame, left), Highway 280 turns southwest to run through the valley behind Forge and Funneltop Mountains to Brevard. It is the main route for visitors from Asheville traveling to Brevard.

Highway 64 comes from Hendersonville (out of frame, left), around this side of Jump Off Rock, headed west to its intersection with Highway 280 and 276, where it turns southwest to Brevard. From there it continues 29 miles to Cashiers, passing behind Three Forks and Toxaway Mountains, and in front of Rocky Knobs.

Highway 276 runs from Cedar Mountain at the NC/SC state line to Brevard where it joins Highway 64 to the junction with Highway 280 near the entrance to Pisgah National Forest. There it enters the forest, passing behind Black Mountain and on this side of Looking Glass Rock, up to Wagon Road Gap (on the Parkway located just before the Pounding Mill overlook), before dropping down the other side of the ridgeline to Waynesville.

Many popular attractions in the national forest are located along Highway 276, including the Davidson River campground, Looking Glass Falls, Looking Glass Rock, Sliding Rock, the Cradle of Forestry, and the "Pink Beds." Spanning the long flat foreground valley on this side of Soapstone Ridge and Funnel Top Mountain, the Pink Beds

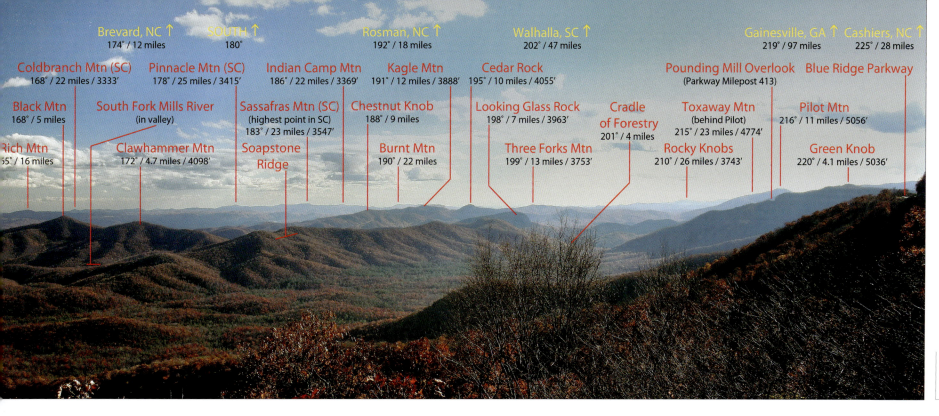

derive their name from the mountain laurel and rhododendron that bloom there in the spring.

Numerous hiking trails also traverse the area including several sections of the popular Mountains-to-Sea Trail. One leg parallels the Parkway, running south from Mt. Pisgah. Near Wagon Road Gap it drops into the foreground valley and climbs across Clawhammer and Black Mountains before descending to the Pisgah District Ranger Station on the Davidson River along Highway 276.

In addition to the Davidson River, the South Fork of the Mills River also results from the creeks draining the steep mountain slopes. It forms in the valley below and flows between Funneltop and Black Mountain, then turns northeast behind that range, and continues on this side of Forge Mountain before joining the North Mills River (both popular trout fishing streams).

See Jump Off Rock near Hendersonville, NC, on page 108 for the reverse view.

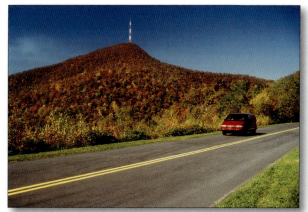

ABOVE: *Mt. Pisgah on the Blue Ridge Parkway, rising to 5,721 feet, has a conical shape and signature communications tower, making it easy to identify at great distances from any angle.*

RIGHT: *This cabin on Highway 276 is part of the Cradle of Forestry, a 6,500-acre tract set aside by Congress to commemorate the beginning of forestry conservation in the United States.*

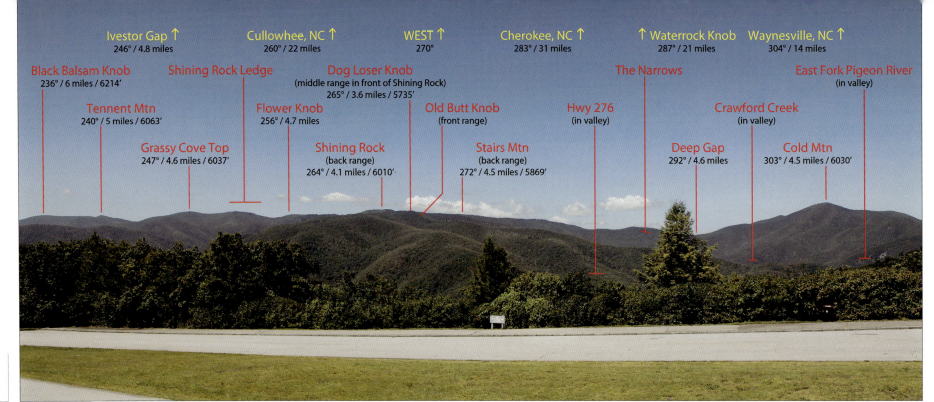

MILEPOST 411.9 Cold Mountain overlook

County, State: On the Haywood/Transylvania County line, NC
GPS Coordinates: N 35° 22.481 x W 082° 47.387
Elevation at Viewpoint: 4,573 ft
Location: Located at Milepost 411.9 on the Blue Ridge Parkway, just north of Wagon Road Gap (where Highway 276 passes under the Parkway).

LOOKING WEST YOU ARE VIEWING THE HEART OF THE Shining Rock Wilderness Area that includes the many peaks along the Shining Rock Ledge from about Tennent Mountain in the south to Cold Mountain to the north. Formed in 1964 as part of the National Wilderness Preservation System, this wilderness is the largest in North Carolina and one of the most popular hiking areas in the state.

Many trails within Shining Rock intersect at Black Balsam Knob, accessed from the Parkway by a dirt road (FSR 816) located just past the Graveyard Fields parking lot (south of here). One of the easier sections of the popular and difficult Art Loeb Trail runs from that road across the crests of Black Balsam, Tennent Mountain, Grassy Cove Top, and Shining Rock to Deep Gap. Creeks drain the foreground slopes to form the East Fork of the Pigeon River (a major tributary of the Tennessee River) in the valley below the overlook.

Paralleling the East Fork along the base of Cold Mountain is Highway 276, which passes under the Parkway just north of this viewpoint. This winding road runs from the entrance of Pisgah National Forest near Brevard (behind the overlook), to Waynesville, located behind Cold Mountain. Tracking along the base of Cold Mountain, 276 wraps around its northern end and behind it to Waynesville and points west. Cold Mountain is the setting of the historical novel (and movie) of the same name, by Charles Frazier.

For a reverse view of this ridgeline, see Haywood-Jackson overlook on page 94.

Waterfall at Graveyard Fields, below Black Balsam Knob. One of the most popular (and therefore overcrowded) destinations on the Parkway, the area offers hiking, creek access, several waterfalls, and backcountry camping.

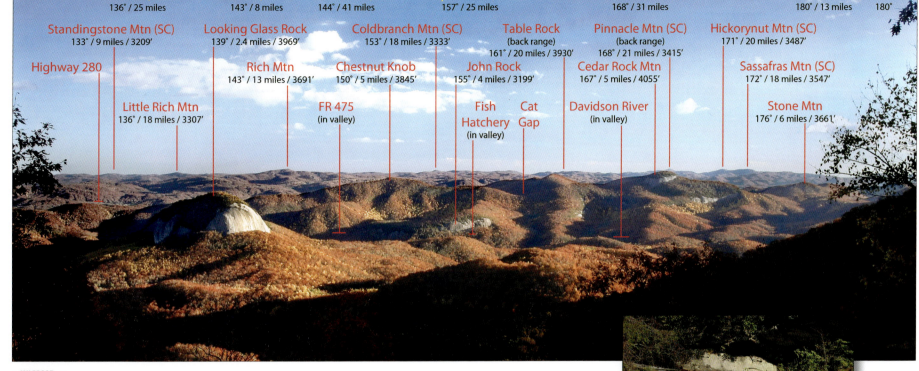

MILEPOST 416.3 Log Hollow overlook

County, State: Transylvania County, NC
GPS Coordinates: N 35° 19.786 x W 082° 49.251
Elevation at Viewpoint: 4,445 ft
Location: Located at Milepost 416.3 on the Blue Ridge Parkway, between the Cold Mountain overlook at Wagon Road Gap and Devil's Courthouse.

THIS OVERLOOK FACES SOUTHEAST OFFERING VIEWS over Transylvania County and Pisgah National Forest in North Carolina toward the low hills of upper South Carolina, which include Sassafras Mountain, the highest point in that state. Other peaks that straddle the state line include Standingstone and Little Rich.

Looking Glass Rock, with its spectacular white granite dome face, dominates the foreground. It is composed of intrusive igneous rock that crystallized from magma, which had cooled slowly below the Earth's surface about 400 million years ago. Over the past few million years, the land around it eroded, revealing the distinctive dome.

A popular rock climbing destination, it offers routes that challenge beginner to expert climber. Day hikers can also reach the top using a 3-mile, moderate-to-strenuous trail, which ascends more than 1,700 feet. The trail starts on Forest Service Road 475, which branches off Highway 276 behind the rock, just before Looking Glass Falls. The Pisgah Center for Wildlife Education and Fish Hatchery (open to the public) are located along this same road, at the base of John Rock, along the Davidson River.

Highway 276 enters the foreground valley from its junction with Highways 280 and 64 at the entrance to Pisgah National Forest, just north of Brevard. It then winds east of the base of the rock, passing Looking Glass Falls (out of frame, left), Sliding Rock, the Cradle of Forestry, and Pink Beds, before climbing out of the valley to join the Parkway at Wagon Road Gap (Milepost 412.2).

Looking Glass Falls, located along Highway 276 in Pisgah National Forest, is one of the most popular waterfalls for visitors to the area due to its innate beauty, easy access, and close proximity to the road.

MILEPOST 420.2 View of Shining Rock Wilderness

County, State: Haywood County, NC
GPS Coordinates: N 35° 19.554 x W 082° 52.920
Elevation at Viewpoint: 5,809 ft
Location: Turn off the Blue Ridge Parkway just south of Graveyard Fields onto Forest Service Road 816 at about Milepost 420.2. Drive the gravel track 1.2 miles to restrooms at the Shining Rock Wilderness trailheads. This view is made about 100 yards north, out Ivestor Gap Trail (gravel road with gate).

This view northwest over the Shining Rock Wilderness is made from the western base of Black Balsam Knob. The long range running across the middle is Lickstone Ridge, which descends from the Parkway near Richland Balsam to Lickstone Bald and Beaty Spring Knob, to end in the valley near Waynesville (on the back side of Beaty). Highway 215, which is the western boundary of the wilderness, runs along this side of Lickstone Ridge in the valley, following the West Fork Pigeon River.

In the valley on the right side of Fork Mountain is Camp Daniel Boone, operated by the Boy Scouts.

Beyond Lickstone Ridge, looking through Double Spring Gap (located between Richland Balsam and Cold Spring Knob), are the Plott Balsam Mountains with Waterrock Knob (along the Parkway), Mt. Lynn Lowry, and Plott Balsam (just visible above Cold Spring Knob). On the range beyond is Big Cataloochee, the high point on the western (far) wall of Cataloochee Valley.

That ridgeline continues north (right) to Mt. Sterling and down to the Waterville Dam along Interstate 40 and the Pigeon River. On the eastern (near) wall, along the Cataloochee Divide, are Purchase Knob and Hazel Top. On the far range is Mt. Guyot, the second highest peak in the Great Smoky Mountains, with Mt. Chapman just to its left.

For the reverse angle from the Parkway near Richland Balsam, see Haywood-Jackson overlook on page 94.

View to the southwest from Black Balsam Knob across Little Sam Knob to Mt. Hardy (left). The remote Shining Rock Wilderness, with dozens of trails crisscrossing the area, is a magnet for day hikers and back-packers. No bicycles or campfires are allowed in the Wilderness.

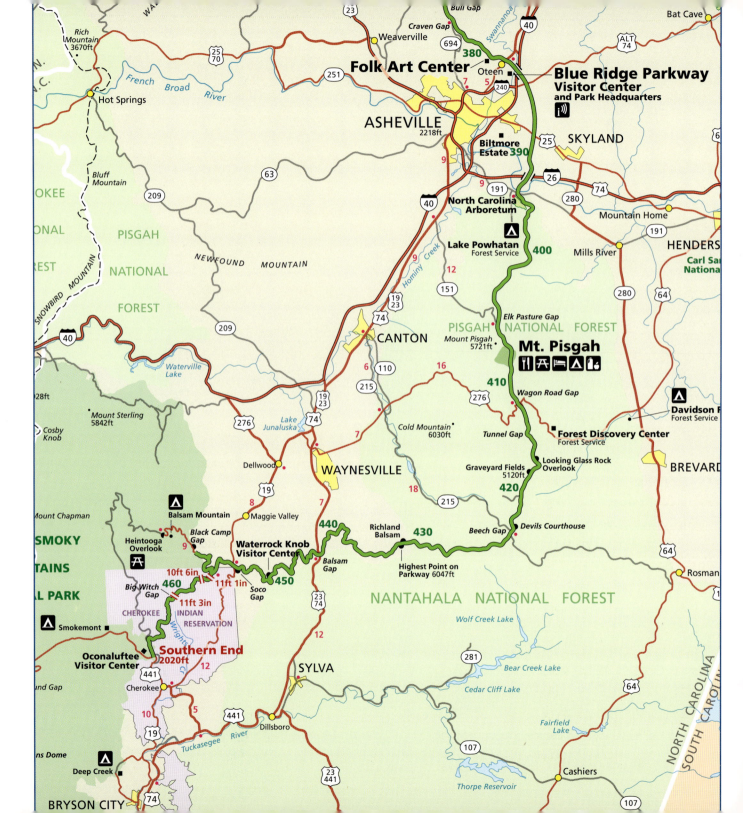

Blue Ridge Parkway overlooks

SECTION FOUR
Looking Glass Rock overlook to Highway 441

Looking Glass Rock overlook—Milepost 417 | Elev. 4492
East Fork overlook—Milepost 418.3 | Elev. 4995
Graveyard Fields overlook—Milepost 418.8 | Elev. 5120
John Rock overlook—Milepost 419.4 | Elev. 5330
Near Devil's Courthouse—Milepost 421 | Elev. 5441 86
Fetterbush overlook—Milepost 421.7 | Elev. 5494 87
    Devil's Courthouse overlook—Milepost 422.4 | Elev. 5462
    Courthouse Valley overlook—Milepost 423.5 | Elev. 5362
Wolf Mountain overlook—Milepost 424.8 | Elev. 5500 88
    Rough Butt Bald overlook—Milepost 425.4 | Elev. 5300
    Spot Knob overlook—Milepost 427.8 | Elev. 5652
    Caney Fork overlook—Milepost 428 | Elev. 5650
    Beartrap Gap overlook—Milepost 428.5 | Elev. 5580
Cowee Mountains overlook—Milepost 430.7 | Elev. 5950 90
Haywood Jackson overlook—Milepost 431 | Elev. 6020 94
    Richland Balsam overlook—Milepost 431.4 | Elev. 6047
    Lone Bald overlook—Milepost 432.7 | Elev. 5635
    Roy Taylor Forest overlook—Milepost 433.3 | Elev. 5580
    Doubletop Mountain overlook—Milepost 435.3 | Elev. 5365
    Licklog Ridge overlook—Milepost 435.7 | Elev. 5135
View from Milepost 436 to Waynesville, NC | Elev. 5190 95
    Grassy Ridge Mine overlook—Milepost 436.8 | Elev. 5250
    Steestachee Bald overlook—Milepost 438.9 | Elev. 4780
    Cove Field Ridge overlook—Milepost 439.4 | Elev. 4620
    Saunook overlook—Milepost 440 | Elev. 4375
    Waynesville overlook—Milepost 440.9 | Elev. 4110
    Standing Rock overlook—Milepost 441.4 | Elev. 3915
    Rabb Knob overlook—Milepost 441.9 | Elev. 3725
    Balsam Gap overlook—Milepost 442.2 | Elev. 3630

The Orchards overlook—Milepost 444.6 | Elev. 3810
Mt. Lynn Lowry overlook—Milepost 445.2 | Elev. 4000
Woodfin Valley overlook—Milepost 446 | Elev. 4120
Wesner Bald overlook—Milepost 448.1 | Elev. 4912
Scott Creek overlook—Milepost 448.5 | Elev. 5050
Fork Ridge overlook—Mileage 449 | Elev. 5280
Yellow Face overlook—Milepost 450.2 | Elev. 5610
Browning Knob overlook—Milepost 451.2 | Elev. 5719
Waterrock Knob overlook & Visitor Center—Milepost 451.2 | Elev. 5719. . . . 96
    Cranberry Ridge overlook—Milepost 452.1 | Elev. 5475
Woolyback overlook—Milepost 452.3 | Elev. 5425 98
    Hornbuckle Valley overlook—Milepost 453.4 | Elev. 5105
    Thunderstruck Ridge overlook—Milepost 454.4 | Elev. 4780
    Fed Cove overlook—Milepost 455.1 | Elev. 4550
    Soco Gap overlook—Milepost 455.5 | Elev. 4570
    Jonathan Creek overlook—Milepost 456.2 | Elev. 4460
    Plott Balsam overlook—Milepost 457.9 | Elev. 5020
Mile High overlook—Milepost 1.3 on Heintooga Ridge Road | Elev. 5250 . . 100
    Lickstone overlook—Milepost 458.9 | Elev. 5150
Bunches Bald overlook—Milepost 459.5 | Elev. 4925 102
    Jenkins Ridge overlook—Milepost 460.8 | Elev. 4445
    Big Witch overlook—Milepost 461.9 | Elev. 4150
    Thomas Divide overlook—Milepost 463.9 | Elev. 3735
    Ballhoot Scar overlook—Milepost 467.4 | Elev. 2550
    Raven Fork overlook—Milepost 467.9 | Elev. 2400
    Oconaluftee overlook—Milepost 468.4 | Elev. 2200
    Oconaluftee Visitor Center on Highway 441—Great Smoky Mountains National Park | Elev. 2040

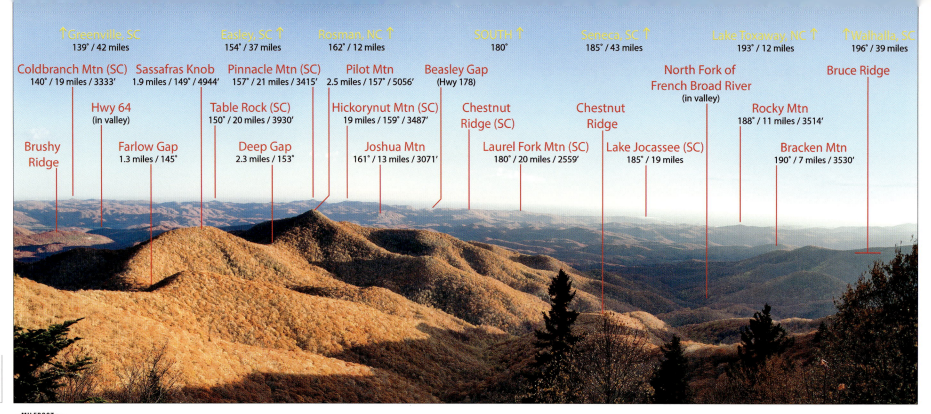

MILEPOST 421 — Near Devil's Courthouse (looking over Pilot Mtn.)

County, State: On the Haywood/Transylvania County line, NC
GPS Coordinates: N 35° 18.425 x W 082° 53.101
Elevation at Viewpoint: 5,441 ft
Location: Located about Milepost 421 on the Blue Ridge Parkway, just north of Devil's Courthouse, between the Log Hollow and Fetterbush overlooks. There is no overlook here, but it can be used to identify peaks seen from Devil's Courthouse.

FROM THIS VIEWPOINT, YOU ARE LOOKING SOUTH over Transylvania County. The popular Art Loeb Trail (30.1 miles), which shares a section of the Mountains-to-Sea Trail, climbs from the Davidson River Campground (out of frame, left) to Pilot Mountain, across the ridge, through Deep Gap to Sassafras Knob and Farlow Gap, before crossing the Parkway north of here. From there it continues to Silvermine Bald (where it tops 6,000 feet), Black Balsam Knob, and Cold Mountain, and then drops to Camp Daniel Boone in the valley behind.

The North Fork of the French Broad River forms on the slopes below the Parkway at the end of Chestnut Ridge and flows south, paralleling Highway 215 to Rosman (located in front of Joshua Mountain), where it joins the West Fork. From there the French Broad turns northeast and continues 117 miles to Tennessee. After merging with the Holston, east of Knoxville, they form the Tennessee River and eventually join the Mississippi to the Gulf of Mexico.

Hickorynut, Sassafras, Pinnacle, Table Rock, and Coldbranch Mountain in South Carolina lie along the NC/SC state line. Sassafras Mountain (in front of Hickorynut), at 3,547 feet, is the highest point in South Carolina, with Hickorynut the second and Pinnacle the third. Further south is Lake Jocassee, a 7,500-acre reservoir created in 1973 by Duke Energy and the state of South Carolina. Its waters come from four rivers—the Thompson, Toxaway, Whitewater, and Horsepasture—all of which originate in western North Carolina.

A hiker rests at the base of the upper falls at Graveyard Fields. The falls is accessed from a trailhead at the Graveyard Fields parking lot, located just north on the Parkway.

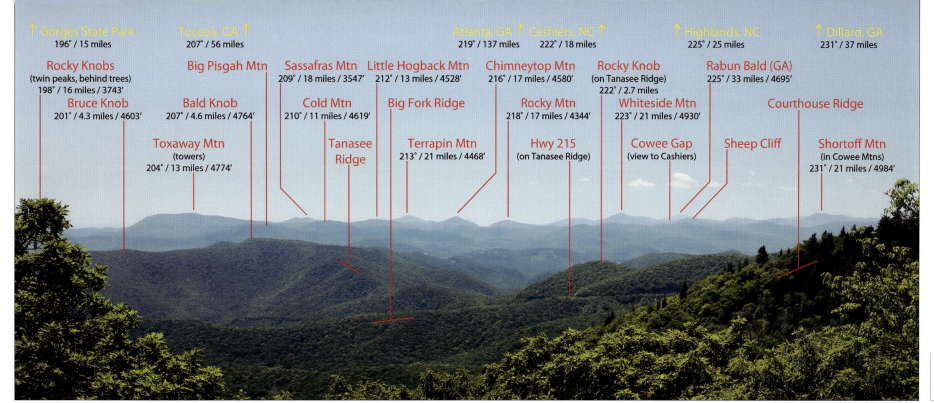

MILEPOST 421.7 Fetterbush overlook

County, State: On the Haywood/Transylvania County line, NC
GPS Coordinates: N 35° 18.252 x W 082° 53.315
Elevation at Viewpoint: 5,494 ft
Location: Located at Milepost 421.7 on the Blue Ridge Parkway just below Chestnut Bald at 0.7 mile, through the tunnel, and north of Devil's Courthouse parking lot.

THIS OVERLOOK, NAMED FOR A BLOOMING EVERGREEN shrub, offers views to the southwest into Transylvania County, toward Cashiers and Highlands in Jackson County, NC, and into north Georgia. Courthouse Ridge, right, runs down from Devil's Courthouse, with Tanasee Ridge behind. The long ridgeline of Tanasee continues to Bald Knob before heading southwest toward Big Pisgah Mountain. Highway 215 travels up along its front side, from Rosman (out of frame, left), behind Big Fork Ridge, and crosses the Parkway at Beech Gap, just south of Devil's Courthouse, before descending to the town of Canton in Haywood County.

Two other main roads traverse the area—Highways 64 and 281. Highway 64 runs west from Brevard to Rosman, passes behind Toxaway and Bald Rock Mountains and in front of Chimneytop Mountain to Cashiers. From there it continues northwest to Franklin then west to Murphy and on to Tennessee. Highway 281 begins at Highway 64 near Lake Toxaway (at the eastern/left base of Toxaway Mountain), and runs between Bald Knob and Big Pisgah Mountain before following the Tuckasegee River to the town of Tuckasegee (out of frame, right).

The headwaters of the French Broad River form on the hillsides below, with the North Fork in the foreground valley following Highway 215 southeast to Rosman, where it joins the West Fork.

For a reverse perspective from Cowee Gap, look at Cashiers Valley from Highway 64 on page 116.

A half-mile trail leads to the summit of Devil's Courthouse, offering spectacular views. Its name is derived from Cherokee and other folklore. One legend has it that the devil holds court in a cave within.

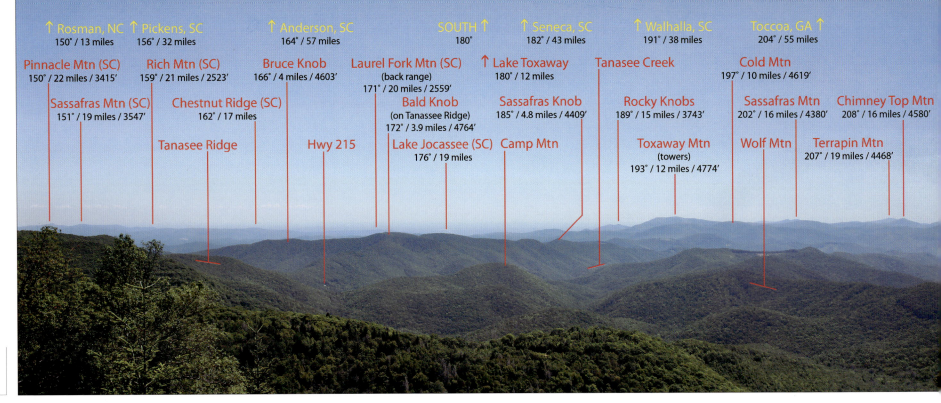

MILEPOST 424.8 Wolf Mountain overlook

County, State: Jackson County, NC
GPS Coordinates: N 35° 18.109 x W 082° 56.050
Elevation at Viewpoint: 5,500 ft
Location: Located at Milepost 424.8 on the Blue Ridge Parkway, just west of Devil's Courthouse.

This view, looking southwest into Jackson County and the Nantahala National Forest, is from Wolf Bald along the Parkway, just west of Mt. Hardy. The long broken line of Wolf Mountain, namesake of the overlook, starts just below (to the right) and runs south toward Cold Mountain (not the more well-known Cold Mountain in Haywood County).

To the east, Tanasee Ridge descends to Bald Knob, and continues south toward Cold Mountain. The Jackson/Transylvania County line follows its ridgeline. Tanasee Creek, a popular spot for anglers seeking brown trout, flows between Tanasee Ridge and Wolf Mountain into Tanasee Creek Lake.

The main roads through the far mountains include Highways 64, 107, and 281. Highway 64 runs east-west from Rosman passing behind Lake Toxaway, and Toxaway and Hogback Mountains, before reaching Cashiers (located between Chimneytop and Whiteside Mountains). From there it heads southwest through Cowee Gap (near Whiteside Mountain) to Highlands (near Satulah Mountain), where it turns northwest. It continues behind Yellow and Shortoff Mountains (in the Cowee Mountain range), and along the front side of Fishhawk Mountain and Jones Knob to the town of Franklin, the seat of Macon County, NC.

Highway 107 runs north-south from South Carolina through Cashiers (where it intersects Highway 64) to Sylva (out of frame, right). Located high in the cool mountains of western North Carolina, the Lake Toxaway/Cashiers/Highlands area is home to many resort communities and is a popular vacation and second-home area for residents of warmer climes, such as Atlanta and Charleston.

After leaving Cashiers, Highway 107 passes the 1,450-acre Glenville/Lake Thorpe Reservoir, located in the valley on this side of Yellow, Blackrock, and Hogback Mountains. Originally built in 1941 by ALCOA, owners of Nantahala Power at the time, the lake was formed by damming the west fork of the Tuckasegee River. Built to provide hydroelectric power for the production of aluminum to be used during World War II, it was originally named for Nantahala Power's first president, J.E.S. Thorpe. Renamed Lake Glenville in 2002, it is the highest lake in elevation (about 3,500 feet) east of the Mississippi, and is owned by Duke Power today.

From there Highway 107 follows the west fork of the Tuckasegee northeast through the town of Tuckasegee, and passes Cullowhee, before ending at Highway 23 in Sylva. Like Highway 107, Highway 281 also runs north-south from South Carolina. After crossing Highway 64 near Lake Toxaway and

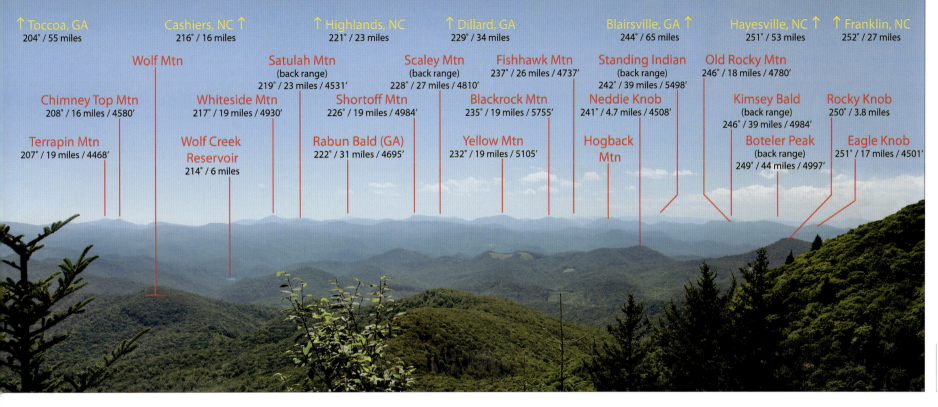

Label	Bearing / Distance / Elevation
↑ Toccoa, GA	204° / 55 miles
Cashiers, NC ↑	216° / 16 miles
↑ Highlands, NC	221° / 23 miles
↑ Dillard, GA	229° / 34 miles
Blairsville, GA ↑	244° / 65 miles
Hayesville, NC ↑	251° / 53 miles
↑ Franklin, NC	252° / 27 miles
Wolf Mtn	
Satulah Mtn (back range)	219° / 23 miles / 4531'
Scaley Mtn (back range)	228° / 27 miles / 4810'
Fishhawk Mtn	237° / 26 miles / 4737'
Standing Indian (back range)	242° / 39 miles / 5498'
Old Rocky Mtn	246° / 18 miles / 4780'
Chimney Top Mtn	208° / 16 miles / 4580'
Whiteside Mtn	217° / 19 miles / 4930'
Shortoff Mtn	226° / 19 miles / 4984'
Blackrock Mtn	235° / 19 miles / 5755'
Neddie Knob	241° / 4.7 miles / 4508'
Kimsey Bald (back range)	246° / 39 miles / 4984'
Rocky Knob	250° / 3.8 miles
Terrapin Mtn	207° / 19 miles / 4468'
Wolf Creek Reservoir	214° / 6 miles
Rabun Bald (GA)	222° / 31 miles / 4695'
Yellow Mtn	232° / 19 miles / 5105'
Hogback Mtn	
Boteler Peak (back range)	249° / 44 miles / 4997'
Eagle Knob	251° / 17 miles / 4501'

Gorges State Park, it travels north toward Cullowhee, passing in front of Toxaway and Cold Mountains to the Wolf Creek Lake/Reservoir, on the east fork of the Tuckasegee River. The lake is fed by Wolf Creek, which forms on the far side of Wolf Mountain, and is one of four lakes built by Nantahala Power and Light in the mid-1950s.

The other bodies of water are the small Tanasee Creek Lake, Cedar Creek Lake, and Bear Creek Lake (the largest of the group at 476 acres). These remote lakes are popular fishing spots (mainly large and small-mouth bass) with public access areas and boat docks. The Tuckasegee River flows northwest from these lakes, in the valley behind Wolf Mountain and Neddie Knob, to Cullowhee, Dillsboro, Bryson City, and into Fontana Lake along the southern border of the Great Smoky Mountains National Park.

See reverse perspective look at Cashiers Valley from Highway 64 on page 116.

ABOVE: *Lake Toxaway, completed in 1903, is the largest private lake in North Carolina, spanning 640 acres. It is located just north of Highway 64, between Rosman and Cashiers. Toxaway Mountain (towers) rises up behind the lake.*

RIGHT: *A couple poses with their cars beneath Bridal Veil Falls. This stunning waterfall is located roadside, 2.5 miles from Highlands, as you head toward Franklin, NC, on Highway 64 (behind Shortoff Mountains, in line with Scaley Mountain, shown above).*

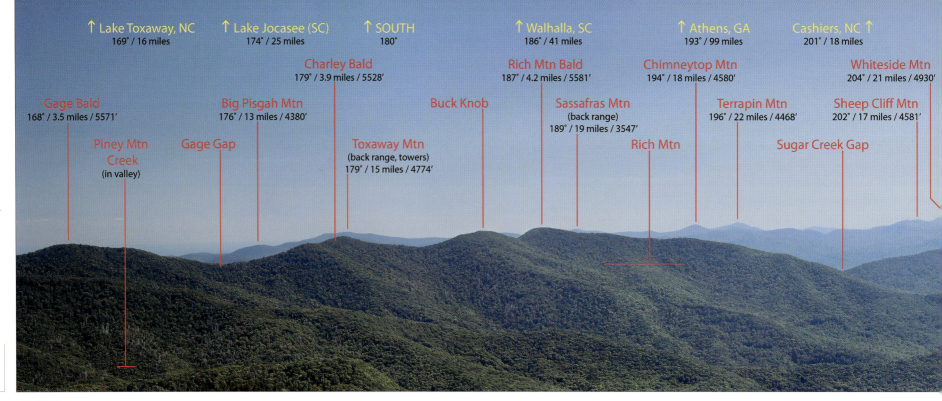

MILEPOST 430.7 Cowee Mountains overlook (1 of 4)

County, State: Jackson County, NC
GPS Coordinates: N 35° 21.331 x W 082° 59.274
Elevation at Viewpoint: 5,950 ft
Location: Located at Milepost 430.7 on the Blue Ridge Parkway, between Devil's Courthouse and the Haywood-Jackson overlook, 0.7 miles east of Richland Balsam overlook.

THE IDENTIFICATIONS FOR THE VIEWS FROM THE Cowee Mountains overlook are shown in four panels on this, and the following three pages. It offers some of the best views to the west along the Parkway between Devil's Courthouse and Waterrock Knob. Within this section the road tracks a north/south compass heading from Wolf Knob to Balsam Gap.

The nearby Richland Balsam overlook is the highest on the Parkway and one of the most visited spots, and while it offers closer views towards Waterrock Knob and the Plott Balsams, as well as Clingmans Dome and the Smokies, it has trees blocking large sections of its westerly view. The Cowee Mountains overlook, on the other hand, has no obstructions making it the superior location for viewing the sweep of the mountains of western North Carolina. Indeed, it is one of the more spectacular vistas along this section of the Parkway, and a great spot for watching the sunset, as it faces west over a series of receding mountain ranges in the Pisgah and Nantahala National Forests.

Behind the Cowee Mountains overlook, on the other side of the road, towers Reinhart Knob at over 6,000 feet, with the Middle Prong Wilderness below, on the Haywood County (eastern) side of the ridgeline traversed by the Parkway. The next pull off on that side of the road is the Haywood-Jackson overlook, offering views to the east over the Shining Rock Wilderness, Mt. Pisgah, and Cold Mountain.

The Mountains-to-Sea Trail runs just below the Cowee Mountains overlook as it continues from Mt. Pisgah and points north along the Parkway to its origins near Clingmans Dome in the Great Smoky Mountains National Park. Many people use sections of this trail both for short walks in the woods and for longer day hikes as it often connects one overlook to the next, paralleling the Parkway all the way to its junction with Highway 441 near the Oconaluftee Visitor Center in the Smokies.

Below this overlook, situated on the eastern edge of Jackson County, one can look down into the Caney Fork section below. Caney Fork Creek runs away to the southwest directly below the overlook, draining the slopes between Rich Mountain on the left and the Great Balsam Mountains on the right.

Looking south across Rich Mountain, the Tuckasegee River, located behind the ridge, connects Wolf Creek, Bear Creek, Tanasee Creek, and Cedar Cliff Lakes. The Wolf Mountain overlook, just north on the Parkway, offers views over those areas.

The Tuckasegee continues northwest from these lake impoundments, passing around the base

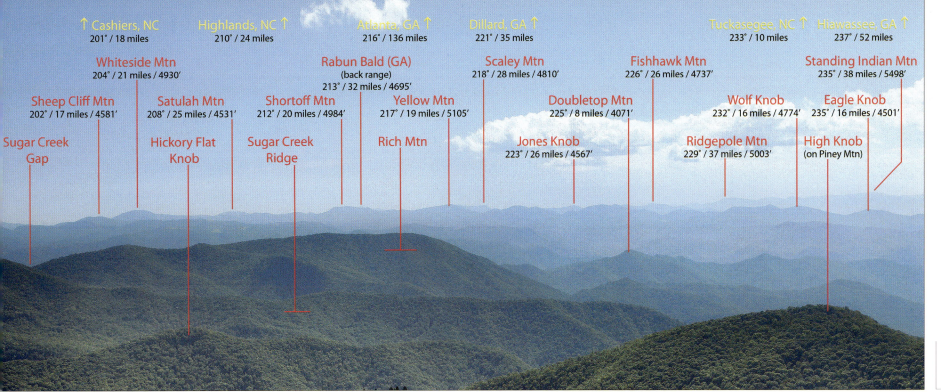

(2 of 4)

of Doubletop Mountain, crossing from left to right in the valley below along Highway 107 to Cullowhee, located at the base of the Great Balsam Mountains. Caney Fork Creek feeds into the Tuckasegee River near East Laport, located between the towns of Tuckasegee, below Doubletop, and Cullowhee.

Hwy 107 originates much further south, branching off Highway 28 north of Walhalla, SC, passing into North Carolina, and running between Chimneytop and Terrapin Mountains to Cashiers, where it crosses Highway 64. Cashiers, located at the base of Sheep Cliff Mountain, and Highlands, near Satulah Mountain, are popular vacation communities. Developers have built numerous golf and recreational communities there, which include High Hampton Inn and Country Club, Burlingame Country Club, Chattooga Club, Bear Lake Reserve, Lonesome Valley, and Sapphire Valley Ski Golf Resort.

Highway 107 continues north from Cashiers,

ABOVE: *Layers of receding ridges accentuated by hazy conditions, combined with an expansive westerly view, make for great photographic opportunities both morning and evening, from the Cowee Mountains overlook.*

RIGHT: *Dry Falls, located 3.5 miles past Highlands on Highway 64 heading towards Franklin, NC. A paved walk leads from the parking lot to the base. Visitors can walk behind the falls, staying "dry," thus the name.*

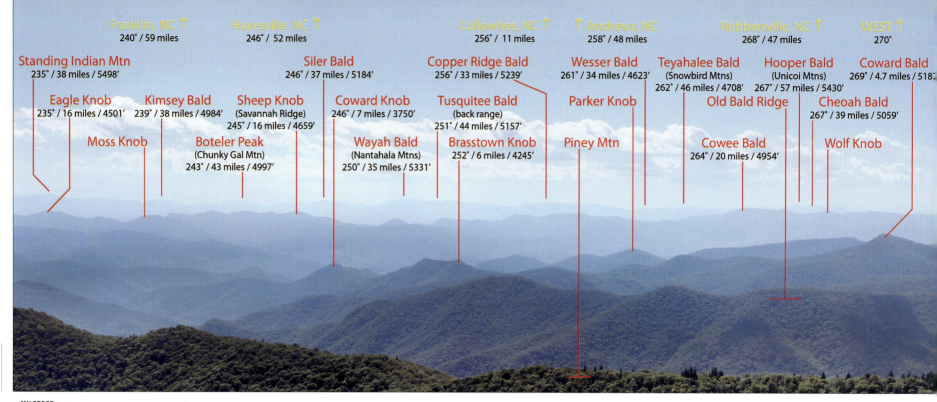

MILEPOST 430.7 Cowee Mountains overlook (3 of 4)

passing Thorpe Reservoir/Lake Glenville, created by impounding the West Fork of the Tuckasegee River, to the towns of Tuckasegee, Cullowhee, and Sylva. Highway 64 heads west from Cashiers passing Whiteside Mountain on its way to Highlands, and continues past several beautiful roadside waterfalls including Bridal Veil, Dry, and Cullasaja Falls. From there it passes between Hogback and Fishhawk Mountains where it turns northwest to Franklin, a popular spot for gem mining, located in Macon County in the valley between Sheep Knob and Boteler Peak.

Several large roads merge at Franklin including Highways 64, 28, and 23/441. Highway 28 runs north to Fontana Lake, while Highway 64 turns west passing between Kimsey Bald and Boteler Peak, to Hayesville and Chatuge Lake. It continues on to Murphy, located behind Tusquitee Bald, before passing into Tennessee. Built along the Hiwassee River, Murphy was incorporated as the county seat of Cherokee County in 1851 and is the westernmost county seat in North Carolina. Founded in 1835 as Huntington, it was the site of Fort Butler, built in 1839 as a staging point along the Trail of Tears, the route of the infamous Cherokee Indian removal to Oklahoma.

Highway 23/441 heads north from its junction with Highway 64 near Franklin, passing behind Sheep Knob on Savannah Ridge and in front of Cowee Bald (in the Cowee Mountains) to Dillsboro (near Sylva) located between the bases of the Great Balsams and the Plott Balsams. There it intersects with Highway 23/74 which runs up between the Great Balsam Mountains and the Plott Balsam Mountains, crossing the Parkway at Balsam Gap, 12.4 miles north of here (but headed south on the Parkway) before reaching Waynesville. Highway 74/441 heads northwest from Dillsboro toward Bryson City and Cherokee.

The Great Balsam Mountains run down from the Parkway near Lone Bald, with Dark Ridge Creek in the valley on the far side along Highway 23/74. Its ranges include Doubletop Mountain, Snaggy Bald, and Coward Mountain, whose ridge runs down from Coward Bald to Brasstown and Coward Knobs.

Looking northwest across the Great Balsam Mountains, the spine of the Plott Balsams is just visible with Yellowface, Blackrock Mountain, Pinnacle Bald, and Perry Top. The impressive Plott Balsams drop from Waterrock Knob (out of frame, right) to the Tuckasegee River and Highway 74/441.

In the far distance, beyond the Plott Balsams, are the Great Smoky Mountains with Clingmans Dome dominating the ridgeline. This undulating ridge runs west, with the NC/TN state line along its crest, from Clingmans Dome to Thunderhead Mountain, along above High Rocks, to Gregory Bald before dropping down to the Little Tennessee River at Deals Gap. To the east of Clingmans Dome is Mt. Collins with Newfound

Label	Bearing / Distance / Elevation
WEST ↑	270°
Sylva, NC ↑	275° / 13 miles
Bryson City, NC ↑	281° / 26 miles
Cades Cove, TN ↑	290° / 49 miles
Cherokee, NC ↑	294° / 20 miles
↑ Maryville, TN	297° / 62 miles
Pigpen Flats	269° / 21 miles / 4715'
Snaggy Bald	280° / 4.4 miles / 5423'
Gregory Bald	283° / 51 miles / 4941'
Perry Top	290° / 14 miles / 5056'
Andrews Bald	294° / 31 miles / 5920'
Mt. Collins (back range)	300° / 32 miles / 6181'
Coward Bald	269° / 4.7 miles / 5187'
Hickorynut Knob	275° / 24 miles / 4646'
Doubletop Mtn	282° / 6 miles / 5481'
High Rocks	286° / 37 miles / 5171'
Piney Mtn	
Pinnacle Bald	296° / 13 miles / 5341'
Blackrock Mtn (Plott Balsams)	300° / 12 miles / 5755'
Stratton Bald	272° / 57 miles / 5335'
Great Balsam Mtns	
Thunderhead Mtn	290° / 14 miles / 5535'
Plott Balsams	
Clingmans Dome	297° / 32 miles / 6643'
Yellow Face	306° / 11 miles / 6033'

(4 of 4)

Gap a bit further along that line, hidden behind the Plott Balsams from here.

The western counties of North Carolina are mountainous and sparsely populated, with timber and tourism being two of the main industries. There are also colleges and universities in the area that provide employment and education including the large (9,500 plus enrollment) four-year Western Carolina University in Cullowhee and two-year Southwestern Community College in Sylva.

At the very western end of the state in Brasstown, located near Murphy, is the historic John C. Campbell Folk School. Founded in 1925, it offers a unique blend of weekend and weeklong year-round workshops in traditional and contemporary arts and crafts. Courses include blacksmithing, cooking, quilting, woodworking, music, basketry, and jewelry.

For reverse view, see Waterrock Knob overlook, page 96.

ABOVE: *Motorcyclists pose for a group photograph at the Richland Balsam overlook just south of Cowee Mountains overlook. It marks the highest point on the Blue Ridge Parkway, at 6,047 feet, and offers similar, but more obstructed views.*

LEFT: *Cullasaja Falls is located 9 miles from Highlands along Highway 64 towards Franklin, NC. It is best viewed from the road, due to very limited parking along this steep, dangerously narrow stretch of highway.*

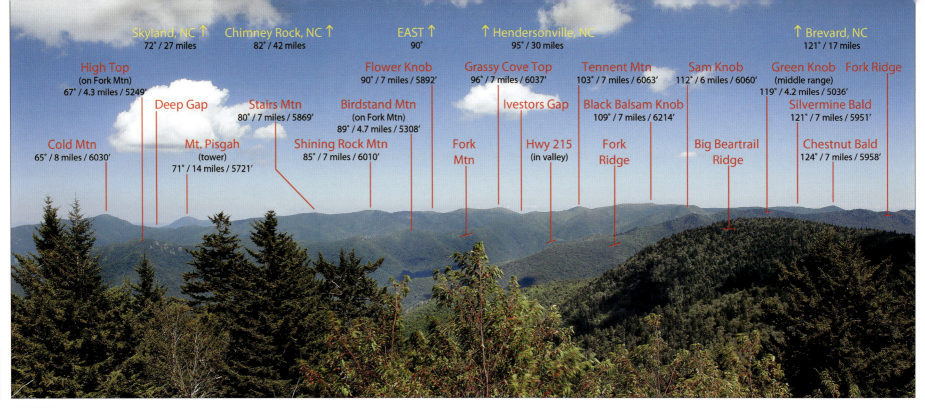

Haywood-Jackson overlook
Milepost 431

County, State: On the Haywood/Jackson County line, NC
GPS Coordinates: N 35° 21.590 x W 082° 59.212
Elevation at Viewpoint: 6,020 ft
Location: Located at Milepost 431 on the Blue Ridge Parkway, between the Cowee Mountains and Richland Balsam overlooks.

LOOKING EAST YOU ARE VIEWING LAND IN THE Pisgah National Forest and the 18,000-plus acre Shining Rock Wilderness Area included within its boundaries. Named for the white quartz outcrop visible near the crest of Shining Rock Mountain, the Wilderness encompasses areas from the Blue Ridge Parkway on the far side of the main ridge, and includes many of the peaks visible from here (including Tennent and Stairs Mountains on the Shining Rock Ledge), as well as the foreground valley down to Highway 215.

Highway 215 climbs to the Parkway from Rosman on the far side of the mountains, crossing to this side at Beech Gap near Chestnut Bald (just south of Devil's Courthouse). From there the highway descends between Green and Sam Knobs, in front of Fork Mountain, to Sunburst (site of an old logging camp) and Lake Logan. Built by Champion Paper in the 1930s, the lake is fed by the West Fork of the Pigeon River, which forms from creeks draining from the mountains in the foreground, and parallels Highway 215 to Canton.

The Little East Fork River forms behind Fork Mountain and joins the West Fork just beyond Lake Logan. Camp Daniel Boone, a large Boy Scout summer camp, is in the same valley as the East Fork, between High Top and Deep Gap. Bordering Shining Rock Wilderness is the 7,900-acre Middle Prong Wilderness (immediate foreground), which is bounded on the east by Highway 215 and on the west by the Parkway.

For the reverse view of Shining Rock Ledge see Cold Mountain overlook on page 80.

Commonly called "Bridge Falls" due to their location at a bridge along Highway 215, these beautiful cascades are located roadside 4.3 miles north of the Blue Ridge Parkway, toward Canton, NC.

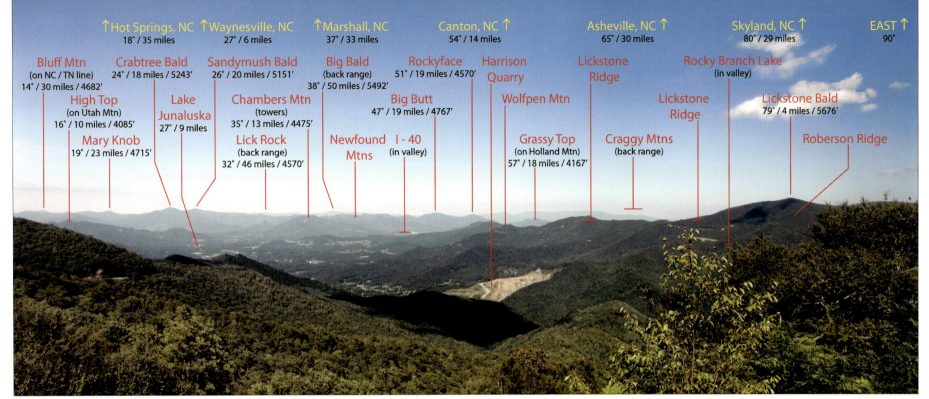

Milepost 436 to Waynesville, NC

County, State: Haywood County, NC
GPS Coordinates: N 35° 24.867 x W 083° 02.461
Elevation at Viewpoint: 5,190 ft
Location: Located about Milepost 436 on the Blue Ridge Parkway at Steestachee Bald. While there is no overlook here, this viewpoint is included because it offers a rare vista to the northeast. Nearby parking is at the Licklog Ridge overlook.

INTERSTATE 40 AND HIGHWAY 19/23/74 run east/west through the main valley in the distance from Asheville, passing along the base of Holland (Canton at its foreground base), Rockyface, Big Butt, and Chambers Mountains. At Clyde (foreground base of Chambers), I-40 turns northwest, passing on the back side of Lake Junaluska and Utah Mountain and in front of Crabtree Bald to follow the Pigeon River to Newport, TN. Highway 19 continues west to Maggie Valley and Cherokee, while 23/74 turns southwest to Waynesville (visible in front of Lake Junaluska), then travels through Balsam Gap to Sylva. The Parkway descends steeply from this viewpoint to the Steestachee Bald overlook (visible below) before passing to the back side of the ridge to Balsam Gap, where it crosses 23/74.

Highway 209 heads north from Lake Junaluska in the valley between Crabtree and Sandymush Balds on the east, and Mary Knob and Bluff Mountain on the west, through the Spring Creek section of Madison County to Hot Springs. Further east on the back range is Sams Gap, where Interstate 26 crosses the NC/TN state line.

On the far right, Lickstone Ridge drops from Richland Balsam on the Parkway, crossing Lickstone Bald. Behind and to the right of the bald is the prominent Cold Mountain, visible from this viewpoint, but out of frame to the right. In the distance beyond Lickstone Ridge are the Great Craggy Mountains that include Lane Pinnacle and Craggy Gardens.

Barn and hay field along I-40 in Haywood County. This rural county was formed in 1808 from the western part of Buncombe County, and includes the towns of Waynesville, Canton, Lake Junaluska, Maggie Valley, and Clyde.

Panorama labels (left to right)

- ↑ Hendersonville, NC — 104° / 40 miles
- Brevard, NC ↑ — 124° / 28 miles
- Greenville, SC ↑ — 135° / 60 miles
- ↑ Rosman, NC — 140° / 28 miles
- Cold Mtn — 102° / 16 miles / 6030'
- Shining Rock — 112° / 17 miles / 6001'
- Steestachee Bald — 119° / 6 miles / 5682'
- Parkway
- Rough Butt Bald — 135° / 14 miles / 5942'
- Rich Mtn Bald — 144° / 14 miles / 5581'
- Coward Bald — 151° / 8 miles / 5187'
- Mt. Pisgah (tower) — 96° / 22 miles / 5709'
- Lickstone Bald — 104° / 10 miles / 5676'
- Grassy Bald — 118° / 6 miles / 5584'
- Richland Balsam — 127° / 11 miles / 6410'
- Mt. Hardy — 132° / 16 miles / 6112'
- Gage Bald — 138° / 14 miles / 5571'
- Snaggy Bald — 146° / 8 miles / 5423'
- Parkway
- Stairs Mtn — 110° / 16 miles / 5791'
- Balsam Gap (in valley) 116°
- Black Balsam Knob — 121° / 18 miles / 6214'
- Fork Ridge
- Cutoff Ridge
- Charley Bald — 142° / 14 miles / 5528'
- Hwy 23/74 (in valley)

MILEPOST 451.2 Waterrock Knob overlook

County, State: On the Jackson/Haywood County line, NC
GPS Coordinates: N 35° 27.568 x W 083° 08.448
Elevation at Viewpoint: 5,810 ft
Location: Located at Milepost 451.2 on the Blue Ridge Parkway. This photo was taken from the eastern side of the parking lot, below the Waterrock Knob Visitor Center, which features restrooms and a gift shop.

WATERROCK KNOB RISES TO 6,292 FEET, THE highest peak along the Plott Balsam mountain range. From this viewpoint, Mt. Pisgah is visible just above Fork Ridge. It is easily identifiable by its conical shape and tall antenna. The Parkway continues from Mt. Pisgah to Waterrock Knob, passing along the far side of Shining Rock and Black Balsam Knob before turning in this direction at Mt. Hardy.

Then the Parkway climbs to its highest point—6,047 feet—at the Richland Balsam overlook, before descending behind Steestachee and Grassy Balds to Balsam Gap, where it crosses Highway 23/74. From this low point, it ascends to Waterrock Knob, passing over Cutoff and Fork Ridges in the foreground. The Jackson/Haywood County line follows the crest of the ridgeline along the Parkway from Mt. Hardy to Grassy Bald, down to Balsam Gap, then across and up to Mt. Lynn Lowry (at the left end of Cutoff Ridge), to Waterrock Knob, with land on this side being part of Jackson County. Haywood County is on the far side of that ridgeline and includes Cold Mountain, Shining Rock, Mt. Hardy, and Lickstone Bald.

Much of the land you see is part of the Nantahala National Forest and Jackson County. Created in 1891 from two adjoining counties, Jackson encompasses 494 square miles and has elevations ranging from 2,000 to over 6,000 feet. The largest town in the county, Sylva (out of frame, right), is located at the western end of the Great Balsam Mountains, as is Dillsboro, the popular tourist town with the famous Jarrett House Restaurant and Bed & Breakfast.

Highway 23/74 connecting Waynesville, the Haywood County seat, to Sylva, the Jackson County seat, runs in the foreground valley in front of the Great Balsam Mountains. Cullowhee, home of Western Carolina University, is located at the west end of that range, just out of frame, right. The Tuckasegee River, popular for its rafting and fly-fishing, flows almost the entire length of Jackson County along Highways 107, 281, and 74/441, the other main road arteries serving the county. The Tuckasegee flows into Fontana Lake, near Bryson City, at the southern boundary of the Great Smoky Mountains National Park.

Whiteside Mountain (far right) sits on the Jackson/Macon County line, while Toxaway Mountain (center, with Lake Toxaway behind) lies on the Jackson/Transylvania County line. The resort community of Cashiers is located in the valley

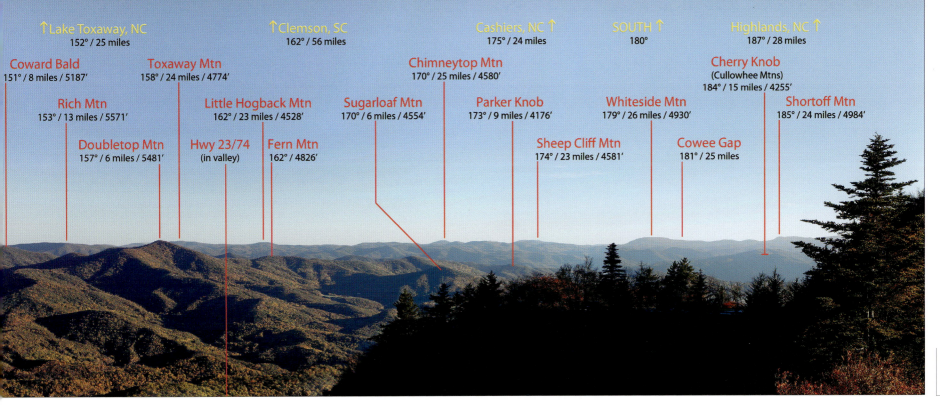

between Whiteside and Chimneytop Mountains, behind Sheep Cliff, along Highway 64.

From the upper end of the parking lot at the visitor center there is a half-mile (one way) strenuous trail to the top of Waterrock Knob, offering great, but not panoramic, views from the peak. The first half of the trail is paved. There are also nice vistas from the west side of the parking lot, offering views (similar to Woolyback overlook on pages 98 and 99) from the Plott Balsams (ridge descending on the left) to Clingmans Dome and Mt. LeConte in the Great Smoky Mountain National Park.

These vantage points to the east and west make this overlook a great spot to enjoy a sunrise or sunset. Picnic tables located on both sides of the large parking lot at the overlook offer visitors a place to sit, relax, and take in the spectacular views.

Compare the scene above with the reverse perspective, Cashiers Valley from Highway 64, on page 116.

ABOVE: *The historic Jackson County Courthouse in Sylva was originally built in 1914. Remodeled and reopened in 2011, it now houses the county library as well as area historic and arts organizations.*

RIGHT: *Vibrant fall colors dominate the foreground ridge in this scene, as viewed from the Blue Ridge Parkway, with Doubletop Mountain behind (left).*

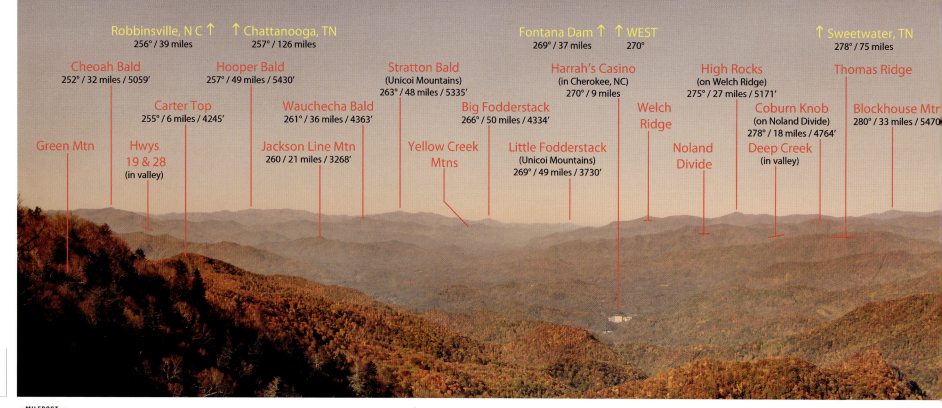

MILEPOST 452.3 Woolyback overlook

County, State: Jackson County, NC
GPS Coordinates: N 35° 28.045 x W 083° 08.524
Elevation at Viewpoint: 5,425 ft
Location: Located at Milepost 452.3 on the Blue Ridge Parkway, between Waterrock Knob and Soco Gap.

LOOKING WEST TOWARD LITTLE FODDERSTACK Mountain, you are viewing along the southern boundary of the Great Smoky Mountains National Park (right) to the Unicoi Mountains along the NC/TN state line. The boundary line runs through Fontana Lake (not visible from here), located at the base of Welch Ridge. This ridge, along with the Noland Divide and Thomas Ridge, rises from the valley floor and runs roughly parallel, north, to the heart of the Smokies.

The large building, prominent above the trees, is Harrah's Casino in Cherokee, located just outside the southeastern edge of the park, on the Cherokee Indian Reservation. Highways 19 and 441 meet near Cherokee, and 441 continues from there, northwest, through the national park, crossing into Tennessee at Newfound Gap and dropping to Gatlinburg in the valley beyond. Highway 19 runs east from Cherokee, climbing up this side of Lickstone Ridge to cross the Parkway just north of here at Soco Gap, before descending to Maggie Valley. Highway 19 continues west from Cherokee to Bryson City, located in front of Jackson Line Mountain in the valley below, and travels west to Andrews and Murphy near the Tennessee border.

Just west of Bryson City, Highway 28 branches off Highway 19 and follows the valley floor to Fontana Lake, passing between the lake and the Yellow Creek Mountains into Tennessee. Fontana Dam, at the end of the 10,000-acre lake, lies 35 miles west of Bryson City. From the dam, the tallest east of the Rockies, the Tennessee River flows through Cheoah Lake, into Tennessee, through Calderwood and Chilhowee Lakes, and the large Tellico Lake, located to the right and behind Little Fodderstack Mountain in the Unicoi Mountains. This range continues south to include Big Fodderstack, Stratton Bald, and Hooper Bald Mountains on the NC/TN state line. The Joyce Kilmer Slickrock Wilderness Area is on this side of the ridge, with Lake Santeetlah and Robbinsville in the valley between Cheoah Bald and Hooper Bald. The Snowbird Mountains are at the edge of the photograph in the distance behind Cheoah Bald.

Deep Creek Campground is between the ends of Thomas Ridge and the Noland Divide. Welch Ridge climbs from the valley to High Rocks, with Hazel Creek draining the valley behind. Cades Cove is on the far side of this ridgeline that ends near Gregory Bald (hidden behind High Rocks). The ridge in front of Welch is the long Noland Divide that extends down from Clingmans Dome to the Tuckasegee River. In front of it is Thomas Ridge that

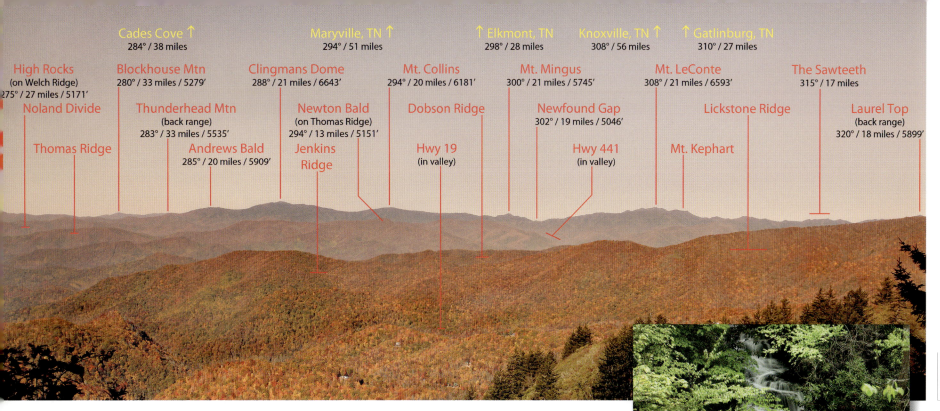

descends from Newfound Gap, with Deep Creek draining the valley between the two ridges.

Viewing northwest over Lickstone Ridge, you are seeing much of the Qualla Boundary, also known as the Cherokee Indian Reservation. On the back range, the "spine" of the Smokies continues from Thunderhead Mountain to Clingmans Dome (observation deck visible with binoculars)—the highest point in the Smokies and the third highest peak east of the Mississippi. From there, the ridge breaks northeast to Mt. Collins, Mt. Mingus, Newfound Gap, Mt. LeConte (actually set back from that ridgeline), the Sawteeth, and Laurel Top. The NC/TN state line runs along this ridgeline from Thunderhead to Laurel Top, as does the Appalachian Trail (AT).

North Carolina's longest trail, the Mountains-to-Sea, is a work in progress, connecting more than 900 miles of existing trails from its juncture with the AT near Clingmans Dome to Jockeys Ridge on the coastal Outer Banks.

ABOVE: *The Great Smoky Mountains Railroad offers several excursions from Bryson City, including one across Fontana Lake along the Nantahala (above) and Tennessee Rivers to the Nantahala Gorge.*

RIGHT: *Soco Falls is located roadside below the Parkway. Take the Cherokee/Hwy 19S exit at Soco Gap and drive 1.4 miles toward Cherokee, park on the road, and follow the short, steep trail to the observation platform.*

MILEPOST 1.3 spur — Mile High overlook (on Heintooga Ridge Road)

County, State: Swain County, NC
GPS Coordinates: N 35° 31.164 x W 083° 10.179
Elevation at Viewpoint: 5,250 ft
Location: Turn right off the Blue Ridge Parkway at Milepost 458.2, just north of the Plott Balsam overlook onto the Heintooga Ridge Road, toward Balsam Mountain Campground. Drive 1.3 miles to Mile High overlook on the left. This road closes in late fall and remains closed all winter.

EARLY MORNING AND LATE AFTERNOON ARE GREAT times to visit this overlook; because it faces north, the strong sidelight helps outline the many mountain ranges. The foreground area is drained by several creeks—Bunches (below the overlook), Straight Fork, and Raven Fork—which all connect near the Big Cove Community on the Cherokee Indian Reservation, before emptying into the Oconaluftee River, whose headwaters form below Newfound Gap.

In the distance you can see the sweep of the Great Smoky Mountains, with Clingmans Dome at its heart (the ramp is visible with binoculars), to Strawberry Knob on the Cataloochee Divide, which is the eastern boundary of this national park. The NC/TN state line and the Appalachian Trail run along the spine of the distant range from Clingmans Dome to Mt. Guyot, before descending to Mt. Cammerer, behind Balsam Mountain, and then down to the Pigeon River and Interstate 40 near Waterville Dam.

Much of this land is part of the Great Smoky Mountains National Park which covers 521,085 acres. Of this total, 276,344 acres are in North Carolina and 244,741 acres are in Tennessee. Dedicated in 1940 by President Roosevelt in a ceremony at the Rockefeller Monument at Newfound Gap, today it is the most visited national park in the U.S. with more than 9.4 million recreational visits in 2010. Mt. Guyot is the second highest summit in the Smokies (after Clingmans Dome) and fourth highest in the eastern U.S. It was named for Arnold Guyot, a Swiss geographer who measured many of the areas peaks around 1859.

Highway 441 (Newfound Gap Road) follows the Oconaluftee River from Cherokee (out of frame, left), passing the Oconaluftee Visitor Center and Smokemont Campground before climbing out of the valley to Newfound Gap (the parking lot is visible with binoculars) on its way to Gatlinburg, TN. It is the main road through the national park and is open year-round, weather permitting. The Parkway ends at Milepost 469.1, where it meets Highway 441, about 10 miles from the overlook.

From Luftee Knob, the Balsam Mountain range runs east and includes Chiltoes Mountain, Cataloochee Balsam, Whim Knob, and Strawberry Knob. These mountains form the southwestern wall of Cataloochee Valley, located on the back side. The Polls Gap trail runs along this ridgeline, as does the Swain (foreground)/Haywood County line.

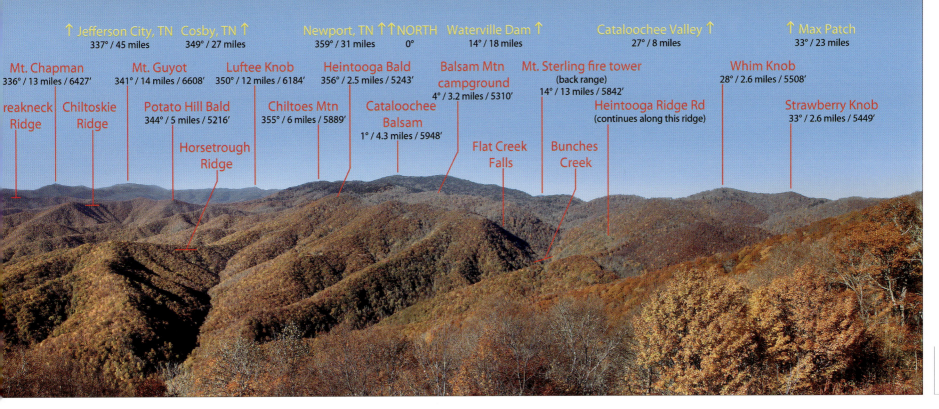

Mt. Sterling, just visible, forms the western wall of Cataloochee Valley, and you can see its lookout tower with binoculars. From there the Mt. Sterling ridge descends to the Pigeon River and I-40.

The Heintooga Ridge Road continues from this overlook for 7 miles to the high-altitude Balsam Mountain campground, and ends 1 mile beyond at a great picnic area (with facilities) in the woods. From there, the adventurous can follow the one-way, dirt, Heintooga Round Bottom road for another 14 miles, winding along Balsam Mountain and down Straight Fork Valley to the Big Cove community and on to Cherokee, for a total of 28 miles (a 1- to 2-hour drive).

There are no facilities or gas on the Heintooga Round Bottom road, and buses, trailers, and motor homes are prohibited, but it is usually passable with a two-wheel drive vehicle in good weather. There are many hiking trails along this densely wooded drive, as well as some backcountry campsites.

ABOVE: *Elk, originally settled in nearby Cataloochee Valley, have now spread across the mountains and can be seen, early mornings and late afternoons, along the Heintooga Ridge Road (above).*

RIGHT: *Erected in 1938, this Masonic Marker on the Heintooga Ridge Road is made up of 687 stones from around the world. The masons have held their annual NC Summer Assembly at this site since 1935.*

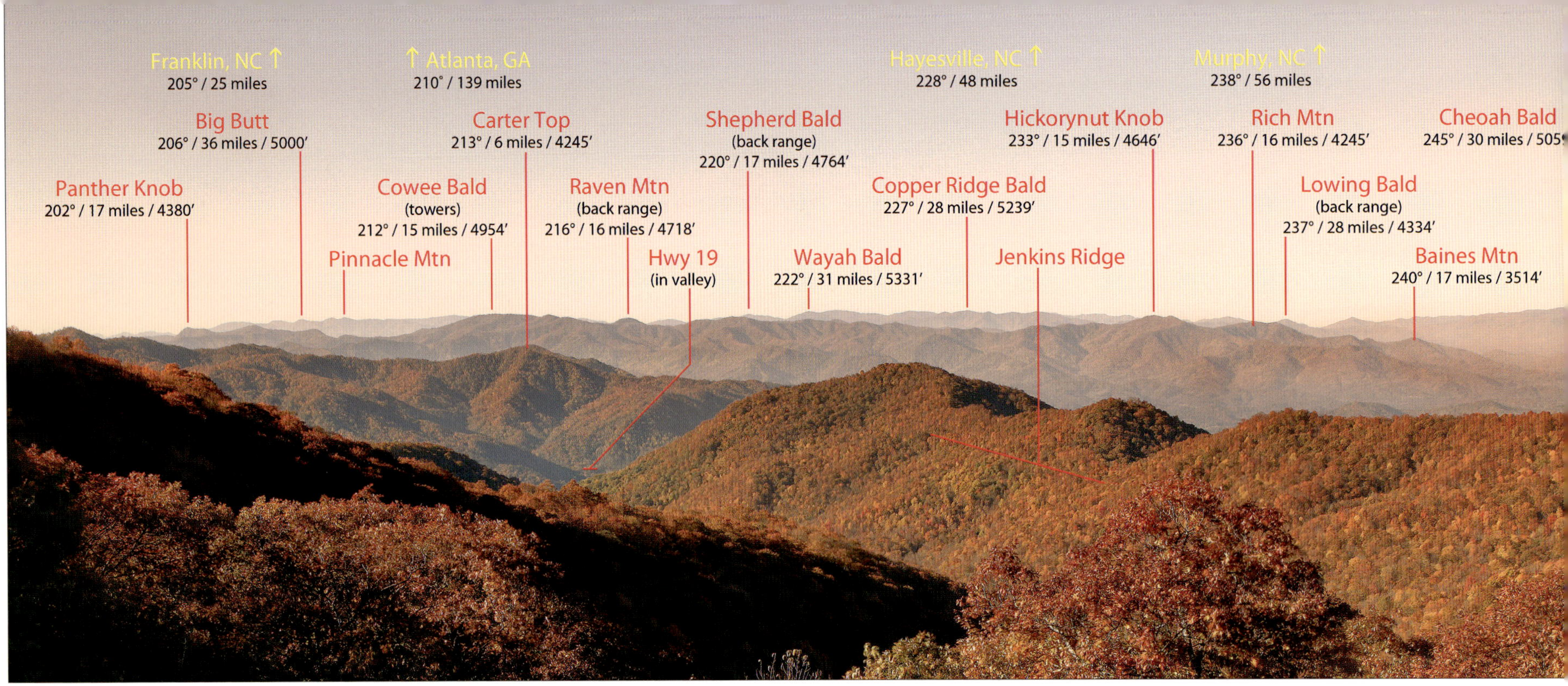

Panorama labels (left to right):

- Franklin, NC ↑ — 205° / 25 miles
- Big Butt — 206° / 36 miles / 5000'
- Panther Knob — 202° / 17 miles / 4380'
- ↑ Atlanta, GA — 210° / 139 miles
- Carter Top — 213° / 6 miles / 4245'
- Cowee Bald (towers) — 212° / 15 miles / 4954'
- Pinnacle Mtn
- Raven Mtn (back range) — 216° / 16 miles / 4718'
- Hwy 19 (in valley)
- Shepherd Bald (back range) — 220° / 17 miles / 4764'
- Wayah Bald — 222° / 31 miles / 5331'
- Hayesville, NC ↑ — 228° / 48 miles
- Hickorynut Knob — 233° / 15 miles / 4646'
- Copper Ridge Bald — 227° / 28 miles / 5239'
- Jenkins Ridge
- Murphy, NC ↑ — 238° / 56 miles
- Rich Mtn — 236° / 16 miles / 4245'
- Lowing Bald (back range) — 237° / 28 miles / 4334'
- Cheoah Bald — 245° / 30 miles / 5055'
- Baines Mtn — 240° / 17 miles / 3514'

MILEPOST 459.5 Bunches Bald overlook

County, State: Jackson County, NC
GPS Coordinates: N 35° 30.956 x W 083° 11.638
Elevation at Viewpoint: 4,940 ft
Location: Located at Milepost 459.5 on the Blue Ridge Parkway between Soco Gap and Cherokee, NC.

IN THE VALLEY BELOW IS JENKINS CREEK, WITH Jenkins Ridge rising up behind and spanning the center of the photos to the right edge. The ridge descends to the valley, left, and ends at Soco Creek and Highway 19, which come down from Soco Gap (out of frame, left) on their way to Cherokee. The Parkway crosses the ridge (right) before winding out of sight on the way to its southern terminus (Milepost 469.1) at Highway 441 between Cherokee and the Oconaluftee Visitor Center.

On the other side of Highway 19 is Carter Top, with the Cowee Mountains behind. This tall range includes Panther Knob, Cowee Bald (tower array visible with binoculars), Raven Mountain, and Shepherd Bald. Franklin lies between these mountains and Big Butt (which is near the NC/GA state line). Beyond the Cowee Mountains are Wayah and Copper Ridge Balds in the Nantahala Mountains. The Appalachian Trail (AT) crosses their peaks before dropping to the valley floor in front of Lowing Bald. There it crosses the Nantahala River and climbs back up the Cheoah Mountains to crest Cheaoh Bald before dropping down to Fontana Lake, located beyond where Thomas Ridge tapers to the valley floor and in front of Big Fodderstack. From there the AT crosses Fontana Dam, before climbing up Twentymile Ridge (hidden behind Welch Ridge) and following the spine of the Smokies to Clingmans Dome (the highest point along its route), before continuing north.

In front, and to the right of the Cowee Mountains, are the Alarka Mountains, comprised of Hickorynut Knob, Rich, and Baines Mountains.

Highways 19 and 74, as well as the Tuckasegee River, continue in the valley at their foreground base to Bryson City. From there the Tuckasegee flows west to join Fontana Lake, while Highways 19 and 74 pass between Baines and Jackson Line Mountains, where the roads merge and continue southwest to the towns of Andrews and Murphy.

The Great Smoky Mountains National Park southern boundary runs from Cherokee, along the base (left end) of Thomas Ridge and Noland Divide, through Fontana Lake, and extends north to include these ridges as well as High Rocks, Andrews Bald, and Clingmans Dome. At this overlook you are just inside the eastern edge of the park and viewing much of the 56,000-acre Qualla Boundary, also known as the Cherokee Indian Reservation.

The Qualla Boundary includes land in several North Carolina counties. Home to the Eastern Band of Cherokee, it is a land trust, not a reservation, as the land is owned by the approximately 14,000

enrolled members of the tribe. The Eastern Band are descendants of those Cherokee who, in the late 1830s, remained in these mountains rather than be forced to march along the infamous "Trail of Tears" to Oklahoma.

Today the Cherokee are noted for their wood carvers, jewelers, and basket makers. The Qualla Arts & Crafts Mutual shop in Cherokee, located next to the Museum of the Cherokee, sells work by many local artists. The town of Cherokee lies at the base and on the far side of Rattlesnake Mountain, with Bryson City (on Highway 19) further in the distance in the valley in front of Jackson Line Mountain.

Highway 441 runs north from Cherokee though the national park, following the Oconaluftee River in the valley between Rattlesnake Mountain and Thomas Ridge before passing the Oconaluftee Visitor Center and Smokemont Campground on its way across Newfound Gap (right of Clingmans Dome) into Tennessee.

ABOVE: *The overlooks at Bunches Bald and nearby Lickstone Ridge are great spots to watch a sunset, as they offer views to the west, over receding rows of mountain ranges.*

RIGHT: *The Museum of the Cherokee Indian in Cherokee, offers visitors a look at tribal history through computer-generated imagery, well-designed exhibits, and an extensive artifact collection.*

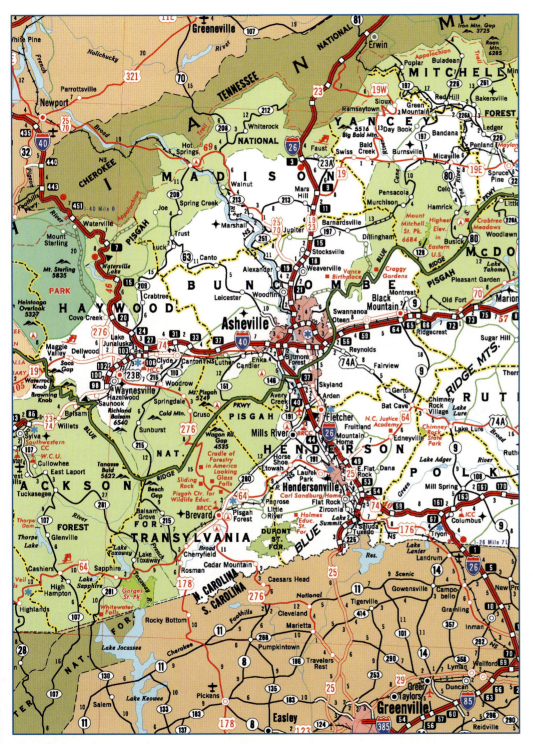

Other WNC Scenes

View from Chimney Rock Park—Elev. 2280. 106

Jump Off Rock near Hendersonville—Elev. 3100 108

View from St. Joseph Hospital in Asheville—Elev. 2223 110

Biltmore House Library Terrace in Asheville—Elev. 2243 112

Craggy Mountain Range from the Asheville Mall—Elev. 2167. . 114

View from I-26 to Craggy Mountains—Elev. 2668 115

Cashiers Valley from Highway 64—Elev. 4300 116

105

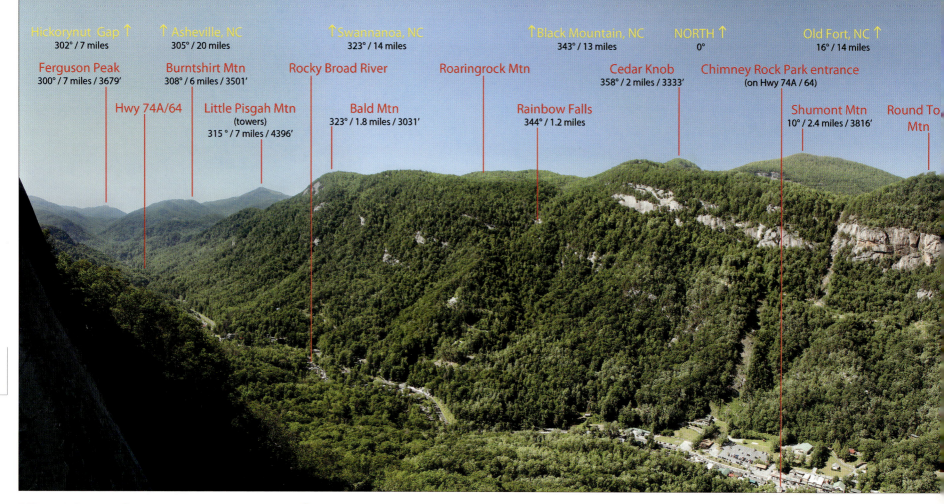

View from Chimney Rock Park (looking north)

County, State: Rutherford County, NC
GPS Coordinates: N 35° 25.967 x W 082° 15.011
Elevation at Viewpoint: 2,280 ft (top of Chimney Rock)
Location: Located 21 miles from Asheville. Take Exit 53A off I-40; take Exit 9 off I-240 onto Highway 74A. From the Blue Ridge Parkway, take Hwy 74A East exit at about Milepost 384.7 near Asheville. In downtown Chimney Rock, turn at the entrance gate and drive to the ticket office.
Visit www.chimmneyrockpark.com for hours and fees.

Looking north from the top of Chimney Rock, you are viewing Hickory Nut Gorge, an 8-mile-long valley carved by the Rocky Broad River. Highway 9, which turns north behind Bald Mountain to Black Mountain, Highway 64 from Hendersonville, and Highway 74A from Asheville converge at Bat Cave and follow the Rocky Broad through the foreground valley. As you climb out of the gorge following Highway 74A toward Asheville, you pass through Hickory Nut Gap (behind Burntshirt Mountain), crossing the Eastern Continental Divide. Rain falling on this side of the divide flows to the Atlantic Ocean; on the far side it flows toward the Gulf of Mexico. Long ago, the Cherokee and Catawba Indians traveling from the mountains to the flatlands, and later drovers taking livestock to market, used this route.

Chimney Rock, as seen from Highway 74A/64 near the park entrance gate, is framed by fall foliage and bathed in warm afternoon light.

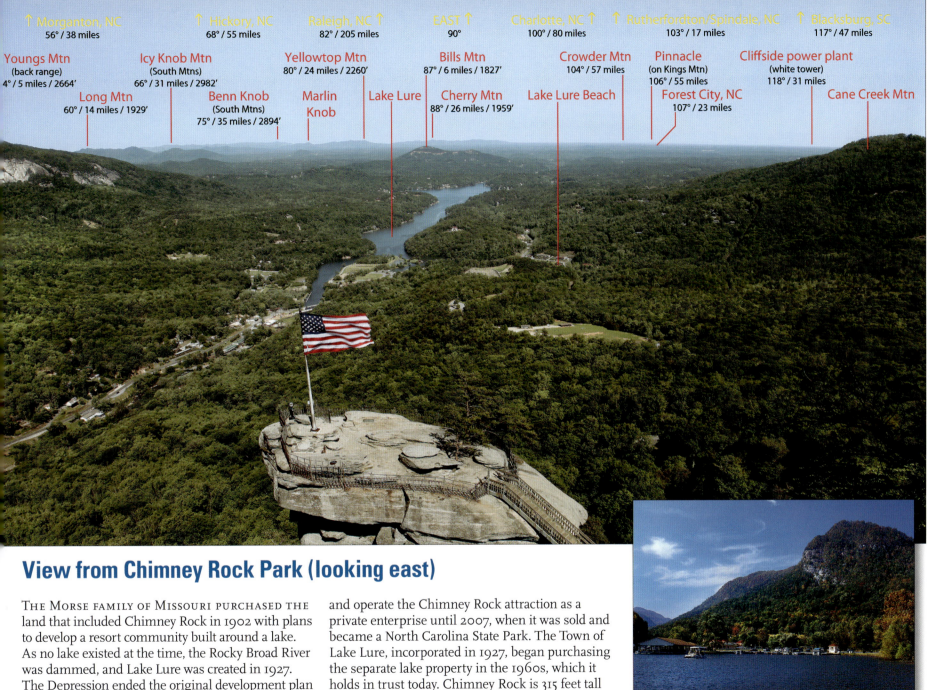

View from Chimney Rock Park (looking east)

The Morse family of Missouri purchased the land that included Chimney Rock in 1902 with plans to develop a resort community built around a lake. As no lake existed at the time, the Rocky Broad River was dammed, and Lake Lure was created in 1927. The Depression ended the original development plan and the family's ownership of the lake, but today lake houses abound, and other developers have built motels, hotels, and resort communities.

Morse family descendants continued to own and operate the Chimney Rock attraction as a private enterprise until 2007, when it was sold and became a North Carolina State Park. The Town of Lake Lure, incorporated in 1927, began purchasing the separate lake property in the 1960s, which it holds in trust today. Chimney Rock is 315 feet tall and about 315 million years old. This view from the stairwell behind the Chimney looks east over Lake Lure and the "thermal belt" lowlands of Rutherford, Polk, and McDowell Counties.

Lake Lure, built in 1927 by the Morse family, was named for its "alluring" beauty. A popular recreational area, it now encompasses about 720 acres, with 27 miles of shoreline.

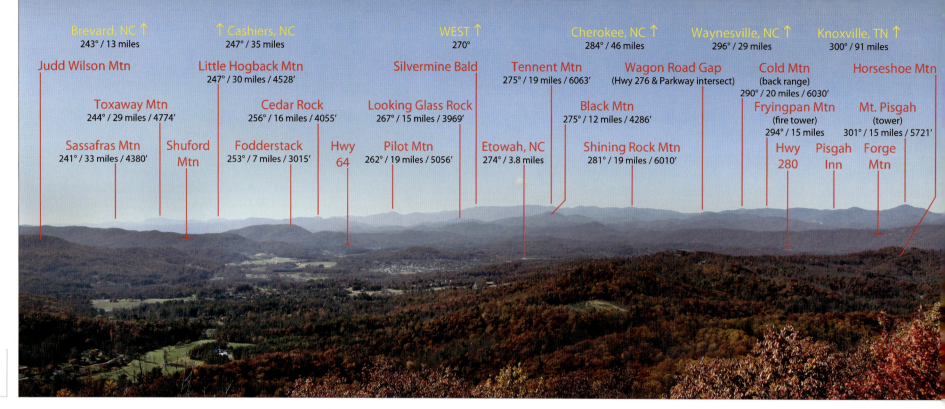

Jump Off Rock near Hendersonville

County, State: Henderson County, NC
GPS Coordinates: N 35° 18.823 x W 082° 31.638
Elevation at Viewpoint: 3,100 ft
Location: From Main Street in Hendersonville turn west on Fifth Avenue and continue about 5 miles. The road becomes Laurel Park Highway about 1.5 miles outside of town. Follow to the top of the mountain where it ends at a parking area and make the short walk to the overlook. Open sunrise to sunset.

THIS EXPANSIVE VIEW TO THE WEST INCLUDES THE sweep of the Pisgah Ridge on the far horizon with the Blue Ridge Parkway running northeast to southwest along its crest. From Asheville in the north, the Parkway climbs out of the French Broad River Valley to Grassy, Ferrin, and Shell Knobs, across Stoney Bald, to Mt. Pisgah. From there it continues past Fryingpan Mountain, Wagon Road Gap, and the Shining Rock Wilderness (between Cold Mountain and Silvermine Bald).

At Silvermine Bald the Parkway turns west and disappears from view on its way to Richland Balsam, Waterrock Knob, and the Great Smoky Mountains. Highway 215 tracks north/south from Rosman, on this side of the range, passing behind Cedar Rock and following the headwaters of the North Fork of the French Broad River to Pilot Mountain. It continues from there, crossing the Parkway just west of Devil's Courthouse (adjacent to Silvermine Bald) to Canton (in Haywood County), on the far side of the mountains.

From Rosman, Highway 64 runs west, passing between Toxaway and Sassafras Mountains to Cashiers and Highlands, then continues through the western part of the state and into Tennessee. Running east from Rosman, it parallels the French Broad River to Brevard (located behind Shuford Mountain) and intersects Highways 280 and 276 just north of town at the entrance to Pisgah National Forest (behind Fodderstack Mountain).

Running west (into the forest) from this junction, Highway 276 follows the Davidson River past the Davidson River Campground and the Pisgah Rangers Station. Further along, just below Looking Glass Falls (at the base of the domed Looking Glass Rock), the river turns east separating from 276 while the highway continues to Sliding Rock, the Cradle of Forestry, and the Pink Beds before climbing to cross the Parkway at Wagon Road Gap. There it drops down the far side of the ridge following the East Fork of the Pigeon River around the foreground base of Cold Mountain to Waynesville (behind the mountain).

Highway 64 continues in this direction from its junction with 280 and 276, between Shuford and Fodderstack Mountains, following the French Broad River into the foreground valley. It passes through the small town of Etowah and around the base of Horseshoe Mountain, then north (right of this overlook) of Jump Off Mountain to Hendersonville

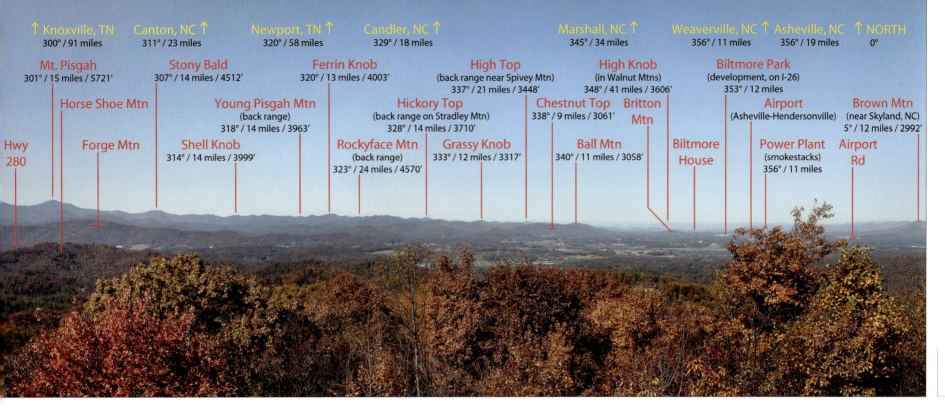

(behind this overlook). The French Broad River also runs along the base of Horsehoe Mountain, but then turns north, passing just east (left) of the Asheville-Hendersonville Airport, power plant, and Biltmore Park on Interstate 26, to cross under the Parkway before reaching Asheville on its way to the Tennessee River.

Highway 280 (Boylston Highway) runs from its junction with Highway 64 and 276 northeast along the foreground base of Forge Mountain to the town of Mills River (in the valley in front of Chestnut Top), where it joins Highway 191 (Brevard Road), which runs north/south between Ball and Britton Mountains connecting Asheville and Hendersonville. The main route from Asheville to Brevard follows Highway 191 to Mills River, then Highway 280 to Brevard.

See, Pisgah Inn (observation deck), on page 78, for reverse view.

ABOVE: *The quaint shops, art galleries, restaurants, and historic buildings along Main Street draw visitors from around the area to downtown Hendersonville.*

LEFT: *Hikers enjoy the early morning view from Jump Off Rock as clouds fill the valley floor. The Pisgah Ridge rises up in the distance, with the Blue Ridge Parkway tracing its ridgeline.*

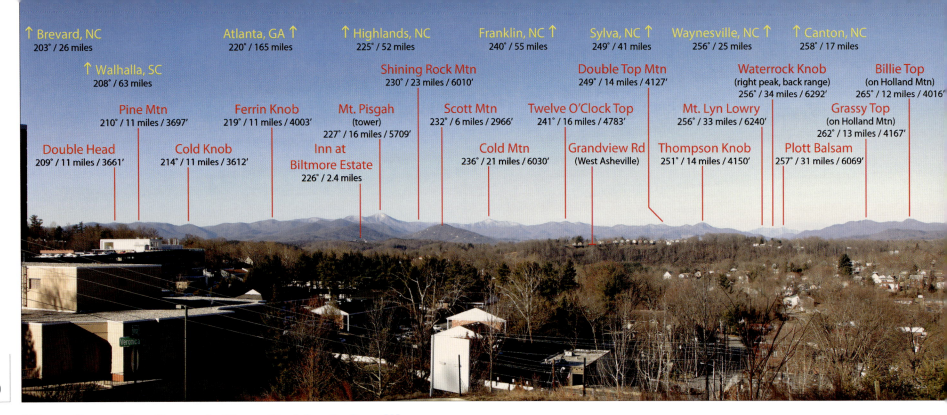

View from St. Joseph Hospital in Asheville

County, State: Buncombe County, NC
GPS Coordinates: N 35° 34.968 x W 082° 32.980
Elevation at Viewpoint: 2,208 ft
Location: Turn off Biltmore Avenue (Highway 25) in downtown Asheville onto Florence Street on the north side of St. Joseph Hospital, and drive 0.1 miles to the top of the hill. There is no parking here, but little traffic as well. This view is useful because it is similar to most from downtown Asheville, looking toward Mt. Pisgah.

Mt. Pisgah dominates the horizon from anywhere around downtown Asheville, and is easily identified by its conical shape and the tall communications tower that rises from its peak. The Blue Ridge Parkway passes through south Asheville (out of frame, left) and climbs to pass along the back side of the ridgeline, left, from Pine Mountain to Cold Knob and Ferrin Knob, to Mt. Pisgah.

From there, the Parkway continues along the ridge behind Shining Rock and Cold Mountain and on to Waterrock Knob in the Plott Balsam Mountains. This range, which includes Mt. Lynn Lowry and Plott Balsam, is visible in the gap between Thompson Knob and Holland Mountain (where Highways 19/23 and Interstate 40 also pass through on their track west to Canton and Waynesville). Often, smoke can be seen rising in this gap from the paper plant in Canton.

In the foreground, left, the roof of the Inn at Biltmore Estate is visible above the trees. The French Broad River runs through the valley just beyond, and winds its way north to Marshall, Hot Springs, and on to Newport, TN. A bit further, at the foreground base of Scott Mountain, is the Biltmore Square Mall, located near the junction of Brevard Road (Highway 191) and Interstate 26.

On this side of Twelve O'Clock Top, Double Top, and Thompson Knob lies Hominy Valley, a rural community traversed by Highway 151, which runs from Highway 19/23 near Candler, to connect with the Parkway just north of Mt. Pisgah.

Closer in, you can see a row of houses hanging off the ridge on Grandview Avenue in West Asheville. The French Broad River, which separates Asheville from West Asheville, is in the valley on the foreground side, with the railroad yard and the River Arts District on this side of the river.

Interstate spur 240 passes through downtown Asheville (just out of frame, right) and joins Highways 19/23 and the future I-26 to cross the French Broad using the Westgate Bridge (1.4 miles in line with Mikes Knob). From there, I-240 runs west to join I-40, which parallels 19/23/74 through the valley, on this side of Spivey Mountain, High Top, The Pinnacle, and Holland Mountain (which includes Billie Top and Grassy Top). These roads, running east-west, then pass through the gap between Holland and Thompson Knob to Clyde, where I-40 turns northwest to follow the Pigeon

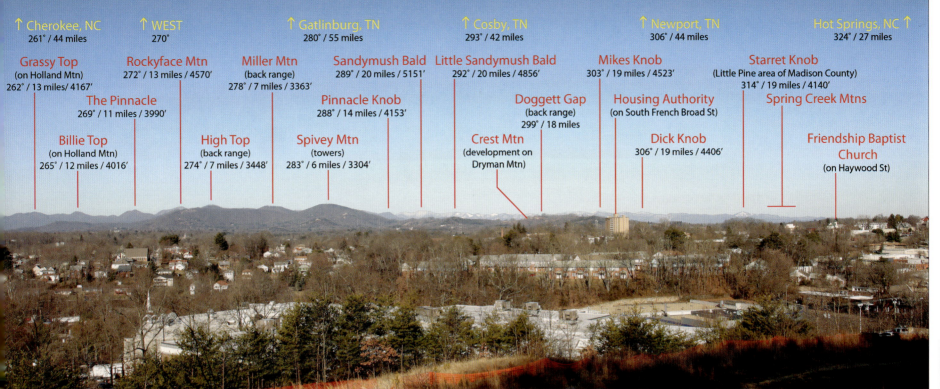

River into Tennessee, while 19/23/74 keep west.

Highway 63 (Leicester Highway) runs from 19/23 (Patton Avenue) northwest around the right end of Spivey Mountain through the Leicester and Sandy Mush communities, located in the valley behind Miller Mountain and High Top. North of Little Sandymush Bald, the road ascends to pass just left of Mikes Knob, crossing the mountain range at Doggett Gap; it then drops to Spring Creek in Madison County. There, Highway 63 ends at Highway 209, which travels north behind the Spring Creek Mountains to Hot Springs. In front of the Spring Creek Mountains is Starret Knob in the Little Pine section of Madison County, with Grassland Mountain to its left.

Closer in the foreground, in line with Doggett Gap, you can see the now completed condominiums at the Crest Mountain development, which also include the Crest Center and Pavilion (not visible) located on Dryman Mountain.

ABOVE: Hundreds of fine restaurants and shops, such as those at the Grove Arcade, draw locals and tourists alike to downtown Asheville.

LEFT: Asheville, surrounded by mountains, is the largest city in western North Carolina. It has a rich architectural heritage with a mix of Art Deco, Beaux Arts, and Neoclassical styles. Mt. Pisgah dominates the horizon, left.

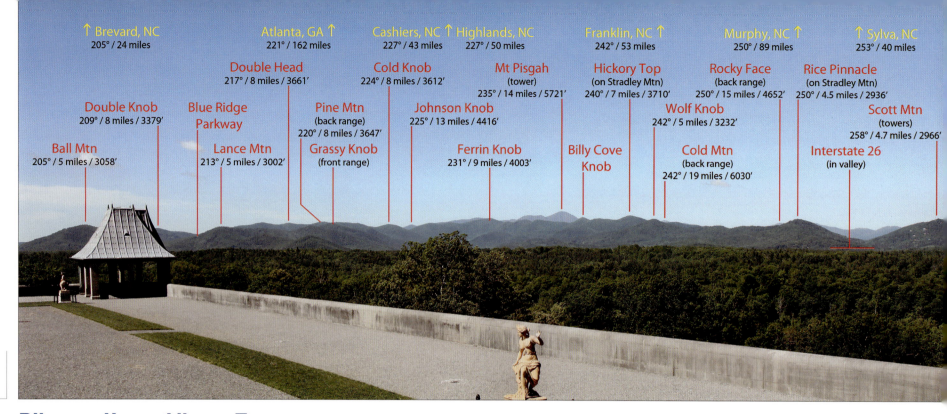

Biltmore House Library Terrace

County, State: Buncombe County, NC
GPS Coordinates: N 35° 32.415 x W 082° 33.201
Elevation at Viewpoint: 2,243 ft
Location: The Biltmore Estate is approximately 4 miles from the Blue Ridge Parkway. Take the U.S. Highway 25 North/Hendersonville Road exit, drive north toward Asheville and follow signs. From downtown Asheville take Hwy 25/Biltmore Ave south to Biltmore Village. This view from the Library Terrace is to the left of the main entrance to the house. Visit www.biltmore.com for hours and fees.

THIS VIEW LOOKS WEST ACROSS THOUSANDS OF ACRES of land that comprise the Biltmore Estate property. At the time the Biltmore House was completed in 1895, George Vanderbilt (1862–1914) owned more than 125,000 acres, including much of what you see from this viewpoint, extending to Mt. Pisgah, the tallest peak in the distance. Fredrick Law Olmsted, who collaborated on the design of Central Park in New York City, designed the estate grounds. Gifford Pinchot was hired to manage the forestlands.

In 1895, Pinchot was replaced by Carl Schenck from Germany, who introduced new scientific management and practical forestry techniques. Schenck noted an interest among the young men he worked with about the importance of maintaining healthy forests, which led him to investigate the possibility of starting a forestry education program. With the permission of Vanderbilt, he established the Biltmore School of Forestry. Established in 1898, this was the first school in America dedicated to training foresters.

After Vanderbilt's death in 1914, his wife Edith sold about 87,000 acres of the estate land to the federal government to form the beginning of Pisgah National Forest. In 1968, about 6,500 of that acreage was designated The Cradle of Forestry in America by Congress to commemorate the forestry school. The remaining land stayed with the estate and today thousands of people visit and tour Biltmore annually, enjoying year-round exhibits and special events.

From the steps of the library terrace you can look across the French Broad River valley and see much of the 8,000 acres of the estate. A section of the river winds through the trees just below this viewpoint. Interstate 26 and Highway 191/Brevard Road run along the far end of the valley in front of Ball and Lance Mountains, past Rice Pinnacle and Scott Mountain. The Biltmore Square Mall, at the junction of Brevard Road and I-26, is located in front of Scott.

The Blue Ridge Parkway climbs out of the valley from the French Broad River, running up along Lance Mountain and on the back of the mountain range to Grassy Knob, Pine Mountain, Cold Knob, Ferrin Knob, Mt. Pisgah and points south. As you start up the Parkway, the Chestnut Cove overlook offers views east over the Avery Creek

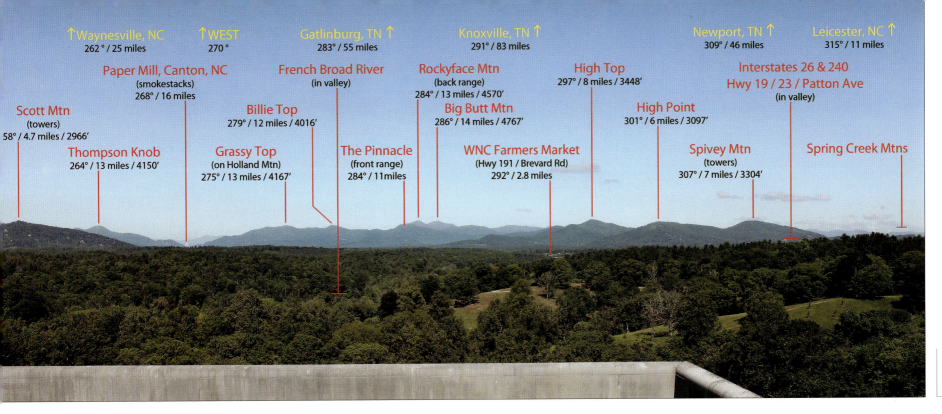

valley, located at the base of Double Knob. A few miles past Ferrin Knob, the Parkway crosses over to the west side of the ridge, offering a look west over Hominy Valley (behind Rice Pinnacle).

Interstate 40 and Highway 19/23 run from Asheville (out of frame, right), along the foreground base of Spivey, High Top, The Pinnacle, and Grassy Top. They pass through the gap between Holland Mountain and Thompson Knob, and continue their route to Canton, Waynesville, and points west.

Highway 191 crosses I-40 at the WNC Farmers Market. In the valley behind High Top, High Point, and Spivey Mountain, are the Sandymush and Leicester communities, with the Spring Creek Mountains of Madison County, beyond.

Compare this photo with its reverse perspective, View of Biltmore Estate and Craggy Mtn. range (from the Blue Ridge Parkway), page 73.

ABOVE: *An aerial view of the Biltmore House with the walled garden and Conservatory, designed by house architect Richard Morris Hunt. The city of Asheville can be seen in the upper right of the image.*

LEFT: *The Biltmore House, framed by fall foliage and photographed in late afternoon light, is reflected in the lagoon behind the house.*

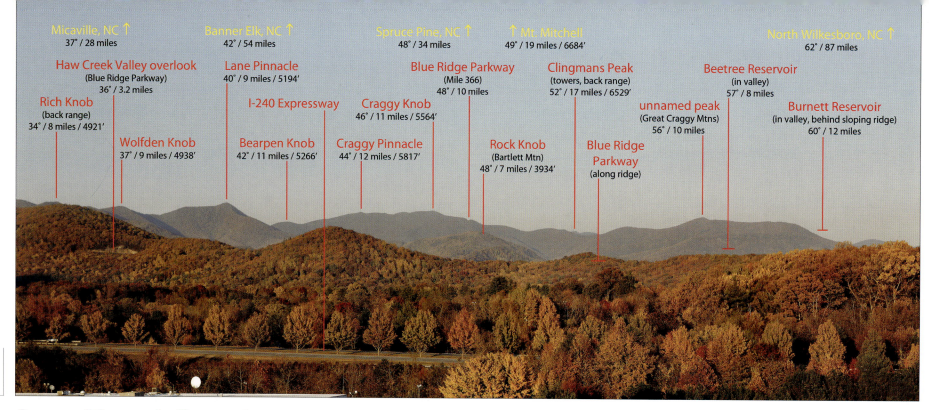

Craggy Mountain Range from the Asheville Mall

County, State: Buncombe County, NC
GPS Coordinates: N 35° 34.823 x W 082° 31.156
Elevation at Viewpoint: 2,167 ft
Location: The Asheville Mall is located on South Tunnel Road near Exit 7 off I-240 in Asheville. This photograph was made from the top level of the parking deck, looking northeast.

THE BLUE RIDGE PARKWAY SKIRTS ASHEVILLE, climbing up from the Oteen community (out of frame, right), across the foreground ridge, and becoming visible at the Haw Creek Valley overlook. The Haw Creek community is in the foreground valley below the overlook, with the Riceville Community on the far side of the ridge.

The Parkway continues to the back range of mountains just below Rich and Wolfden Knobs, Lane Pinnacle, Bearpen and Craggy Knobs, before traveling around to the far side of the mountains at about Milepost 366, to the Craggy Gardens Visitor Center. From there it winds in front of Mt. Mitchell, the highest point in eastern America, and Clingmans Peak (not to be confused with Clingmans Dome in the Great Smoky Mountains), before turning northeast toward Grandfather Mountain (47°, 57 miles) and Boone.

A large bowl-shaped valley below Clingmans Peak (front side), between Craggy Knob and The Pinnacle (hidden behind unnamed peak in Great Craggy Mountains), forms the Asheville Watershed, which feeds the man-made Burnett/North Fork Reservoir, the main water supply for the Asheville area. The much smaller Beetree Reservoir, once the city's primary drinking water source, is now a backup supply. In the foreground is the I-240 Expressway, a loop off Interstate 40 offering access to Asheville. It runs parallel to business Highway 70 through this section of east Asheville.

For reverse perspective see, Haw Creek Valley overlook, on page 72.

The Buncombe County Courthouse (left) and Asheville City Hall (right) are centerpieces of the city's vibrant downtown. They hint at the variety of architectural styles prevalent throughout the city.

↑ Old Fort, NC 130° / 26 miles
↑ Black Mountain, NC 146° / 20 miles
↑ Chimney Rock, NC 152° / 33 miles
↑ Tryon, NC 160° / 48 miles
Asheville, NC/SOUTH ↑ 180° / 18 miles

Carter Mtn
Barnardsville, NC 144° / 7 miles (behind Carter Mtn)
Lane Pinnacle 154° / 14 miles / 5194'
Frosty Knob 160° / 9 miles / 4236'
Chestnut Knob 171° / 10 miles / 3845'

Bullhead Mtn 136° / 14 miles / 5899'
Craggy Pinnacle 142° / 14 miles / 5817'
Snowball Mtn 148° / 13 miles / 5341'
Rich Knob 159° / 14 miles / 4921'
North Knob 167° / 10 miles / 4045'
Bill Cole Mtn (front range) 172° / 8 miles / 3278'

Locust Knob 133° / 14 miles / 5489'
Craggy Dome 140° / 14 miles / 6056'
Craggy Gardens Visitor Center (Blue Ridge Parkway)
Jess Knob 152° / 11 miles / 4386'
Nofat Mtn 157° / 4.8 miles / 3002'
Middle Mtn 163° / 9 miles / 4111'
I-26
Brittain Mtn 174° / 10 miles / 3556'

View from I-26 to Craggy Mountains

County, State: Madison County, NC
GPS Coordinates: N 35° 51.915 x W 082° 31.996
Elevation at Viewpoint: 2,668 ft
Location: This photograph was made from the first "Scenic overlook" (about 1.5 miles after Exit 9), as you climb Interstate 26 to Sams Gap, just after Highways 19/23 split off to the right, past the town of Mars Hill, NC. There is a small covered deck and parking lot at the overlook.

LOOKING SOUTHEAST TO THE GREAT CRAGGY Mountains, the Blue Ridge Parkway runs along the crest, climbing up from Asheville to Rich Knob, Lane Pinnacle, the Craggy Garden Visitor Center (building visible with binoculars), Bullhead Mountain, and Locust Knob. Just past Locust Knob the Parkway turns east on its way toward Mt. Mitchell (hidden, out of frame, left), highest point in the eastern U.S. The Asheville Watershed and Burnett Reservoir are in the valley on the far side of Craggy Dome. There is a great view of this range, with Mt. Mitchell visible, higher up at the NC Welcome Center on the opposite side of I-26, accessed from the eastbound lanes from Tennessee.

Nestled among the foreground mountains are the rural farming communities of Barnardsville, Beech Glen (in front of Nofat Mountain), and Paint Fork (behind Frosty Knob). The town of Weaverville lies at the south end of Brittain Mountain along I-26 between Asheville and Mars Hill. This section of I-26, completed in 2003, replaces Highways 19/23 as the north-south corridor from Asheville to Kingsport, TN. Highway 19 and 23 split off at the bottom of the hill (foreground). Highway 19 runs in front of Carter Mountain and continues east to Burnsville while Highway 23 (out of frame, left) roughly parallels I-26 to Tennessee.

For reverse view see Craggy Gardens Visitor Center (looking west), on page 69.

Aerial view of I-26 construction at Sams Gap, 1998. The first interstate highway in North Carolina to be designated a scenic byway, it is also the largest project ever undertaken by the NC Department of Transportation.

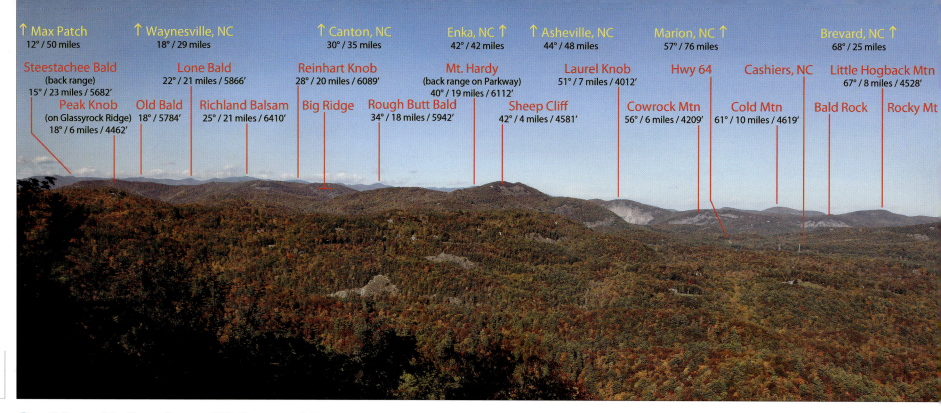

Cashiers Valley from Highway 64

County, State: Jackson County, NC
GPS Coordinates: N 35° 05.529 x W 083° 08.785
Elevation at Viewpoint: 4,300 ft
Location: From Cashiers drive 4.6 miles west on Highway 64 toward Highlands to Cowee Gap. Note the brown "Wildlife Viewing Area" sign and a small pull-off on the right. This is a very dangerous place to cross the road as it is in a curve, hidden from traffic. It is best to go just past the curve and turn around at Whiteside Mountain Rd., park, and walk back.

From this viewpoint at the Jackson/Macon County line you are looking east over Cashiers Valley. The large bare rock face, center, is Laurel Knob, with Pilot Mountain just visible behind. The smaller bare faces are Cowrock and Bald Rock Mountains. Cold Mountain (not to be confused with the more famous one in Haywood County) lies in the distance between, at the Jackson/Transylvania County line.

The Blue Ridge Parkway runs along the far range of mountains to the northwest from Mt. Hardy (near the Wolf Mountain overlook) to Rough Butt Bald, Reinhart Knob, past the Cowee Mountains overlook to Richland Balsam (highest point on the 469-mile-long track of the Parkway), and Lone, Old, and Steestachee Balds. The Jackson/Haywood County line runs along the same crest with the towns of Canton and Waynesville in the valley on the far side.

Cashiers (pronounced CASH-ers by locals) lies in the foreground valley (tall metal tower) at the intersection of Highways 64 and 107. Highway 64 runs east/west to town from this viewpoint, winding its way down along the front of the closest ridgeline, left. From there it continues behind Rocky Mountain and in front of Toxaway Mountain to Brevard. Highway 107 tracks north/south through the foreground valley from Sylva (out of frame, left) through Cashiers before running behind Timber Ridge and in front of Sassafras Mountain, to Walhalla, SC (out of frame, right). The Whiteside Cove community, home of many of the area's original settlers, starts on the far side of Timber Ridge along 107 and runs through the valley at the base of the eastern face of Whiteside Mountain.

In the summer months the population of Cashiers (elevation 3,484 feet) swells from 2,500 to over 10,000 as part-time residents, fleeing the heat of southern locales such as Atlanta, Charleston, and Florida, fill up the numerous gated communities and golf resorts. One of these popular retreats is located at Lake Toxaway, which sits in the valley behind, and to the right of, Toxaway Mountain.

Another popular destination, the High Hampton Inn, sits at the foreground base of Chimneytop Mountain. This historic resort hotel was built on land originally purchased in the 1830s by Wade Hampton III, from South Carolina. Hampton served as a Confederate General in the

Civil War and as governor of the state during the later Reconstruction years.

The current inn was completed in 1933 by E.L. McKee, a wealthy businessman and industrialist from Sylva. Families have been staying at the Inn for generations, enjoying its many amenities and rustic setting. Today, Will McKee, grandson of E.L. McKee, manages the 1,400-acre property, which includes most of Chimneytop and Rocky Mountains.

Waterfalls are abundant in the surrounding mountains, and from this viewpoint all waters flow southeast into the Savannah River Basin. This 10,577-square-mile expanse includes land in southwestern NC, western SC, and eastern GA. The Gorges State Park is located on Highway 281, which runs south off Highway 64 behind Chimneytop Mountain, with Whitewater Falls further south near the NC/SC state line.

For the reverse perspective, look at Cowee Mountains overlook, page 91.

ABOVE: *The High Hampton Inn, located in Cashiers near Rocky Mountain (center), offers golf, boating, and much more, and has been a seasonal retreat for generations of families visiting the cool mountains of western North Carolina.*

RIGHT: *Whitewater Falls, at 411 feet, is the second highest cascade east of the Rocky Mountains. It is one of over one hundred falls located in the surrounding mountain counties.*

Resources

TOP: *Late afternoon light adds a warm face to this old barn in Henderson County, NC.*

BOTTOM: *Henderson County is one of the largest producers of apples in the state.*

Maps

Detailed Guidemap to the Blue Ridge Parkway and Surrounding Area. Published by Outdoor Paths Publishing; *www.oppmaps.com*, and available in most Parkway and area outfitting stores. They include three maps that cover the complete route of the Parkway: the Northern Section—Milepost 0–123; Central Section—Milepost 106–269; Southern Section—Milepost 269–469.1.

DeLorme Atlas & Gazetteer™ for North Carolina and Virginia, one volume for each state.

National Geographic Trails Illustrated maps. Offering numerous ones that cover the region, corresponding to the Parkway, including #773/New River; #779/Linville Gorge & Mt. Mitchell; #780/Pisgah Ranger District; #789/Lexington Blue Ridge Mts. (George Washington and Jefferson National Forests).

National Geographic, TOPO! Outdoor Recreation Mapping Software© for North and South Carolina and Mid-Atlantic (discontinued in 2012).

Blue Ridge Parkway two-sided foldout paper map by the National Park Service.

Recommended Books

Adams, Kevin. *North Carolina Waterfalls: Where to Find Them, How to Photograph Them.* John F. Blair Publisher: 2005.

Barr, Peter J. *Hiking North Carolina's Lookout Towers.* John F. Blair Publisher: 2008.

Bernstein, Danny. *Hiking North Carolinas Blue Ridge Mountains.* Milestone Press: 2012.

Bernstein, Danny. *Hiking North Carolinas Blue Ridge Heritage.* Milestone Press: 2009.

Blouin, Nicole, Logue, Victoria and Frank. *Guide to the Blue Ridge Parkway.* Menasha Ridge Press: 3rd Edition, 2010.

Colbert, Judy. *Virginia Off the Beaten Path®, 11th: A Guide to Unique Places (Off the Beaten Path Series).* GPP Travel: 11th Edition, 2011.

Fussell, Fred C., with Kruger, Steve. *Blue Ridge Music Trails of North Carolina: A Guide to Music Sites, Artists, and Traditions of the Mountains and Foothills.* UNC Press: 2013.

Hall, Karen and the Friends of the Blue Ridge Parkway. *The Blue Ridge Parkway (Postcard History Series).* Arcadia Publishing: 2006.

Pitzer, Sarah. *North Carolina Off the Beaten Path®, 10th: A Guide To Unique Places (Off the Beaten Path Series).* GPP Travel: 10th Edition, 2011.

Simmons, Nye. *Best of the Blue Ridge Parkway: The Ultimate Guide to the Parkway's Best Attractions.* Mountain Trail Press: 3rd Edition, 2008.

Websites

Biltmore Estate, Asheville, NC: *www.biltmore.com*

Blue Ridge Music Center: *www.blueridgemusiccenter.org*

Blue Ridge National Heritage Area/Parkway info: *www.blueridgeheritage.com/attractions-destinations/blue-ridge-parkway*

Blue Ridge Parkway Foundation: *brpfoundation.org*

Blue Ridge Parkway home page: *www.blueridgeparkway.org*

Blue Ridge Parkway site by National Park Service: *www.nps.gov/blri/index.htm*

Camping reservations: *www.recreation.gov* to reserve a campsite, or call 877-444-6777

Chimney Rock Park: *www.chimneyrockpark.com*

Eastern National (bookstore and visitor center operations): *www.easternnational.org*

Folk Art Center, Asheville, NC: *www.southernhighlandguild.org*

Friends of the Blue Ridge Parkway: *www.friendsbrp.org/index.cfm*

Geographical Names Information System (GNIS) website: *geonames.usgs.gov/pls/gnispublic/f?p=132:1:1894214150214714*

Grandfather Mountain State Park, Linville, NC: *www.ncparks.gov/Visit/parks/grmo/main.php*

Mt. Mitchell State Park: *www.ncparks.gov/Visit/parks/momi/main.php*

Mt. Pisgah Lodge, Milepost 408.6: *www.pisgahinn.com*

NC Minerals Museum, Spruce Pine, NC: *www.blueridgeheritage.com/attractions-destinations/museum-of-north-carolina-minerals*

North Carolina Arboretum, Asheville, NC: *www.ncarboretum.org*

Virginia is for Lovers/Parkway info: *www.virginia.org/blueridgeparkway*

Virtual Blue Ridge/Parkway Guide: *www.virtualblueridge.com*

Phone Numbers

Parkway, emergencies, accidents, fires: 800-727-5928
Parkway information, weather, road conditions/closures: 828-298-0398
Biltmore Estate: 800-411-3812
Blue Ridge Music Center, Milepost 213: 276-236-5309
Blue Ridge Parkway Visitor Center/Asheville: 828-298-5330
Chimney Rock Park: 828-625-9611
Folk Art Center, Milepost 382: 828-298-7928
Grandfather Mountain: 800-468-7325
Mabry Mill Restaurant/Gift Shop, Milepost 176.2: 276-952-2947
Moses Cone Memorial Park, Milepost 294: 828-295-7938
Mt. Mitchell State Park, Milepost 355.4: 828-675-4611
Mt. Pisgah Inn/Restaurant, Milepost 408.6: 828-235-8228
Northwest Trading Post, Milepost 259: 336-982-2543
Peaks of Otter Lodge (reservations), Milepost 86: 866-387-9905
Recreation.gov camping reservations: 877-444-6777
Virginia's Explore Park Visitor Center, Milepost 115: 540-427-1800

For Future Editions of This Book

While I have made every effort to be as accurate as possible, there may be some errors, due to the overwhelming complexity of a task like this. If you happen to find any mistakes, please contact me by email at barnwellphoto@hotmail.com, because I would be interested to know for future editions.

Elevations of area cities (US Geological Survey figures)

Virginia cities

Fancy Gap, VA	2,894 ft
Floyd, VA	2,493 ft
Lexington, VA	1,063 ft
Lynchburg, VA	630 ft
Roanoke, VA	935 ft
Rocky Mount, VA	1,132 ft
Staunton, VA	1,391 ft
Waynesboro, VA	1,293 ft

North Carolina cities

Asheville, NC	2,129 ft
Black Mountain, NC	2,398 ft
Boone, NC	3,218 ft
Brevard, NC	2,224 ft
Burnsville, NC	2,825 ft
Cashiers, NC	3,484 ft
Cherokee, NC	1,985 ft
Chimney Rock, NC	1,093 ft
Hendersonville, NC	2,159 ft
Linville, NC	3,665 ft
Mount Airy, NC	1,099 ft
North Wilkesboro, NC	988 ft
Sparta, NC	2,930 ft
Spruce Pine, NC	2,559 ft
Sylva, NC	2,044 ft
Waynesville, NC	2,746 ft
West Jefferson, NC	2,976 ft

Feet to Meters Calculation Chart

500 feet = 152.4 meters
1,000 feet = 304.8 meters
1,500 feet = 457.2 meters
2,000 feet = 609.6 meters
2,500 feet = 762 meters
3,000 feet = 914.4 meters
3,500 feet = 1066.8 meters
4,000 feet = 1219.2 meters
4,5000 feet = 1371.6 meters
5,000 feet = 1524 meters
5,5000 feet = 1676.4 meters
6,000 feet = 1828.8 meters
6,5000 feet = 1981.2 meters
7,000 feet = 2133.6 meters

Biltmore Estate, one of the most popular tourist destinations in North Carolina, draws thousands of visitors a day, with visitation peaking during the fall color season.

Also by Tim Barnwell

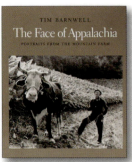

The Face of Appalachia:
Portraits from the Mountain Farm
2003
ISBN 0-393-05787-9

The culmination of more than 25 years of work, the book features photographs showcasing scenes of daily life, such as farming, hunting, religious activities, working with oxen and horses, and making traditional crafts. More than 100 photographs are combined with the author's conversations with the subjects, providing an insight into the lives, family histories, and personal dreams of the hardworking, proud, and resourceful men and women of this unique area of the country.

The rugged and remote mountains of the southern Appalachian region have served to isolate and preserve the last vestiges of life as it once was throughout rural America. Transcending their geographical origins, Barnwell's photographs record this way of life, and remind us how our forefathers lived for generations, with seemingly little change, in the decades before modern industry, roads, technology, communications, and now the information age, transformed the country. The book includes a preface by museum director, writer, and curator Sam Gray, and an introduction by photographer George Tice, author of more than 17 books of photography.

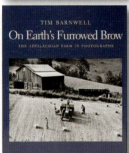

On Earth's Furrowed Brow:
The Appalachian Farm in Photographs
2007
ISBN 978-0-393-06267-0

The images in this book span the seasons, showing scenes of farm life at each time of the year and how these seasonal activities shape the lives of the subjects. Many of them are living as their parents and grandparents did, in close-knit communities bound by heritage, kinship, and faith. Set against the breathtaking backdrop of the Appalachian Mountains, more than 100 timeless black and white photographs provide a window onto a world that is quickly fading. Portraits of people in their homes and at work in the fields illuminate the richness and rhythms of everyday life.

The images are complemented by oral histories derived from conversations between Barnwell and his subjects. This union of photography and text honors the heritage, humor, and wisdom of these genuine and hardworking people. The book includes a foreword by John Ehle, author of 17 books, including *Winter People* and *The Journey of August King*.

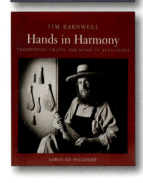

Hands in Harmony:
Traditional Crafts and Music in Appalachia
2009
ISBN 978-0-393-06815-3

This unique book explores folk music and traditional handcrafts. Eighty evocative black and white portraits are combined with biographies and oral history interviews, along with a music CD, to celebrate those involved in the music and craft communities in and around the southern Appalachian region. Barnwell's portraits speak to the beauty and uniqueness of the handmade object and their creators, and to the musical heritage carried forward by those performing the original folk songs of this region. Portrayed here are craftsmen making pottery, blacksmithing, weaving, and other timeless crafts. They share the spotlight with musicians playing all manner of traditional instruments, from the Dobro guitar to the fiddle, including Doc Watson, David Holt, Ralph Stanley, Earl Scruggs, Bill Monroe, Jerry Douglas, and Pete Seeger. The accompanying CD includes 21 old-time fiddle and banjo tunes, a capella ballads, blues, and folk songs, which showcase the talents of many of the musicians portrayed.

The book includes a foreword by Jan Davidson, Director, John C. Campbell Folk School.

Published by W.W. Norton & Company: New York and available in three different editions: Trade hardback (at local bookstores, on-line, and at *barnwellphoto.com*), limited edition with clothbound embossed slipcase, and special edition with slipcase and mounted photographic print (only from *barnwellphoto.com*).